The GODDESS of WAR

The
GODDESS
of WAR

A TRUE STORY OF PASSION, BETRAYAL
AND MURDER IN THE OLD WEST

Dennis McCown

SANTA FE

Sunstone books may be purchased for educational, business, or sales promotional use.
For information please write: Special Markets Department, Sunstone Press,
P.O. Box 2321, Santa Fe, New Mexico 87504-2321.

Book and Cover design › Vicki Ahl
Body typeface › Minion Pro
Printed on acid-free paper

_____

Library of Congress Cataloging-in-Publication Data

McCown, Dennis, 1950-
  The goddess of war : a true story of passion, betrayal, and murder in the Old West / by
Dennis McCown.
    pages cm
  Includes bibliographical references and index.
  ISBN 978-0-86534-899-8 (softcover : alk. paper)
  1. Texas Hill Country (Tex.)--Biography. 2. Hardin, John Wesley, 1853-1895--Friends and
associates. 3. Texas Hill Country (Tex.)--History, Local. 4. Texas--History--1846-1950.
5. Murder--Texas--El Paso. I. Title.
  F392.T47M35 2012
  976.4'0610922--dc23
  [B]
                          2012038321

_____

WWW.SUNSTONEPRESS.COM
SUNSTONE PRESS / POST OFFICE BOX 2321 / SANTA FE, NM 87504-2321 /USA
(505) 988-4418 / ORDERS ONLY (800) 243-5644 / FAX (505) 988-1025

For Beulah, Hazel, and Grace

"When you finally find time to research your own family's history, it's already too late."

—Joyce Capps, at her home at Deer Creek,
San Saba County, Texas, May 1998

CONTENTS

ACKNOWLEDGMENTS

"Thank you," I told her at the end of the interview.
"No. Thank you," she answered. "It's about time
someone looked into this."

B y tradition, an acknowledgments page is to honor those who supported a work in progress. I must necessarily break new ground here. The researching of this story involved not only those who encouraged, but those who actively discouraged its production. For a time, my sources dried up faster than waterholes in a Texas drought. To be fair, I have to admit there is great pain, anger, and sadness in these pages that has not lessened over the last hundred years, and so, to those who desired this research never see the light of day, I offer a wish that through this book the ghosts of the past may finally be laid to rest.

That said, the author wishes to recognize the following individuals, for as every historian knows, a book like this could never have been written without the help of many people.

I first heard part of this story from members of the Jennings family. Years passed, however, before I had a chance to look into it. Though that version proved inaccurate, it provided a framework upon which to research the truth.

I very much appreciate the help of Thomas and Wilda Fay Jennings, Glenn and Dorothy Wilkins, Sharon Allen, and Ruth Jo Martin, who gave so generously of the family information and photos they had gathered and preserved over the years, plus Rodger Barnes who freely shared his mother's life-long collection of Williams family data and who hosted an important gathering of Williams researchers. Other descendants have generously shared family information, including Beauregard Lee II, John McPhee, John G. Belcher, Dolly Close, Sheri Mitchell, Jerry Kemp, and genealogists Tyre Harris Brown IV and Doris Johnston, who both provided important insights. Several historians have offered sources and encouragement. Chief among these was Joyce Capps, who was unafraid of asking hard questions; plus Chuck Parsons and Leon Metz, both of whom took an early interest in my work. I must also thank Rick Sherman of the California Genealogical Society, who helped achieve a major breakthrough; Laura Sigaud and Pat Lindsey of Austin Community College, who acted as my sounding boards as the research developed; Jim Bradshaw at the Nita Stewart Haley Memorial Library, whose careful cross-indexing of names mentioned in interviews and letters led to so many discoveries; Steve Davis and Mandy York at the archives at Texas State University for help with photographs and the Hardin Collection; the volunteer staff of the Family History Center, Oak Hills Stake; Pam Risvold, who used her network of genealogical researchers to access information I was unable to get on my own; Judge Charles Chapman of Haskell County, Texas, who took it upon himself to dig through county records to locate what I needed; Dr. Debra Pauline Shipman, Maria Celeste Costley, Juanita Arellaño, and Petra Ringel for invaluable translations; Miguel Bonilla Lopez, Secretario General del Instituto de la Judicatura Federal, and Carlos Baez Silva of the Instituto, for their help accessing case files from the Mexican Supreme Court; historical researcher Joe Sonneman in Juneau, Alaska, and genealogist Nancy Ehlers in Sacramento, California; the San Saba County Historical Commission, who gave me an opportunity to present this story for the first time; historians Rick Miller and Bill Cummins; Dr. Charles Wukasch who helped interpret research dealing with the Wends; the volunteers at the Texas Wendish Heritage Society in Serbin; the volunteers at the Gonzales County Records Center and Archives; Donaly Brice and the staff of the Texas State Archives; David Baskin at the Texas State Genealogical Library; Dr. Bob La Perriere of the Old City Cemetery Committee in Sacramento, who opened up the Mortuary Office and allowed me to read through files on New Helvetia; Richard Gold, Division Chief of Records in the Bexar County District Clerk's office for locating an important case file; Eva Murphy at the Massachusetts State Library; Eddy County Manager Stephen Massey, and Robert G. McCubbin, Robert DeArment, Jim Earle, Gene Riggs, John Robinson, and J.W. McNellis for photos.

I must also offer a very special thanks to NOLA, the National Association for Outlaw and Lawman History, Inc., of which I was a proud member, for NOLA provided a substantial grant that enabled me to go to California and complete my research.

The last few years of my work on this narrative involved personal lessons. Assisting me were three fine doctors, Dr. Mark T. Brown, Dr. Shannon Cox, and Dr. J. Dudley Youman III, all of whom helped me through difficult days. As every writer knows, getting close to finishing is not an option. These doctors made it possible for me to complete my work, and I am forever grateful. Also in this regard, I'd like to thank Roni Bankus for her advice and encouragement.

Finally, I would like to acknowledge my deep appreciation to the hundreds of private citizens, county and district clerks, grounds keepers and cemetery managers, archivists, librarians, researchers, genealogists, secretaries, museum staff, and others who so patiently took time to answer the questions, letters, and calls of a writer from far away. Without the thousands of hours these people provided narrowing leads, copying, and offering suggestions, I could never have pieced the whole story together.

Thanks.

—DRM

PREFACE

There is something sweet about an old lady vague about her age, but there is something peculiar about someone who equivocated so consistently her own children never knew with certainty when she was born. Such a situation leaves an outsider with the idea the old woman had secrets to hide.

So it was with Laura Blanche Jennings, who was born on the eighth of March. Her birth year was probably 1891, but this is difficult to prove. The one salient date Laura could never escape from, however, was 1895, a time in her life too well documented for her to deny. There is a well known photograph of her and her mother from that year. Laura appears to be much closer to four than three in this photograph.

For this and other reasons, the eighth of March 1891 is probably accurate, but it matters little, for whatever the year, Laura's birth was the unifying moment for six pioneer clans: the Jennings, Williams, Lewis, Hardin, Knight, and Mrose families. Each of these clans was rooted in religion and tradition. Each had a patriarch and a good mother. Each had an extended family and a circle of friends, and they lived in a critical period in American history: the Late Frontier and the beginning of the Modern Age.

As these families struggled to raise their children and reach material success—all within a strong moral and religious framework—events conspired to set them back. They did produce offspring who made them proud, but children from these families were raging disappointments whose lives were filled with scandal, despair, and heartache. Theirs is a story of sex, money, betrayal, abandonment, theft, alcoholism, kidnapping, gambling, lynching, rustling, bigamy, murder, abuse, prostitution, arson, corruption, fraud, and conspiracy. It is a story of a childhood ripped out by the roots. It is a story of six little towns struggling to survive. It is a story of money and poverty; power and death; truth and what became history. It is the story of two of the most famous murders of the Old West. Though this is an awful chronicle of three young women from Fredonia, Texas, scarred forever by the scandals of their youth, it is also a remarkable saga of a child's resilience and a father's stubborn love. At the same time, the story is so horrible some of it has been ... until now ... a dread secret within these families for a hundred years.

One family produced a flirt so headstrong and willful she broke her parents' hearts, then her heart was broken by an adulterous husband. Another family produced a sociopathic murderer who, it is claimed, killed another man just for snoring. A third family produced an arrogant and abusive son who had one shining moment of courage and determination, then sank into a long life of disappointments. Still another family had a daughter throw her life away on a whim—not just once but three times—then go on to betray everyone who loved her and spend her remaining years in guilt. The fifth family had a son leave, become a success, but be murdered before he could return home in triumph, and the last family adopted and lost the only child they ever wanted and loved.

And the woman who united the fates of these six extraordinary pioneer families was Laura Jennings. This is her story.

It is also the story of her mother, Helen Beulah Mrose, one of the most enigmatic figures in the history of the American West. Until now, researchers have not been able to do more than speculate on where she came from and went, but for eleven incredible months she was at the fulcrum of history. Her story is a tragic lesson of what might go wrong in a person's life, and it is an example of what every parent knows in his or her heart: Who is treasured more, the hardworking son who does favorably and produces a strong and loving family? Or the ne'er-do-well who tears his family apart in controversy? In the end, it must be admitted, we agonize and grieve over young lives wasted more than we celebrate the good. It is not something wrong with us. The truth is in some families the exceptional child is not the best child, but the worst.

—DRM

A NOTE TO THE READER

The narrative you are about to read is based on legends told among the residents of southwestern San Saba and northern Mason counties in the central Hill Country of Texas. The author used these contradictory stories as a foundation from which to seek out historical facts, based on primary sources such as documents, interviews, letters, and newspapers as available; secondary sources such as books when necessary.

To construct this story was like putting together the pieces of a vast, complicated puzzle. The author has taken care to preserve as much of the chronology as possible. More research will have to be done by serious historians—especially in Mexico and California—but for the general reader, this is as close to the way things happened as possible.

As you read, remember the individuals in this story were common people, with real lives. They had no concept they were living one of the last, great adventures of the Old West. Two of these people thought to write their memoirs, but both lied shamelessly throughout. All the rest are remembered only through dusty records, cracked photographs, and faulty memories of the still-living. The people in this story are dead and gone, but most of them felt at the time they had ruined their lives, damaged their families irreparably, scandalized their peers, and must and ought not to be remembered.

With this in mind, it is important for the reader to understand that instead of telling this story through the experiences of its most famous character, the author has chosen to develop the narrative on unconventional lines. In this story, there are five characters: an aging gunfighter, a beautiful woman, a good cowboy, an angry husband, and a darling little girl. In the end, the stories of the woman and the girl are what mattered, but the encounters these people had that led to El Paso in 1895 changed the history of the Old West. Though this is a story of two violent murders, it is also a tale of survival, redemption, and perseverence.

—DRM

PART ONE
A Beautiful Woman, An Angry Husband, and A Little Girl

"San Saba [County, Texas] was a tough place to start a family."

—"Sonnie" Jennings, conversation,
September 1999

1
THE OUTLAW COUSIN
1874–1887

"I am a wolf and it is my night to howl."[1]

Five miles northeast of Georgetown, Texas, was a little village called Berry Creek, established in 1846 when Captain John Berry built a gristmill here. Attracted by fertile land at cheap prices, a large group of relatives and in-laws of the Williams family built farms between the North Fork of the San Gabriel River and Berry Creek.

In early June 1874, members of these families gathered at the home of Judge James N. Lemond.[2] Nothing is known about the reasons for the gathering, but one curious fact has emerged: most of the menfolk were missing, and of those gathered at the Lemonds' that day were an inordinate number of women and children from the Williams, Lemond, and Ellison families. Toward evening, riders appeared on the horizon to the northwest.

In the way of such things then, the assembled group noticed the riders were better mounted than most, for they were riding long-legged, deep-chested horses, poor choices for cowboys, but fast mounts for outlaws and lawmen. Lawmen these were not, however, for there was something about the way they twisted around in the saddle to check out the horizon behind them that caused the women to move the children inside. As Judge Lemond stepped out to the fence, the women hesitated on the porch to get a look at the riders, then they, too, went in. Guns were probably loaded; children were shooed away from windows and doors.

Without dismounting, the armed riders parleyed with Judge Lemond, and it was obvious something was amiss. The riders were not moving on. In fact, they dismounted, keeping their horses between themselves and the horizon, and after a while, the menfolk shook hands as an agreement was made.

Things did not look good to those in the house. Someone was assigned to lead the horses to the barn. Another was sent to water and feed them. By the time Judge Lemond came in, the womenfolk knew the visitors were there to stay. The riders had to be fed, but no one invited them inside. The mood was grim, the children scared, the women mystified. As the barn doors closed in the fading light of evening, it could be seen the horses tethered inside were not unsaddled. The children were hustled off to bed, but the adults sat up in the dark, not a light in the house, not a light in the barn. It was the custom to sleep on the porch in good weather. On that night, however, no one went outside. Most probably, Judge Lemond did not sleep.

About four a.m., birds began to stir in the light of the false dawn, and the barn door creaked open. The horsemen emerged cautiously, and after a quick slug of stale coffee brought from the house, the men mounted and rode stiffly away. At dawn the household was up, the chores were done, and a rousing breakfast provided. Now was the time for questions, and Judge Lemond explained the encounter to his guests. Not only did the hospitality of the frontier demand the outlaws be received the night before, he told them, but one of the riders was kin, a distant cousin of his sister-in-law.

Times have changed. Not only do modern people brag about kinship to outlaws, they often invent such kinship. Not so with those who lived with them. It was a smaller world a hundred years ago, and a person could not live his life without one of the great outlaws galloping through, and so it was with these riders in the night. Over the years, the story of the encounter with the outlaws was recounted as family history, not adventure.[3] Having an outlaw in the family was a scandal the Lemonds were not proud of, but one they did not deny.

As the families gathered at the Lemonds understood the term, the main outlaw that night was a *cousin*. While we in the modern world think of such kinship as extending only to the children of our uncles and aunts, such was not the case then. Being a cousin involved not only biological cousins, but spouses, in-laws, and "removed" cousins.[4]

Judge Lemond and his wife were kin not only to pioneers of Texas like the Williamses, Akes, and Ellisons, but also to the Longleys and Browns. Judge Lemond's sister-in-law, Nancy Brown Lemond, was a cousin of Anastasia Brown, who had married George Culver Tennille in Gonzales County. The marriage did not last, and George Tennille later married Amanda Billings. Their daughter,

Sarah Tennille, married Joseph Clements, whose first cousin was the notorious John Wesley Hardin. On the run in Texas for the violent murder of Deputy Sheriff Charlie Webb in Comanche five days earlier, it was Hardin, and at least one other man, who had called upon this distant relationship for shelter.[5]

Among the womenfolk at the Lemonds that night was twenty-eight-year old Ann Eliza (née Ellison) Williams, together with her son, eight-year-old David Alonso, and daughter, two-year-old Helen Elizabeth.[6] Though Helen was quite young, of one thing we can be sure: as she grew up and heard the story of the encounter with the outlaws retold at family gatherings, she remembered it. This simple event, seen through her impressionable blue eyes, was to be one of the most momentous in her life.

It was not, however, the only encounter her family had with the outlaw Hardin. Helen's uncle, A. C. "Dick" Williams, and other family members lived near Prairie Lea, fifty miles southeast. We know nothing of their encounter with Hardin a day or two later, but it was probably similar to what happened at the Lemonds' home. Still another encounter between the extended Williams family and Hardin occurred near Cost in Gonzales County.[7]

About this time, Hardin rode into Luling and entered Reuben Jacobs' store. "Reuben [...] thought it was a holdup, laid out his wares, and said to Hardin, 'Help yourself. It's on the house.' Hardin replied, 'I am not a thief. I will pay you in gold,' which he did. Hardin warned the storekeeper not to tell anyone he had seen him or he would return and kill him...."[8]

Hardin was not the only outlaw in the family. In addition to Jeff and Will Ake, related to the Williams family through the Barneses, there was rustler Ben Lemond and train robbers Samuel Dawson "Kep" Queen and John Tolivar Barber. In addition, there were at least three other desperadoes in the family: Bill Longley, Clay Allison, and A.J. Williams.

A.J. (Andrew Jackson) Williams was born in Milam County, Texas, in late 1847. His parents, Curtis and Elizabeth Williams, died prior to 1860. Taking custody of A.J. and his sister Martha Ann, Curtis' brother Aaron Williams, Jr., raised his adopted niece and nephew like his own children.

In 1878, Dick Williams, one of Aaron's sons, acquired land and interests in Eastland County, a hundred miles north. About the same time, A.J. Williams acquired land in neighboring Shackelford County; he also appeared in nearby Jones County, where he registered cattle and hog brands. Williams married at least twice.[9]

Arrested for theft of a cow on March 21, 1882, he was convicted and sentenced to two years in prison, but on December 24, 1883, Texas Governor John Ireland pardoned him.[10] Williams' troubles, however, were not over. In Jones County authorities charged him with another theft of cattle in July 1885. Soon afterward, he tried bribing an officer, in this case the new sheriff of Jones County, George Scarborough.[11] Williams obtained bond on this case, but he skipped out, and it was not the first time he had done so. Adella Barnes, A.J.'s grandniece, wrote, "I found ... a court order dated July 18, 1874 listing Aaron Williams, N.P. Ellison, and A.C. Williams as sureties for bond of A.J. Williams ... [who] did not appear in court and [the men] had to forfeit the bond."[12]

Williams was found guilty on February 10, 1885, but he filed for a new trial and was found not guilty on May 1, 1886.[13] On February 4, he was charged with the theft of three cattle; on the tenth he was charged with stealing two more, and just two days later, stealing another two. In each case, he obtained continuances or was found not guilty.

Meanwhile, some Williamses appeared in New Mexico. The Lincoln County War was over; Billy the Kid was dead. Cattlemen from Texas relocated to southeastern New Mexico in large numbers. Several Williamses moved to what would become Eddy County. A.J. Williams decided to let things cool and departed for New Mexico himself in 1885. On April 20th, W.H. Smith, a justice of the peace, signed an order requesting his extradition.[14] On April 27, 1885, Acting Governor Barnett Gibbs specified the fugitive be delivered to George Scarborough, as agent for the State of Texas.[15]

Scarborough rode the train to a small town in New Mexico, rented a horse and headed for the ranch. Williams seen [sic] him coming and took off. George run him for several miles, but his horse was no match for Williams'. He come [sic] back to Abilene, turned in his report, and said he would get him next time....

When he got word again he shipped his thoroughbred horse by

train and rode the train with him. He rode out to the ranch and Williams saw him again. But this time he run him down.... Williams refused to stop [and] George shot his horse. Williams fell and George had him handcuffed before he could get up. [16]

Scarborough took his prisoner back to Texas. Concerned about the security of his jail, Scarborough delivered him to Sweetwater, but a month later Williams grabbed Sheriff Bardwell from behind. During the ensuing melee, several prisoners escaped, but Williams was recaptured. In 1886 Williams was returned to Jones County but was found not guilty. The case for bribery was still pending.

A year later, Williams encountered Sheriff Scarborough in a saloon called "The Road to Ruin" in Haskell County.

Its sign was "Q.T. Saloon" till a one-legged sign painter came along and wanted to paint a sign. They were sorry for him and wanted to help him. Draper [one of the owners] asked what sign he wanted to paint. They sat down together and sketched off a few signs. The two men finally drew a large key with the letters [WHIS] on it, with "The Road to Ruin" under that...

A bar to joy which home imparts
A door to tears and aching hearts;
A bar to heaven, a door to hell,
Whoever named it, named it well.[17]

Another account says, "Haskell has the reputation of having ... one of the best and most honest signs ever put over a saloon door, to truthfully notify its customers of its nature. A doorkey with 'Whis' written across it, signifying whiskey was followed by the words, 'The Road to Ruin' ... a sign that faithfully told the traveler who entered those portals where the road ended. And I used to see on a road east of town a mile post that read '5 miles to Hell,' which doubtless referred to this sign."[18]

George Scarborough and his brother Will were relaxing in the Road to Ruin on Saturday, October 15, 1887. Scarborough "was facing a mirror with his back to the door when he saw Williams come in. Williams drawed [sic] his gun. But George whirled and drew his gun and killed him."[19]

A newspaper reported:

Geo Scarborough, sheriff of Jones County, and his brother shot A.J. Williams, in a saloon, the Road to Ruin. The trouble grew out of an old grudge in which Williams was indicted for trying to bribe an officer, and George Scarborough was the principal witness. Williams went to [the] Road to Ruin saloon, where Scarborough was writing a letter, with a double barrel shotgun in his hand, when Geo. Scarborough and his brother both began shooting Williams with revolvers, George shooting three times and his brother two. Williams lived only about fifteen minutes.[20]

A different account said Scarborough "wheeled and emptied his pistol at Williams before Williams could fire at all."[21]

Still another version said, "Scarborough was in the 'Road to Ruin' saloon, writing a letter, when Williams came in with a cocked double barrel shotgun and threw it down on Scarborough. Scarborough's brother, who was near, rose and drew his revolver, which attracted Williams' attention, and George Scarborough rose and grabbed Williams and he and his brother shot him five times, killing him instantly."[22]

The Williams family was outraged by the death. Reported the *Luling Signal*, "Mr. A.C. Williams was in the city last week trying to get the full particulars of the killing of his brother A.J. Williams at Haskell a few days ago, by Sheriff Scarborough of Jones County. He stated that if his brother had been killed in honorable combat it was all right, but if he had been murdered, he proposed to do a brother's part by him."[23]

It was not a hollow threat. Dick Williams was a tough man from a tough town. When he rode north to look into the death, it's unknown how many men he took with him, but any one of his family would have been a match for George Scarborough. Nothing seems to have come of it, however, and there's not a hint of what he learned or did after visiting Haskell.[24]

The shooting of A.J. Williams in Draper and Baldwin's Road to Ruin Saloon led to another killing two days later. "W.M. Carter, while drinking, took up the quarrel with J.L. Baldwin, charging Baldwin with unfairness and mistreatment of Williams. This led to another shooting in which Carter was killed."[25]

Today, the shooting of Carter is better known than the shooting of Williams, but it points out the fact the Road to Ruin was a hazardous joint. Of four fatal shootings in Haskell during the frontier period, three happened inside the saloon and the other just outside.

At any rate, related by blood and marriage—and explaining their relationships as "cousins" in what is today an outmoded way—the outlaws in the extended Williams family suffered a bad twelve-year period from 1878–1889.[26] Of those allied with the family, first to go was Brown Bowen, hanged; Sebe Barnes, shot to death; John Wesley Hardin, sent to prison; and Bill Longley, hanged on October 11, 1878. Ben Lemond died in April 1883. Clay Allison died in an accident July 3, 1887. A.J. Williams was shot to death on October 15 of that year. Kep Queen was killed by a posse near Claremore, Oklahoma, on November 16, 1888. John Barber was killed in December 1889. It is apparent there was an "outlaw gene," or at least an outlaw tradition within the family, which was to continue with one more outlaw, the most fascinating and mysterious of all. One day, the *El Paso Herald* would call her "The Goddess of War."

2
LOST CREEK
1889–1894

> "[I]t was probably half Steve's fault, half [Helen's]
> fault, and half Miss Mary's fault."[1]

Established soon after the Civil War, Fredonia, Texas, was set between the San Saba River to the north and the Llano River to the south. Among the first settlers was the Michael Jennings family.[2] Michael, a tall, red-haired man, was born in 1840 in Westport, Ireland. At seventeen, he had moved to Scotland to learn stonemasonry, and when 27, he returned to Westport and married twenty-five-year-old Bridget Kearney. The couple returned to Scotland, where a son James was born in November 1867.

After the O'Jenningses emigrated to the United States, they settled in Jerseyville, Illinois, north of St. Louis. A son, Stephen Kearney Jennings, was born there November 5, 1869, as well as two daughters named Mary Ann, one in 1870, the other in 1874.[3]

By the time of the 1870 census, Michael and Bridget Jennings were farming. At first, they did well, but economic conditions stagnated. Since Texas had once been an independent country, there were no huge tracts of federal land within its borders. To encourage settlement, the state instituted a program similar to the federal Homestead Act. The plan was widely advertised, and though the Jenningses were illiterate, they became inflamed with "Texas fever."

In 1876, Michael, Bridget, sons Jim and Steve, daughter Mary Ann, and Michael's brother Austin traveled to Round Rock, Texas, where they bought wagons, horses, and supplies. Michael had been granted 160 acres in San Saba County, with the stipulation he live on the land three years and make improvements. While the Jennings family waited for the tract to be surveyed, they set up camp near Lost Creek, a half mile north of Fredonia.

The camp was short of the actual acreage assigned, and when the surveyor told them they'd have to move, Michael misunderstood. He persuaded the surveyor to plat the land they were on, unintentionally settling for a smaller piece than he'd been granted, yet one including part of Lost Creek.[4] Michael scrawled his mark on the paperwork on December 8, 1877.[5] The land was in the extreme southwestern corner of San Saba County. Michael's brother obtained 80 acres nearby. Soon afterward and a mile north, a man was killed and scalped by Comanches.

At that time, Mason County's Hoo Doo War simmered around them. Some neighbors were refugees from a range war to the east on the Yegua, plus the little town of Lampasas had erupted into the bloody Horrell-Higgins Feud. Rustlers and outlaws were everywhere, leading to what started out as a vigilante action and devolved into the San Saba Mob. And, every full moon in the summer and fall might bring Comanche raiders.[6]

Even so, the family worked their land peaceably. At first, they lived in a soddy, a temporary house guaranteed to leak in a rain and drip dust when dry. Michael set himself and his son James to building a house and stone fences to enclose their fields. The project took years, and when complete, they had the largest, finest house for miles. With a well enclosed as part of the structure, the structure was one of few to have indoor water. Their third son, Michael Joseph Jennings–"Little Mike" or "M.J."–was born here in August 1880.

The Jenningses were self-reliant and hardworking. Michael had an excellent voice and may have played the violin. They enjoyed dances, barn-raisings, and other activities with their neighbors, but they were also rigid Catholics who believed Protestants were doomed to hellfire. Since activities of a pioneer settlement involved funerals and marriages, it's possible the Jennings family was excluded from some occasions.

Today, we like to believe the pioneers were generous, friendly, and cooperative, but the opposite was often true. Isolation on the frontier could lead to unremitting suspicion. It could take years for a settler to be accepted by an established community. Sometimes, frontier society turned on its own in times of trouble. This was the dark side of living as a pioneer. No one wanted to get involved in problems that didn't concern them. While many settlers were successful, others were shattered by the experience. The isolation, fear, and hard work, plus a lack of support could break those less hardy.

An example of this negative frontier experience—which later affected the Jenningses indirectly—occurred fifteen miles north of their homestead, near Richland Springs. Here, the family of Daniel and Margaret Harkey had settled, but in 1869 Margaret died. Daniel died three weeks later, leaving thirteen children orphaned.

Sarah Harkey Hall recalled, "Aunt Nancy Harkey came to where we were [....] 'If [we] only lived near you we could help [...] but we live so far it will be impossible for me to come [....] This is the most heartrending scene I've ever witnessed. Thirteen children inside of one month left orphaned [...] the youngest not a month old, the oldest seventeen ...."[7] Having said that, the aunt departed.

The family of orphans, led by the oldest, Joe, and twelve-year-old Sarah, did okay at first, but in the summer, the vicinity was raided by Comanches. The Harkeys escaped, but they lost their livestock. "Joe, finding it difficult to feed and clothe us by his day labor, enlisted as a Texas Ranger [....] How it grieved me to see him saddle Old Charley, our family horse, and take the last blanket our dear mother's hands had woven, and leave us [....]"[8]

Somehow, the Harkeys survived, but in her heart, Sarah was bitter. "There were others near us that could have helped us, that showed no help."[9]

This dark side of the frontier would affect the Jennings family too. Isolated by religion and intolerance, the Jennings children had hardheaded, surly attitudes. Jim, the eldest, had almost no childhood; he farmed and had cattle. Mary Ann, who never married, grew so mean-spirited, acid-tongued, and tough that grown men feared her, but she ruled the homestead. Steve Jennings, who worked at ranching and cowboying, became very hard, but Mike Jr., who worked at the stockyards in Fort Worth, grew to be "pure Irish mean."[10]

By 1884, the hardworking Jenningses had fields outlined with stone fences. They had cattle, hogs, and horses. Though they tended to be aloof, they were among the leaders of the community. Two signs point to their prosperity: Austin Jennings married Aba Pratt on October 11, 1885, and on May 31, 1887, Jim, Michael, and Bridget became American citizens. The family flourished while their neighbors suffered; a likely explanation for this is their stone fences. The Jenningses did not make claims for stolen stock, while neighbors' losses mounted.[11] Violence surrounded them on every side. It was so dangerous a neighbor, Ed

Hartman, was murdered when "he went out of the house after sundown for the first time in nine years." [12]

New settlers including the Ellison and Williams families moved to Fredonia in 1886 to farm. One of these, Bill Williams, was a hardworking man, but he lacked patience. He would nearly kill himself planting and haying, but when it came to long-term projects, he couldn't follow through. A great pioneer, he was doomed to leave what he had started to others, beginning with his childhood in Arkansas and ending in California sixty years later.

Born November 21, 1838, in Conway County, Arkansas, Bill (W.C. or William Crawford) was one of four sons of Aaron and Betsy Williams. His father, reportedly the first cousin of Abraham Lincoln through Lincoln's mother, Nancy Hanks,[13] moved to Texas on the advice of kinsmen. He first settled near Brownsboro, in Caldwell County. His son, Bill Williams was seven years old at the time.

During the Civil War, Bill and his brothers fought for the Confederacy.[14] When their neighbors got into the cattle business after the fighting, the Williams clan benefited. The Chisholm Trail passed near their farm. Small ranchers like them contributed cattle to be driven north. Some outfits chipped in cowboys to look after their interests, but there is no evidence any of the Williams boys went "up the trail."

The cattle drives had begun after the Civil War, and by 1872, the Ellison and Dewees Cattle Company was driving hundreds of thousands north. There was little incentive for owning land. The range was open and unfenced. Some Ellisons owned tracts of a few hundred acres, mostly at river crossings like the San Marcos River ford at Martindale, but most of the family spent money on homes and luxuries.

The Williams family was different. Controlling land was important, for they were farmers, not drovers. Their farms at Brownsboro were not especially fertile, but for twenty years they struggled. Then on January 26, 1865, the Ellison and Williams families were joined when twenty-six-year-old Bill Williams married seventeen-year-old Ann Eliza Ellison. Ann Eliza was the daughter of Catherine and Nathaniel Powers Ellison, uncle and namesake of the famous drover N.P. Ellison. About two years later, Aaron Williams and three of his sons moved to Williamson County. Their kinsmen, the Akes, Lemonds, and Berrys, had found an opportunity along Berry Creek, northeast of Georgetown. Here, on November 1, 1872, Bill and Ann Eliza Williams had a baby whom they named Helen Elizabeth.

In the mid-1880s, however, the Ellisons realized they should have invested in land rather than cattle, as barbed wire was closing the free range. The cattle business had changed; railroads were stretching into Texas. There was no need for cattle drives, and the Ellisons were frozen out of using land and access they had enjoyed for a generation. Ann Eliza Williams' father gathered his resources to buy a farm at Adullam, southwest of Fredonia. Bill Williams followed his father-in-law's lead and bought land near Blue Stretch, east of Fredonia. By 1885, forty-six-year-old Bill Williams and his thirty-seven-year-old wife Ann Eliza—together with their children Lon, Helen, Sally, Kate, and Lewis—were settled in a new home on the northern border of Mason County.

A half-mile north of Bill Williams' farm lay the Jennings homestead. The never-telling waters of Lost Creek divided the two farms; today, Highway 71 divides the properties, but more than that divided the settlers. The Jennings family had arrived during hard times. They had stone fences around their land and their hearts; they had survived hard times by being harder. Their farm was thriving. The family worked, slept, and bled with uncommon self-reliance, and they had learned to mind their own business. Violence was a fact of life. No one was safe, and the Jennings family, in the middle of the violence, suffered nothing. Because of this, there is no doubt they were connected to the San Saba Mob. Ranchers to the north and west suffered losses; hangings and shootings were common all around; mob members met on moonlit nights in nearby Voca, yet the Jennings family milked cows, planted cotton, minded hogs, and kept their mouths shut. They had learned something on the frontier: silence and perseverance were the best ways to survive violent times.

For gregarious newcomers like the Ellisons and Williamses, the Jennings family probably seemed clannish with little time for frivolity, yet their farmstead had indoor water, a shingled roof with decorative lightning rods and flower beds that went beyond practicality. The family was there to stay, and as testimony to their hard work, the Jennings house survives to this day. The well-to-do Williams family lived in a board-and-batten farmhouse, which is long gone.

The Williams and Ellison families, however, were confident in their heritage as Texas pioneers. The newcomers must have seemed as alien to the Jenningses as the Jennings family seemed to them. In the Jennings clan's view, the Ellisons and Williamses were untested newcomers who bought what they hadn't carved from the wilderness. They talked big and lived easily, especially after Nathaniel Powers Ellison and his wife died, and the Ellison land, money, and home passed to Ann Eliza Williams. As a result, the Williams family tripled its lands and value in a year and a half.

Lost Creek dwindled to a trickle in the drought of 1886 but continued to flow. It was here the younger generation reached out. It probably started as kids throwing rocks at each other over the creek. Before long they were sharing swimming holes. The Jennings boys were too young to go "up the trail," but they dreamed of being cowboys. Jim, Steve, and Little Mike acquired horses and the equipage of cowboys. They whooped and hollered, and it only requires a bit of imagination to visualize the day a dashing Steve Jennings galloped down to Lost Creek and looked across at a blossoming Helen Williams. Their acquaintance turned to passionate teenage love. There may have been sex too, but even Mike and Bridget Jennings had been unmarried lovers once.

At this time, Steve Jennings was a young cowboy with black hair and pale eyes. "Steve's eyes were blue, I believe, but they maybe was gray. I remember you could see his pupils all the way across the yard."[15]

Steve was close to six feet tall and barrel-chested. Like all cowboys, he swaggered rather than walked. He was not well educated, but he was not stupid. A good-looking man, he had a streak of vanity. He liked good horses almost as much as he liked being seen on them. When he bought clothes, he took care of them. He did not go to town in muddy boots or sweaty shirts like the farmers did.

While he was full of promise, however, he was a dreamer, easily discouraged. He was hypercritical of others but blind to his own faults. He was penny-pinching, yet spent beyond his means. He was also profane. "I remember how he could cuss! He didn't say, 'Goddamn' the way the oldtimers did when they was mad [...] He could make it sound dirty by saying "God" and then stutterin' for seconds before he would say, 'DAMN!' Somehow the way he did it, it sounded worser [sic] than anyone else I knew."[16]

If Steve's life had turned out with half his promise and a third of his dreams intact, he would have been a middling rancher with no more debt and no less cattle than anyone else. There were many like him, born too late to be drovers, but in time to homestead and start a herd of their own. The young men of the 1880s were the old men of the 1940s; though they hadn't done it themselves, they were close enough to have heard it. Because of this, this generation passed on a heritage wistfully regarded through rosy lenses today. Steve Jennings could have been one of those calloused, hard-bitten, crusty oldtimers beloved by historical interviewers, if only he hadn't been crusty, calloused, and hard-bitten as a youth.

Helen Williams, though a teenager, was already turning men's heads. A beautiful young woman, she had dark blonde hair, blue eyes, and a personable character. She could make strangers feel like friends. Raised in a loving home, she was sweetnatured. She was an excellent horsewoman and could shoot well. Educated, she had good handwriting and could cipher. She loved music. At this time she was about five feet four inches tall and weighed around a hundred and ten pounds, a teenager swelling into a fashionable 1890s vamp.

A farm girl with potential, Helen probably would have matured into a grand old dame of Mason County society, but she had flaws. Spoiled by her parents, she was impressionable and sentimental. She was, it must be admitted, an incorrigible flirt, and she became an alcoholic later in life. Like all teenagers, she demonstrated the certitude of immaturity, and sadly, she never developed beyond that. And she liked sex, not a character flaw today, but questionable a hundred years ago.

Worse matches than that of Steve Jennings and Helen Williams were made at the time, and some worked out. The Jenningses were reluctant at first, but the Williamses seemed like a good family. In the end, the Jennings clan put their skepticism aside. For their part, the Williams and Ellison families were interested in the prosperity of the Jennings farm. Steve, they must have thought, might inherit a good stake someday. While both families embraced the idea of marriage, however, there are hints neither set of parents had any choice in the matter. Steve and Helen were on their way to a relationship that needed to be legitimized by marriage.

The stumbling block to the union was religion. The Williamses were Protestants; the Jennings family was Catholic, and they were adamant no child could be born without the blessing of the Catholic church. The Williams family swallowed its pride, and sometime in 1888 or early 1889, Helen Williams became a Catholic. She and Steve became engaged.

Despite this forthcoming happy occasion, violence still raged nearby. On February 16, 1889, two men, Charles Smith and Asa Brown, were hanged by vigilantes a mile from the Jennings homestead. The governor offered a $500 reward.[17]

A month later, on March 13, 1889, nineteen-year-old Steve Jennings and sixteen-and-a-half-year-old Helen Williams obtained a marriage license in Mason. According to family tradition, Father Petrus McMahon married them at the Jennings farm.[18] Bill Williams proudly recorded in his bible, "Stephen Jennings & Helen Williams was [sic] married March the 21st, 1889." The newlyweds filed for a homestead,[19] but strangely, it was for 80 acres, not the 160 allowed married couples.

Not much is known of their married life. As anyone in Texas can tell you, it's hard to make a living off eighty acres. Helen's family had done their pioneering forty years before, and she was unprepared for the hardships of living in a soddy far from friends and family. Every day was an adventure; every day was numbingly the same. There was too much to do; there was nothing to do. Steve got work on a ranch forty miles away; Helen, living alone, became desperate. Her parents allowed her a chance to grow; the Jenningses meddled without shame, especially Steve's harpy sister, Mary Ann.

Early on, Helen got pregnant. The harshness of her life wore on her in untold ways, and the baby did not live. Bill Williams recorded its passing in his bible, "Virgin Mary was borned [sic] February the 11, 1890. [L]ived only three hours, when the blessed little one left this world to dwell with angels. Thursday Feb the 13, 1890."[20] The baby's grave is marked by crinum bulbs that put out a bit of growth in the spring but never have flowers. It's unknown if Helen planted the bulbs; a similar stand of crinums is near the Jennings homestead near Fredonia.

For a seventeen-year-old girl, the baby's death, her own harsh life, and her disillusionment may have been too much. She may have complained. Raised to survive hard times, Steve may have demanded better of her, and his overbearance seemed harsh. The romance was over. Helen may have petitioned her parents for relief, but neither they nor Steve's gave her much sympathy.

Something had to give; but, unfortunately, it was Helen's family. Her brother Lon, a loving support during her childhood, moved his family to Mayhill in James Canyon, part of the Peñasco River country of southeastern New Mexico. The date for this move is obscure, but appears to have been between 1890 and 1892.

Meanwhile, Helen's parents were interested in irrigation possibilities and land speculation along the Gila River in southern Arizona and in a farming community called Cartwright, a few miles northwest of Phoenix. Bill Williams and his wife moved to Arizona in mid-1893 and were unable to help Helen further.

It was about this time Helen became pregnant again; this time she delivered a healthy baby girl. Bill Williams recorded her birth, "Laura Blanche Jennings borned [sic] March 8, 1891."[21] Laura's birth was one of few bright occasions for Helen. Marriage with Steve was a disaster. The problem was not poverty or immaturity. There was also abuse, though of what sort is unknown. Helen—trapped spiritually by a church that demanded her submission, by in-laws who didn't understand her, by a family ever more distant—had no recourse.

Certainly, Steve abused her. He persecuted her spiritually, verbally, and emotionally. He mistreated her, stifled her tears, and deprived her; he may have physically abused her too. No one alive today will speak of the abuse, but it's obvious something awful was happening between Steve and Helen Jennings out there in the thorny hills of Texas. It's hard to imagine how that kind of situation could be treated with indifference, but there was no one around to hear this lonely wife's complaints. In the Old West, "domestic violence was draped in a veil of silence, serving to protect abusers from exposure to the community."[22]

Because of this, Helen had no choices. To be fair, there are rumors she brought some of it on herself. Old-timers recall stories she was flirtatious as her marriage fell apart. Was it revenge? Was it her natural character coming out? If the rumors are true, Helen abused Steve her own way. In this case, it's not important who started the abuse; it simply doomed the marriage.

Despite the conflict, Helen became pregnant a third time. Again, something went wrong. Remembered in family tradition as Brian, the baby had difficulty breathing, and Helen begged Steve to get a doctor. All versions of the story agree Steve considered the cost of a doctor before declaring the baby would get better.

Bill Williams wrote, "In remembrance of one that was borned [sic] July the 1, 1893, lived only 24 hours when the blessed little one left this world to dwell with the happy ones which has [sic] gone before. He rest [sic] in the city of the dead at Union Band. He was baptised [sic] in the name of Jesus Crist [sic] which [sic] has cleansed him from all sin. Buried July the 3, 1893."[23]

This baby, buried to the right of his sister Virgin Mary, would get an expensive headstone. Was it Steve's way of making amends ... or Helen's way of making him pay? Because the birth and death dates are wrong, the stone may have been an afterthought.

The death of Brian Jennings, however, was pretty much the end of the marriage. Steve and Helen were in open warfare, and little Fredonia, Texas, was rent apart in controversy. The Williams family was out in Arizona, but there were in-laws and friends to take their side. The Jennings family was among the most respected in the area, and they had allies too. Though most people had a tendency to mind their own business, there were fights and shunning—social death in a little community. The Jenningses would not give an inch: the fault was Helen's they declared. Without her family's support, she must have agonized over what to do.

By this time, of course, Helen was a different person than she had been four years earlier. No longer a wide-eyed bride, Helen was an experienced frontier wife, and her experience hadn't come from having babies—any teenager could do that. No, her experience didn't come from getting what she expected or needed. It came from losing babies she really wanted, from rejecting a spouse she once desired, from surrendering innocence she ached to keep. Helen had given up too much, and she must have decided to get it back. It was time to strike out on her own.

Divorce was not out of the question.[24] Without her family to advise her, there was little she could do, and she filed against Steve Jennings in Mason,

Texas, in March 1894. Her lawyer was probably J.T. Stapleton, the only attorney in Fredonia.[25] The case was continued until the fall term of the court, where, on October 1, 1894, a motion was filed, "Now comes the plaintiff in this case and moves the court to dismiss the same."[26]

The papers for the case are mysteriously missing, but they could go a long way toward explaining what Helen was thinking. By abandoning her suit, she gave Steve an opening. Even more important, did she herself appear in court, or by attorney only? This is crucial, but there's not a hint in the records. Whatever happened next must have been horrible, and soon afterward, Helen took her daughter Laura and rode away. "She came one night and borrowed a horse from my family, [the Millers,]" a rancher said years later, "but they never got it back."[27]

Helen believed her brother's family was on the upper Peñasco River northwest of Eddy, New Mexico,[28] but they were actually in Cartwright, Arizona.[29] Various other kinsmen were in Eddy County though. Surely these relatives would shelter her until she could get to Arizona. An obvious question is why didn't she head east to Georgetown, Texas, to the safety of her grandfather's home? It's possible she did just that, then caught a train west. With a young daughter to worry about, it seems likely, but one interviewee[30] stated she arrived in Eddy by horse, and if true, Helen undertook an epic ride four hundred miles across West Texas in the cold and wind of early winter to reach the safety of her family in New Mexico.[31] It was the act of a desperate woman.

Whatever really happened, the day Helen rode away with her three-year-old daughter Laura on the saddle in front of her, the Jennings family lost its soul. In that tiny town, neighbors blamed the Jenningses for the failure of the marriage. In Helen and Laura's place was left rumor, innuendo, and gossip from afar, yet it was these that were to become the legends of Fredonia.[32] Helen Jennings, this beautiful and remarkable young woman, had touched their hearts, tried to bring a clannish family out of its shell, and raised everyone's passions to a fever pitch, yet with her final, angry departure, she created a hole in the Jennings family that has not healed to this day. So it was that when she rode to New Mexico on a borrowed horse, she was gone forever but could never be forgotten.

PART TWO
The Good Cowboy & The Beautiful Woman

"[T]o show you what [New Mexico] was like they
told a story about a tough guy who got killed
there, and as soon as he got to hell, he wired back
for his overcoat."

—Teddy Blue

3
MARTIN MROSE
1856–1892

"[N]early all the oldtime men of his day are gone
out over the narrow dim trail, and those living
have got a lot of dead horses buried in some place,
having been rode to death, just a few jumps ahed
[sic] of the law."[1]

As Helen Jennings and her three-year-old daughter traveled toward New Mexico, it must have seemed a good move. The Territory of New Mexico was booming. The desert was being turned into productive farmland; ranches were enormous; talented men were on the verge of greatness. One of these was an extraordinary cowboy named Martin Mrose.

"I met a real cowpuncher," an old man recalled one day. "[H]is name was Martin Marose[2] [sic]—a Pole who was raised down around Georgetown, Texas. He must have weighed around a hundred and [eighty] pounds and was pretty well put together. A crackerjack of a cowpuncher; could ride and rope like he'd been doing it a hundred years." [3]

Another cowboy said, "[I] think he was from [the] old country. Bohemian, I think, big fellow, light complected [sic], light haired, blue eyed. One of my best friends, great friend of Dave Kemp, the sheriff at Eddy. Had a little bunch of cattle. Bought and turned herds loose, more of a horse man than anything else. [...] Very likable fellow."[4]

Still another said, "He was a good cowman and a good cowboy and everybody liked him."[5]

"He was a full-blooded Swede."[6]

"My grandfather called him El Aleman, [the German.]" [7]

"Martin [Mrose], a Bulgarian cowpuncher [...] was placed in charge...." [8]

"Martin Mrose was a Swede. ... [I] knew of him for years and [...] we would meet here on the [Halagueño Ranch.] He worked for them and then started an outfit of his own." [9]

"I knew Martin Mrose. He used to have horses and cattle down there below Mescalera Valley. [...] He was a dar[n] good fellow. Mrose's ranch was right up above Seven Rivers on the east side." [10]

"I remember Martin Mrose well. [...] He impressed me as a [...] Swede. [...] He was a big, light-complected [sic] fellow. [...] He was in the cattle business. He had got quite a bunch of cattle there on the river [near Eddy.]" [11]

For years historians have assumed Martin Mrose was a Pole from St. Hedwig, Texas. There are reasons for this misconception. First, it's near San Antonio, and there is a claim he was from the vicinity. Dee Harkey wrote, "Martin Morose [sic] was a Polander. His people came in a bunch with other Polanders to Karnes County, Texas, right after the Civil War, and settled on little farms together. It was known as Polander settlement."[12] Another time Harkey said, "Martin M'rose [sic] was [...] raised close to Helener, [sic] where there was a Polander settlement."[13]

Another reason St. Hedwig is suggested is there was a family there with a surname similar to Mrose's. Though this family appears to have used "Maros" most often, there are uses of the spelling M-r-o-s and M-r-o-z, both often confused for the spelling of Martin Mrose's last name.

The Maros family is documented in church records, censuses, and county records, and it is clear Martin Mrose was not one of the sons of Valentin and Barbara Maros,[14] but this opens up a new question: If not St. Hedwig, where was he born?[15] There is an outside chance he was born and raised in San Antonio, but the St. Michael's parish, predominately of Poles and Irish, did not maintain consistent record keeping until 1866. The same is true for the Poles of Bandera, Texas, so if his origin was either of these two settlements, it would be hard to prove.

Another possibility exists, however.[16] A Wendish couple, Matthaus and Hannah Mrosko (also spelled Mroske) arrived in Galveston, Texas, in 1854 from Durrbach, Prussia. Though they came from the same area of central Europe, the Wends differed from the Poles, for they were Protestant, which in their case meant Lutheran.[17] The Wends were a diverse group, speaking German as well as Polish and Wendish.[18] In Texas, the suffixes -ko, -ka, -ky, or -ke were routinely dropped from Wendish, Polish, and Czech names. In this case, the name Mros, meaning "frost," resulted.

The Mroskos bought land in Lee County. They were active in the church at Serbin, and they are buried in the Wendish cemetery there. Old-timers recognize the name Mrosko, the same as the Polish recall Maros at St. Hedwig. Like the St. Hedwig family, the Mrosko family is well documented in Serbin birth records,[19] and it is doubtful Martin Mrose was from this family, but the large population of Wends provides the most intriguing lead.

A much bigger group than the Poles, the Wends were a determined lot. Between fifteen hundred and two thousand Wends settled in the Serbin area alone; the largest group, five hundred strong, landed in December 1854 at Galveston, Texas. By ox cart and on foot, the Wends traveled 200 miles to Serbin where they established a school, a church, and a cemetery.

Unfortunately, the Wends had to learn the limited farming methods popular in Texas at the time. Cotton was the cash crop; corn was food, made into "corn dodgers." Wheat and barley, staples of Central Europeans, did poorly in the heat and soils of that part of Texas, while potatoes, turnips, cabbage, and other produce familiar to the immigrants were "buggy" in Texas. It took time to learn American methods and acquire proper tools.

One agricultural method the Wends were familiar with worked well, however, and that was the raising of swine and geese. The vast agricultural pipeline that supports modern swiniculture and the poultry industry did not exist then, but hogs and geese could be grazed in a semi-wild state in the oak forests near Serbin, feeding on mast and wild plants until harvest. The Wends proved adept at this, and before long every farm had geese and pigs aplenty. Smokehouses were everywhere, and the Wends found a ready market among their American neighbors.

As the Wends struggled to establish themselves, a disaster struck in the form of drought. One of the most terrible in Texas history, it started in the early summer of 1855 and lasted 14 months.[20] Sometime during this period, specifically between January 3 and April 23, 1856, Martin Mrose was born.

For the struggling Wendish colony, the stresses facing it were great. Racially different from nearby German immigrants, the Wends began to divide, some attending a German church because they spoke German, others maintaining a Wendish church at Serbin. Another problem facing the colony was not all Wends had settled in Serbin proper. While Serbin remained the cultural heart of the Wendish enclave, other Wends branched out to the north. One Wendish settlement was Paige. Other settlements associated with the Wends were Fedor, Dime Box (and Old Dime Box), Warda, Loebau, and Giddings.

Unfortunately, just as these settlements were taking off, the Civil War intervened. On top of that, drought returned from 1862–1865. The economy stagnated with the loss of trade, a shortage of goods, and a lack of labor. Not trusted by their Confederate neighbors, isolated from their kin back in Germany, beset with shortages of seeds, livestock, and manufactured goods, the colony teetered on the edge. Martin Mrose's childhood must have been rough. From an early age he was assigned chores, but at the same time, he was educated like all Wendish children were, for schooling was an important part of their culture.

By 1879,[21] twenty-three-year-old Martin Mrose had made his way to Live Oak County. Conditions must have been harsh. Dee Harkey said, "Martin Morose and Elic Tulic [...] wanted to learn to ride wild horses and be cow punchers. They were [... directed] to Malon McCowan,[22] who had plenty of young horses. I was breaking horses at McCowan's when they came. They made McCowan understand what they wanted. He put them at his horse camp, where his corrals were, gave them a little grub, ropes, and hackamores, and asked me to teach them to work and ride horses. McCowan did not pay them anything for their time. This horse camp was close to where I was staying with Mr. Stapleton, my school teacher.[23] I spent all my spare time breaking horses for Mr. McCowan. I was with these two boys almost every day for three or four months."

Another time, Harkey said, "McCowan [...] wanted to put M'rose, a big [h]usky fellow, with me to learn the cow and horse business. Martin stayed with me about three years and [...] McCowan wouldn't pay him anything. After he had been with me about three years he learned to talk English and was a big, rough Polander." [24]

Although there are many inconsistencies in Harkey's memories of Martin

Mrose, one of the oddest is Mrose's age. In 1880, Harkey was 14. Mrose was 25, and he would have been much bigger than Harkey. Harkey should have been awed, but in his reminiscences, he speaks of Mrose as a peer. Harkey was also changeable whether he knew Mrose three months or three years, but in light of later events, three months is likely.

A bigger discrepancy, however, is who taught whom to ride. Martin Mrose is known to have been in Live Oak County, Texas, in 1880. Despite a later claim by Milton Phillips in 1895 that Mrose came to New Mexico in 1884, there are documents suggesting he was there as early as 1880. Mrose was hired by the Eddy-Bissell Cattle Company as a "top hand," an ostler, a man good with horses.[25] Numerous accounts credit him with being an outstanding cowboy, a bronc-buster, and an excellent horseman. One lifelong cowboy said that he "could ride and rope like he'd been doing it a hundred years."[26] Another said, "Martin seemed to display more 'horse sense' than the average cowhand. He would take a green bronc and cut and rope cattle and the colt would do most anything a seasoned cowhorse would do for the average cowboy."[27]

If Mrose learned to ride in 1879, it is unlikely a year later experienced cowboys would mistake him for a great horseman. At the same time, Harkey had little experience with horses. His sister, Sarah Harkey Hall, in her account of the Harkey's childhoods is quite clear only her oldest brother, Joe, had a horse, and he was rarely home.[28] Where Dee Harkey would have gotten experience breaking horses is a mystery, but it suggests Mrose taught Harkey to ride, not vice versa.

Mahlon McCowan is known to have raised hundreds of horses at a time. He surely did not do this alone, especially since he lived so close to the *bandidos* of Mexico. He would have had a dozen or more cowboys working for him. It's unlikely he needed a fourteen-year-old kid to break horses. Martin Mrose was probably one of the experienced ranch hands working for McCowan, and a young Dee Harkey worked for free to gain experience.

Even so, Harkey continues his narrative, "One morning, Martin Morose asked me if he could ride Red Bird. I told him I didn't care, so he rode him off, and I never saw him again until I came to Eddy in 1890."[29] Horse stealing in those days was a serious offense, but Harkey treats it lightly.[30]

This recollection is also wrong. If Mrose worked for Mahlon McCowan in 1879, he did not run far with this allegedly stolen horse, for the 1880 census recorded him only four miles away working for John and Bennett Sparks. That would suggest the horse wasn't stolen after all.

It is important here to remember there was no term for what we know today as "cowboy." There were "stock men," "cattle tenders," and "herders." Specialized positions were "drovers" and "cow punchers." The heyday of the great cattle drives was on, and there was status attached to working with cows. If one couldn't own cattle, one could work with them. There was adventure and money working in this career, but few of the big outfits would hire someone "off the street," as it were. There was one thing lacking: a horse and tack.

After the Civil War, a cowboy might need staking, but by the 1880s, cowboying had become a profession that required equipment. A horse, saddle, bridle, hackamores, hobbles, lassos, slicker, and saddle blanket were prerequisites. A gun of some sort—and percussion pistols were used as well as Sharps rifles—was becoming *de rigeur*, but boots hadn't assumed the features we accept as "cowboy" yet. A Mexican sombrero was as common as a Stetson, a poncho as common as a duster, woolly and shotgun chaps were as common up north as *armitas*, chinks, and batwings down south. It was a considerable investment to achieve a rig that, depending on the value of the mount, might exceed three hundred dollars. Martin Mrose, whether he rode off with Red Bird illegally or not, had such a rig. It shows considerable determination.

From 1880 to 1883, there is not much mention of Martin Mrose, but, undoubtedly, he was using the skills of a cowboy: roping, branding, riding. He cared for horses in all kinds of weather. He worked his way through Texas heat and blue northers. He met drought and flood, snake and wolf, tornado and dust devil. The life of a cowboy, though romanticized now, was a life of unending toil, and Mrose worked on the hardest ranges in America, the Brush Country of South Texas and the desert of New Mexico. It's likely he went on a drive or two before 1880. If so, he trailed cows a thousand miles or more through dust, wind, thirst, and privations of every sort. He met the encroachment of mesquite thickets, and he saw the start of fencing of private range, water, and crossings. There was much to be learned, and it's apparent from the accounts of the old timers that not many young cowboys made it a career.

What today are demonstration skills—bulldogging, roping, and bronc riding—were day-to-day drudgery for a cowboy then. All in a day's work were nursing sick cattle, mending harness, and delivering breached calves. Most cowboys could not only rope a longhorn by its horns, but by its back heels. A cowboy could overpower the animal, light a fire, heat a branding iron, brand, castrate, and notch the longhorn's ears before riding on to other chores. Many cowboys personalized their gear with conchos and decorative leather, some wove horsehair lariats and quirts, and others made horn accessories, but as a whole, cowboys had little leisure time. For the most part, what they had, they used up. Saddles were worn out, boots discarded, ropes got busted. Not much remains of equipment used during a career in the saddle, and that's true of the men themselves too.

For many, the end of roundup season meant unemployment. Sweeping a saloon, cutting hay, or drifting around was the norm. For the lucky ones, there was a job in the big outfits, but off-season work was as likely to be digging irrigation ditches as tending cattle. With the beginnings of fencing, a cowboy might spend weeks digging postholes and stretching wire.

Somewhere between can't and couldn't,[31]a cowboy maintained friendships, learned to shoot, visit the whores, or drink whiskey. Such a life reduced a man to the elementals. It taught loyalty to those who are good to you, stoicism in the face of privation, patience in the face of adversity. Only the best survived such a life, and it's clear Martin Mrose not only survived, but thrived. In light of his later career, he was not only competent, he was great in the saddle. He was an excellent roper. He learned to shoot well. He mastered ranching as well as cowboying, and before long, he was considered a "top hand."

Mrose learned in harsh south Texas where to be a "brush-popper" was difficult. Teddy Blue said, "The country south of San Antone is brush country, [...] mesquite and cactus and thorn and I don't know what else, but I know everything that grows has thorns on it except the willows, and some of them are an inch long."[32]

Another cowboy said of the brush poppers, "[T]he brush hand almost daily exerts as much skill and grit as any rodeo star [....] Nobody ever sees the brush popper in action. When he does his most daring and dangerous work he is out of sight down in a thicket. [...] No ditch digger ever exerted himself more or sweated more profusely than a brush hand in a thicket on a hot day."[33]

And somewhere in this brush country or on the sweaty cattle trails north to Kansas, the rancher and promoter C.B. Eddy recruited Mrose to work on the range in New Mexico and Colorado, "he being recommended as a good man to break horses for working cattle. [Mrose] came up on the train with [... a] party [... of cowboys] to Pecos and they were all put at work [...], Tom Fennessey in charge of the outfit, a trial herd which was sent to Colorado. Martin was a peaceable young [man] who could not talk plain English at this time."[34]

It was a wonderful opportunity, and for a young Wendish cowboy from Texas, it was a good time to move to New Mexico.[35]

4
THE VVNS
1881-1893

"The ranch [...was...] a natural feedlot at the center
of perhaps 60 square miles of lush mountain
grass...."[1]

Longhorns, crosses of English breeds from the East Coast and feral cattle from Mexico, were all over south Texas by the 1860s. Despite the animals' bony build, eastern markets demanded beef after the Civil War, and by 1868, cattle that were bought for a few dollars in Texas sold for twenty, thirty, or even more in Kansas. Between 1867 and 1887, cattle were trailed north to railheads in Kansas and to ranges in Colorado, Wyoming, Nebraska, the Dakotas, and Montana. It was a time we fondly remember as the Golden Age of the Cowboy.

While the buyers were interested in weight at the end markets, the cattle were usually bought at a set price per head. A savvy buyer would keep abreast of the latest prices per pound back East, then negotiate at the pens per animal. The sooner a herd got to Kansas, the longer the drovers had to negotiate. Low prices might be better later, and cattle grazed in a river bottom near the railhead might be more marketable after they fattened.[2]

For the drovers, the wait was unbearable. Months away from home while following a slow herd, and having subsisted on a diet of dust, fire-blackened beef, hard *tasso* jerky, cornbread, molasses, and spicy Texas beans, the cowboys were looking forward to baths, clean clothes, and an easy ride home. Trail bosses, caught between the desire to sell quickly and the option of better prices later, worried over a decision that could mean thousands of dollars, this in the day when a common cowboy made thirty to fifty dollars a month.

But there were troubles coming for the cattle drives. In every area through which herds passed, local cattle died. The problem was attributed to "Texas fever." Longhorns were not dying of the disease, and cattlemen noticed longhorns couldn't pass the disease on to local cattle if they had wintered in the north.

The cause of this was poorly understood then. It was a disease called *bovine piroplasmosis.*

> "Cattle first contracting the disease as calves do not become sick and develop an immunity that persists for as long as [it] remain[s] in their blood. [...] In contrast, animals first infected as adults often die. [...] However, the cattle fever tick can be killed by even moderately low temperatures and cannot survive the winter more than a few hundred miles north of the mouth of the Rio Grande. So Texas cattle wintered in the North were no longer dangerous to native cattle."[3]

There was talk of a safer, national cattle trail through Oklahoma, western Kansas and eastern Colorado to avoid the problem, but instead, the pioneering diversion of the Goodnight-Loving[4] Cattle Trail occurred. Starting in Concho County, Texas, the trail branched off the Western Cattle Trail and crossed the plains to Horsehead Crossing on the Pecos River. From there, the trail followed the river through eastern New Mexico and then to Colorado and points north.

Though the Pecos River had notoriously foul-tasting water and steep banks, it was fed by a number of tributaries in eastern New Mexico. The land here was short-grass prairie, perfect for ranching, but even with distinctively branded cattle, the trouble with herds on the vast plains was they invited rustling. The trick was to catch and brand a calf before it could be marked. One man recalled, "While rounding up the last herd in No Man's Land we found many cattle with their eyes sewed up and staples driven through their feet to prevent them following their stolen calves."[5] Killing the cows was an even more common procedure. "The Rustlers always figured [...] as long as they got the calf, it matters little who got the cow."[6]

Rustling was not a serious crime. According to New Mexico statutes, unlawful branding was only a fourth-degree felony; with so much money to be gained, some men began to steal. "Progressive" cowboys throwing "a wide loop" were not altogether condemned. It showed pluck to rustle and begin a herd of one's own.

A remarkable admission of rustling came from longtime cowboy, Fred S. Millard, who said, "I can count all the men on my fingers that never branded anything but what they knew was theirs and probably have a finger or two left...." As to why he gave up putting his own brand on other men's cattle, Millard explained, "I married in 1896 and since that time I have been straight."[7]

No fences, free-range cattle, quick money at the end of the trail all contributed to rustling. To protect their herds, cattlemen had to control vast ranges, trails, and water holes. Few locals had the resources, but outsiders did. English investors and New York bankers poured money into the cattle industry.

One of these was the Eddy-Bissell Cattle Company, run by two New Yorkers, C.B. (Charles Bishop)[8] and J.A. (John Arthur) Eddy.[9] Their father, John Eddy, had been in the leather business but had branched out into hops, cotton, and banking. His neighbors, also involved in these enterprises, were the Amos Bissell family; the two families were allied in their enterprises.[10]

The Eddy brothers grew up prosperous, well-dressed, and well-placed, yet they did something unusual: they went west and lived as cowboys. They must have been good at it too, for they didn't stand out as dudes in the cowtowns of Abilene and Ogallala. No one seems to know when they went West, but by 1878, they dressed the part and "walked the walk." They could ride, and did so over huge distances. They could socialize with cattle buyers and cowboys. They must have been in Wyoming, Nebraska, Kansas, and Texas, and they explored New Mexico and Colorado carefully.

In 1878 the firm of Amos Bissell & Sons and the Chemical Bank of New York[11] provided the Eddys with startup money, and the Eddy-Bissell Cattle Company was born. They would burn **VVN**, a brand registered on August 1, 1881.[12] Two years earlier, J.A. and C.B. Eddy had established the "High and Lonesome" ranch along Rye Slough at the northwest base of Black Mountain, 20 miles west of Cripple Creek, Colorado. "The ranch is [...] remote and isolated [....] The grass is up to a horse's belly in summer and early fall; but so is drifting snow in winter and early spring."[13] It also had access to government land.

Different than most of their competitors, the Eddys had a plan. The cattle business was not yet an industry; it produced cows in an erratic supply and quality. The Eddys' purpose with a New Mexico operation was to produce an annual "crop" of twos and threes: two- and three-year-old cattle strong enough to drive north, young enough to be "tender," and small enough to pack on weight as they were fattened for market. These New Mexican cattle were destined for two drives annually, one starting in late March after the first roundup, the other in May or early June.

"Roundups [...] continued until late fall. [M]any cowboys rode as much as 100 miles each day. [...A] cowboy in those days had to ride and ride straight up, sixteen hours a day."[14]

James F. Hinkle, a governor of New Mexico, said, "From 1885 and for about ten years thereafter it was just cattle, nothing more—only a fight to hold your own. The roundups started with the first green grass, usually in April, and continued until November and it was ride and ride hard all the time."[15]

The drives could take three months. At the end of the trail, nutritious alpine grasses were bursting from the moist ground. It was perfect for fattening cattle, and waiting for all this beef were the rich mining districts. "Colorado was one big mining camp. [...] And all the camps were 'short on meat and long on grass.'"[16]

Ranchers on the plains east of Denver could not drive cattle over the Front Range. Herds coming from the south, however, came up the Arkansas River to Cañon City and could reach South Park and the mining camps. Some of this route was the Goodnight Trail. The Eddy Diversion, a pioneering route through Trinchera Pass, which branched off the main trail to avoid tolls through the more westerly Raton Pass, was extensively used.

In June 1880, the Eddys set their plan in motion by buying cattle from Dodge City, Kansas. They paid premium prices at the "end" of a Texas drive and in competition with Eastern cattle buyers, and it was at this time the Eddys hired their best cowboys. Tom Fennessey joined the outfit there; another the Eddys employed was Martin Mrose, hired as an ostler for the horses. Fennessey and Mrose would remain friends the rest of their lives.

None of that first herd of Kansas cattle was used to stock VVN ranges in New Mexico; the cattle were fattened and slaughtered to create the market in Colorado that would fuel Eddy operations later. Though the Eddys hadn't planned on a New Mexico ranch in the beginning, they used the profits from their first drives to purchase herds in New Mexico. In 1881, the Eddys bought a large ranch headquartered at Clayton Wells in southeastern Lincoln County. They called their ranch Halagueño, [17]located east and northeast of Loving's Bend, where cattleman Oliver Loving and one of his cowboys had once beaten off an attacking force of Apaches. Loving died of his wounds; the incident was fictionalized in Larry McMurtry's novel, *Lonesome Dove.*

The Halagueño Ranch was established near the end of the Lincoln County War. Later, J.A. Eddy would tell his grandchildren Billy the Kid stayed at the ranch.[18] One old-timer recalled it "was nothing much more than a cattle ranch headquarters at that time […] set out on a forty mile square flat of sand and chinnery and stretched out as far as the eye could see."[19]

By 1882 or 1883, the Eddys were ready for the first drive of their New Mexican cattle, using their own cowboys. At first, such cattle were worth two or three dollars a head in startup costs, but brought $50-100 at the slaughterhouses in Colorado. A typical herd of twos and threes might have run about 1,500 animals driven by ten cowboys, a wrangler, a cook, and a trail boss. Deducting costs and losses, a herd at destination was worth about a hundred thousand dollars; the Eddys drove two herds a year for ten years. The profits were enormous.

As the money came in, the Eddys acquired another ranch at the foot of Black Mountain, the IM Ranch. This ranch was used for haying and year-round feeding operations. The IM would make three Eddy spreads, each with a different purpose. Halagueño, in New Mexico, supplied the "calf crop" and feeder cattle; Black Mountain controlled the summer grazing; the IM Ranch gave the Eddys a place to hold cattle until better prices prevailed.

There were problems at Black Mountain, however. "In 1883 rustling and changing of brands created hot feelings among the Black Mountain ranchers and those of the Arkansas River region. The murder of rancher Ed Watkins of Salida in that year touched off bad feeling[s] that existed for ten years throughout the area. The IM Ranch on Badger Creek near Black Mountain was the center of much of the trouble."[20] Watkins had changed brands on cattle, and all of his stock was hidden on the IM Ranch. Shortly thereafter, Watkins was hanged at Cañon City, Colorado.

"The final outcome of the investigations was that almost all of Watkins' cattle were discovered to bear brands which had been changed. No one ever tried to repossess the cattle which had been run off the Watkins place by the South Park ranchers."[21]

Black Mountain was also the scene of one of Colorado's most enduring legends. A grizzly bear named "Old Mose" had preyed on South Park cattle for years. Incredibly, there was a standing reward for this grizzly for thirty-five years, which suggests not one bear but several. Nevertheless, Old Mose successfully outwitted and killed hunters who came after it until 1904, when a bear hunter chased it for two months before finally bringing it to bay. When the bear was butchered, over one hundred bullets were found in its body.

Though both the Eddy brothers "went up the trail," their trust in the men they'd hired increased, and they came to rely on Martin Mrose as one of their best cowboys. The typical cowboy of the day "went up the trail" once or twice in his lifetime. Truly great cowboys like the Ellisons, Dewees, Goodnights, and others may have gone up the trail five to ten times. It seems clear Mrose went up the trail once—and sometimes twice—a year for twelve or thirteen years, and he did it not as a dusty cowboy trailing cows endlessly over the plains, but as trail boss, scouting ahead for water and grass, worrying about bedding the herd for the night, struggling to make time and getting the herd to Colorado safely. His stamina, horsemanship, leadership, and courage, therefore, were far above ordinary. Mrose may have been one of the best cowboys to ride the planet, and the Eddys trusted him with an uncommon amount of responsibility.

Both the state of Colorado and the territory of New Mexico conducted censuses in 1885. C.B. Eddy was recorded in Lincoln County, New Mexico, with a crew of cowboys including Tom Fennessey. It was June 1885, too late to start another herd north, so that means the year's second herd had already departed. Meanwhile, in Park County, Colorado, Martin Mrose was enumerated on June 1,1885.[22] The census suggests Mrose was the summer foreman. Obviously, he had gone up the trail with the season's first herd and was conducting business associated with the disposition of the cattle. A second herd was en route and possibly already in Colorado. What is significant about this is J.A. Eddy was not listed on the census.[23] Mrose was alone and in charge of the ranch.

Answering questions "with a 'Maybe yes' or a "Maybe no,'"[24] Mrose established his reputation during this period. One of the cowboys who worked for him was Nub Jones, a son of Heiskell and Barbara Jones of Seven Rivers.

[W]e were short-handed on [a] trail drive for the VVNs. Martin was trail boss, and not supposed to work. […] We were gone nine months. We celebrated my sixteenth birthday at Walsenburg, [Colorado.] We went to a saloon and I saw Bob Ford, who claimed he killed Jesse James. There was a lot of drinkin' an' he an' Martin matched, but there was plenty of men and they separated them.

We shipped the twos and threes from Walsenburg to some feed lots in Missouri. That left us with the big steers. […] Mornings we took time about goin' off alone with the steers. […] It was my time to take the herd out, and there was a blizzard on. It was a reg'lar norther. The steers wouldn't head into it. […] I was hankerin' to get back, for I was nearly froze. When I got [close] to the fire[,] I just fell off my horse. […] Cold as I was I could see that Sparks was mad about something. […] As I come [sic] to the fire Sparks grabbed a spade used for putting coals on the oven. Hughes Kile reached 'round to his bedroll, got his .44, and shot Sparks. I stretched him out on his bedroll, and the fool quit breathin'!

They cut a slit in his coat and got out the roll of money. They stepped off ten paces, dug a hole, and buried it. They said they'd been gamblin' and Sparks had won all the money.

They sent for the undertaker and the doctor, but neither came. […] I was still wonderin' what to do when the justice of the peace came out. He sat on the tongue of the wagon and talked to us. Martin [Mrose] had cleared out. Hughes Kile stood hitched [i.e. arrested]. I told just how it happened. […] That left me alone in camp. I took the bedrolls and went to sleep. At first the snow covered me and I was comfortable. But the wind began to blow and it drifted off me. I was awakened by Martin beating me with the double end of a rope. He dragged me toward an old abandoned depot, whippin' me to keep me staggering along. When we reached the building we found some kindling, coal, and an old potbellied stove. We built a fire and went to sleep. That night several sheep herders lost their lives, and hundreds of cattle either froze or drifted before the storm [....][25]

A.P. Black, another drover for the VVNs, remembered the Bob Ford incident differently. He recalled:

> [Mrose] had the first herd [that spring] and I trailed a few weeks behind. When his herd got to Cripple Creek most of the boys rode into town for a little amusement.
>
> Bob Ford run a 'honkey-tonk' and dance hall in Cripple Creek at the time, so Marose [sic] decided he'd ride in to take a look at the man who killed Jesse James. I guess he never thought a hell of a lot about Mr. Ford, for after taking one look at him, he whipped out his six-shooter and chased Ford down the middle of his own dance floor and ran him into a room in the back end of the building.
>
> Just as Ford slammed the door, Marose slammed a couple of shots through the middle of it, but the victim escaped. When Marose told me about that he figured Ford was 'still a runnin'.'"[26]

Martin Mrose was certainly someone to be reckoned with. "On one occasion, instead of Martin going with the horses, he was to go back [to New Mexico] on the train. Dave Walker, on relating his departure said that Martin was without a coat and had about five hundred dollars in bills sticking out of his shirt pocket. 'I suggested that he put his money out of sight. 'Maybe no,' replied Martin. 'I would like to see some jeester reachin' for that.'" [27]

Mrose seems to have had a fun side, too, though his humor—like all cowboys'—was a bit rough. A.P. Black recorded his unusual training methods for a cow pony.

> I didn't see Martin till [sic] late that fall, and the salt grass along the Pecos River had frosted. [...]
>
> I took care of the stock mares that winter and Martin looked

after the saddle-horses. Our camps weren't more than about five miles apart, so we got to see a lot of each other.

Riding up along the rim of the cap-rock one day, I saw the damnedest commotion about a mile below. I couldn't figure out what it was, so I decided I'd better go see what was going on. After I found a place where I could get down and got close enough to the rumpus, I saw a horse, saddled and bridled, fighting a two-year-old heifer. The horse on one end of the rope and the heifer on the other. Martin was sitting crosslegged in the sand smoking cigarettes and taking it all in. It was a horse he'd just broke and hadn't rode more than a few times.[28]

Though Mrose wasn't a gifted visionary or a skilled promoter like the Eddys, he understood what the Eddys were doing. On September 13, 1883, Mrose homesteaded two tracts totaling 160 acres just west of the Eddy ranch.[29] Notice of his final proof on the land was published in *The Fairplay Flume* on April 2, 1885. Mrose's land was along Rye Slough and controlled access onto Black Mountain. He built a cabin and a fence, a fence that may have closed off the Eddy's legal three-sided fencing of a large section of government land. Mrose also homesteaded land near Artesia, New Mexico,[30] and he contracted water from the Pecos Irrigation and Improvement Company's Northern Canal. As the last part of his plan, he bought a ranch across the Pecos River, in the Alacran Hills east of La Huerta. It's apparent from these moves he intended to capitalize on the Eddys' scheme to raise cattle in New Mexico, move them to Colorado to fatten them, and sell them to meat markets in the mining camps. Like other investors, he had hitched his star to the Eddys' coattails.

5
THE WOMAN AND THE COWBOY
1894

"La forijida, la niña, y [el] caballo muerto."[1]

About October 1894, Helen and Laura Jennings arrived in New Mexico after trekking across West Texas to escape Helen's abusive husband, Steve Jennings. Helen "was very beautiful. She was [...] very poor [....] She came to Eddy [...] to wait for her family, but they never came for her. [... M]y grandfather called them '*la forajida, la niña y caballo muerto.*'"[2]

Fleeing an abusive husband, this desperate woman, with no money and a small child in tow, was likely to attract questions. Undoubtedly, her skittish behavior won her no friends; she was vague about her origin and where she was going. She may have told different stories to different people. None of this would be unusual for an abused woman on the run, but in a tightly knit community like Eddy, it seemed suspicious. For this reason, it is necessary to understand Eddy.

In the 1880s the Pecos River drainage was one of the best open cattle ranges available. Grass extended twenty miles west of the river and a hundred miles east. Because of this natural bounty, cattlemen like the Eddy brothers developed immense ranches, but the "endless" grass resource was soon used up. The range was overstocked by 1884. The worst year, 1886, was the "Big Die-off," when more than 35% of the cattle in the Pecos country starved. In 1888 a serious drought struck.

A colony of Mormons had once tried irrigation at Double Crossing but had given up midway through the project. Ex-lawman Pat Garrett proposed to improve on their plans but didn't have the personality or connections. The Eddy brothers did. Despite dwindling grass, drought, and blizzards, VVN operations thrived. The Eddy brothers' purchase of Clayton Wells, the first hand-dug wells east of the Pecos River, and their emphasis on fattening cattle in Colorado provided a stability to their operations that impressed investors.[3] More than that, while Garrett talked of money, the Eddys thought in terms of capital. Garrett understood there would have to be ditches dug; the Eddys knew dams would have to be built. Garrett thought of involving El Paso people; the Eddys went to Switzerland for their first major investor.

Lincoln, the county seat, was a hundred miles away, which made conducting legal business difficult. The Eddys successfully petitioned the New Mexico Legislature in 1889 to separate the area from Lincoln County. The new county was named Eddy.

On October 31, 1887, the Pecos Valley Land and Ditch Company was organized.[4] A small dam and the Halagueño Ditch were constructed to attract investors, after which the company reorganized as the Pecos Irrigation and Investment Company, which began a massive project of development that would involve building hundreds of miles of railroad, establishing towns, constructing the largest dams in North America, and digging irrigation canals to supply one of the largest irrigated farming regions on earth.

When finished, the Northern Canal was 35 miles long, six feet deep, and 35 feet wide, all hand-dug. The Eddy Dam and much of the canal system were completed in 1891; the McMillan Dam was finished in 1893; the railway, which reached the new town of Eddy on January 10, 1891, was pushed through to Roswell in mid-1895.

Engineers and surveyors poured into the area; many had worked on irrigation projects in San Saba County, Texas, and would work in the Imperial and San Joaquin valleys of California. For historians and genealogists, the connection between these points is significant. Read the obituaries of settlers of Fresno, California; they were born in Texas. An example is Lon Williams, Helen Jennings' brother. Born in Caldwell County, Texas, he lived in Fredonia, then tried the Rio Peñasco in Eddy County, moved to Cartwright, Arizona, and finally ended up south of Fresno.

Other Texas people who came to Eddy were Todd Barber and Elias Gibson Queen, both related to Helen Jennings. Still another Texan to put down roots in Eddy County was David Leon Kemp. Described as a "man that if he owed you a dollar he'd pay ya and he was truthful,"[5] Kemp was liked in Texas, and his reputation preceded him to New Mexico. It's certain he was involved in law enforcement prior to the establishment of Eddy County, and as soon as the new county had elections, he became sheriff.

Seven Rivers, established in 1879, was the first town in Eddy County, named for seven springs, each with its own stream, which came together and drained into the Pecos. Cowboys referred to parallel streams as "ladders." Ranchers in the Seven Rivers area incorporated a "7" as part of their brand.[6] This is the origin of Martin Mrose's brand: Seven Ladders.

Seven Rivers was one of the most violent towns in the Old West. Residents claimed they could read newspapers at night by the light of gunfire. Contrary to recent academic theories the West wasn't violent, of the first 57 internments at the cemetery, none was from disease. Nearly half of the adult male skeletons analyzed during the moving of the cemetery revealed their owners had died of bullet or knife wounds.[7] One old-timer recalled, "Seven Rivers [...] used to be an awful tough place [....] There was somebody killed there every few days."[8]

C.B. Eddy, however, wanted the county seat for the new Eddy County to be a better place. He moved his headquarters from Clayton Wells to La Huerta; he may have coerced the workers involved in the irrigation projects to vote for a new town called Eddy to be the county seat. The town site was laid out in March 1889 and incorporated in 1893. Although it was intended to be "dry,"[9]the town was christened on September 15, 1888 by Lillian Greene, who, ironically, broke a bottle of champagne near the Guadalupe Ford of the Pecos River.

> "Eddy was evidently not the staunch nondrinker that legend would have. His usual address while staying in New York was the Union Club. This establishment [...] contained a popular and well-stocked bar. Staunch prohibitionists of the time did not frequent such establishments if they had other choices [.... T]here is a very intriguing telegram from Charles B. Eddy to the Superintendent, Terminals, Kansas City: 'Will you kindly send aboard my car tonight on No. 3, 6 bottles of Overholt or Wilson Rye Whiskey.'"[10] Another hint of the Eddys personal tastes is from Francis Tracy. The Eddy brothers, he said, "were bachelors, with no idea of marriage, were pretty good sports and while by no means dissipated were always ready for a good time."[11]

Though restrictions against the sale of alcohol may have originated with company manager J.J. Hagerman and the model of Colorado Springs, another reason for the Eddys' restrictions may have been their father, a lifelong proponent of temperance. So, even though the Eddys may have drunk alcohol themselves, they were determined the town be dry.

Early settlers had confidence in these restrictions. Bragged an editor, "The board of supervisors let a contract this week to Luscious Anderson to erect a calaboose or jail [...] built of 4 x 6, securely spiked together, with a concrete floor. Constable Smith will mark out the soft spots for the drunks and disorderlies—fortunately, however, Eddy has but few of either."[12]

Like many early residents, Sheriff Kemp was a teetotaler. In fact, Kemp's main vice was chewing gum. A woman recalled, "[He] said that [if] you chewed gum you'd stop and think ... before you spoke. ... And they'd tease him, and ... you know Dave was a violent opposer of liquor, and he told my dad, 'Course you can't drink whiskey when you was chewing gum.'"[13] *The Eddy Argus* said Kemp was the only sheriff that didn't use tobacco, alcohol, or profanity.

Though Kemp didn't drink, he recognized an opportunity when he saw it. He formed a partnership with Tom Gray, and they erected a tent on the north edge of Eddy called Wolfton or Temptation to serve "liquid hardware" to laborers working for the irrigation company. The saloon was called the Lone Wolf; it was in a tent, its bar was planks laid across barrels, and it had a stuffed wolf as figurehead. Selling "medicinal whiskies," Dublin stout, and Schlitz beer, the two men were doing well by April 1890.

Alcohol is more stimulating in the presence of other vices, however, and the Lone Wolf was short on entertainment. "Bart" Nymeyer, the county surveyor, bought a plot a mile-and-a-half south of Eddy that became Phenix, New Mexico.[14] The little town's motto was "A little nonsense now and then is relished by the best of men."[15] The spelling Phenix is on the original plat, but it was also called "Oasis of the West," "Hagerman City," "Ragtown," or "Jagville." Pronounced "fen-iks" by old-timers, the sintown was where gamblers, saloonkeepers, and whores concentrated within an easy walk of teetotaling Eddy.

On May 7, 1892, *The Eddy Argus* reported the first saloon, W.A. Bennett's

The Legal Tender. C.F. McDonough opened a music and concert hall, complete with a carpeted supper room, a band, and dancing girls. Jube Johnson, a black violinist, was at Philbrick's Saloon producing some of "the best music ever heard in Eddy."[16] The Wigwam offered bartending services of "Little Joe," billed as one of the best "mixerologists in the country."[17] As Wolfton's revenues declined, Kemp joined Ed Lyell in erecting an enormous saloon in Phenix called the Silver King, the grandest of all.[18]

Reelected sheriff in November 1892, Kemp tried to regulate the saloon district of Phenix. The impetus seems to have been an annoying rock-throwing incident. "For some time, as the train has journeyed through Phenix on its southward trip, the passengers have been endangered by rocks thrown at the cars by person or persons unknown."[19] Difficulty catching the culprit resulted in the appointment of W.T. Williamson as a special deputy in Phenix.

The appointment was a smart move. Legitimate businesses were attracted to Phenix, and by 1895 there were a thousand people there. There was a book dealer as well as bookies; a blacksmith and a goldsmith; a druggist as well as opium dens. Chinese restauranteurs, Mexican laborers, a Jewish dentist, "Arab" peddlers, Swiss immigrants, and black railroaders rubbed elbows in the little town. Constable William H. Smith lived in Phenix with his Mexican wife. W.M. Earhart, a cowboy from the Las Cruces area, relocated to Phenix, and Texas gunman Ben Thompson's son and brother, both gamblers, lived there too. [20]

Phenix was unruly, and the most notorious area was Casanova Alley, which had saloons and painted ladies. Naked prostitutes, it was claimed, accosted men on the streets. The hack service transporting drunks back to Eddy sometimes rolled the men for their wages. There were shootings, knifings, and robberies, and they only got worse through 1893 and 1894. Kemp and his men–hampered by jurisdictional problems and an uncooperative court system–lost ground in Phenix.

In reaction, the citizens of Eddy County elected a slate of "law and order" officers in November 1894. The incoming sheriff, J.D. Walker, promised to get control, but if one studies contemporary accounts, it's obvious he was quickly outgunned. Before long, Phenix was the wildest town in North America. Not helping the situation any, John Denson, a violent ne'er-do-well, arrived in town and was appointed a special officer, "having alleged authority from his cousin, Constable William Smith."[21] On June 1, 1894, shortly after his arrival, Denson killed Con Gibson in the Silver King Saloon. Gibson was an ally of Sheriff Bud Frazer of Pecos, Texas, who was involved in a feud with an ex-deputy named Jim Miller. Denson and Gibson exchanged words. "Gibson told Denson to 'take a last drink' preparatory to being killed. Denson took the drink, saying it would not be the last. Then, according to the witnesses, Gibson put his hand to his waist to draw his pistol and was shot in the head."

The saloon owner, Ed Lyell, and Constable Smith disarmed Denson and examined Gibson's body. Gibson's pistol had hung up in his suspenders, so the shooting was ruled self-defense. The wounded man lingered for three days before expiring. *The Eddy Argus* commented on June 8, 1894, "Phenix might be a safe place for a man to visit, if there were no armed officers there."

After the shooting, Denson went on a rampage. His cousin, Mannie Clements, tried to escort him from Eddy, but Denson was then arrested in Midland, Texas. Later, he returned to Phenix to rape an old woman after assaulting her husband.[22] On October first he was arrested for flashing a gun. Finally, on December 20, 1894, Denson pulled a gun on Phenix Marshal Lon Bass. While Bass was restrained, Denson burned him with a cigarette. Bass wounded and arrested his assailant outside Philbrick's Saloon in north Phenix a few minutes later.[23]

As bad as anyone in Phenix, however, Dee Harkey assaulted a young black woman who worked at a nearby restaurant. This led to an incident where the restaurant's owner shot at Harkey as he advanced on him with a meat cleaver. A grand jury decided the two men had "bluffed one another...."[24] Harkey pleaded guilty to assaulting the girl and was fined $5.

Harkey was also charged in Socorro and in Chaves counties, New Mexico, with pulling a pistol in a threatening manner. In Eddy County in 1899, he was charged with the same offense, pleaded guilty, and was fined again. Harkey was also charged under the Edmunds Act,[25] a federal statute used in a morality crusade against the sinners of Phenix. Though few of the "cohabiting" couples seem to have been fined or convicted, their arrests necessitated a trip to the nearest federal court. Some of the arrestees may not have drifted back to Phenix after their hearings, so it was a minor influence in cleaning up Phenix.

It was about this time Helen and Laura Jennings arrived in Eddy. They were broke and had no prospects after their journey from Texas. Martin Mrose, who was becoming a prominent rancher and investor, however, was intrigued. "[He] got in with a woman at Eddy who had a child 2 or 3 days [sic] old. Walker Bush and Dave Kemp owned [a] sporting house out of town, and Martin picked her up out of this house. [...] His wife was from down in Texas somewhere. Fellow named Lyles, from Dallas, [...] run Dave Kemp's sporting end and [I] think he brought her up from down there."[26]

Dee Harkey disagreed, saying, "I am not sure whether [she] was one of these whores out here. I rather think she was a San Angelo girl."[27] The San Angelo comment is the closest anyone in Eddy County ever made to the truth about Helen Jennings.

Martin Mrose, however, didn't hesitate. He was at the point of being prosperous. His ranches, horses, and cattle were going to make money. He was ready to settle down. He and Helen married in November 1894.[28] Rumors persist they were married at the Silver King Saloon, partly owned by Mrose's friend, ex-sheriff Dave Kemp.

No civil record exists for the marriage. It was not mentioned in contemporary newspapers either. This was a confusing time for the newlyweds, with enforcement of the Edmunds Act in progress and accusations of rustling and other crimes being made, but we can assume they were, in fact, married. That no wedding license was recorded is not unusual, but it suggests they were married by a Catholic priest. Helen had converted to Catholicism at the time she married Steve Jennings. Unfortunately, Catholic records for St. Edward's parish at Eddy do not exist prior to 1896.

Marriages were often spur-of-the-moment,[29] and people were only then getting used to applying for civil licenses. An example is the marriage of Frances Plowman and John C. Queen. Married in 1899, Mrs. Queen could still display her wedding certificate in the 1940s. "[I]t is the only proof of my marriage. In those days—not too long after Eddy was carved out of Lincoln County—it was not customary to obtain a wedding license."[30]

Wedding licenses, county seat, and a courthouse were signs of civilization in the Pecos valley, and the village of Seven Rivers was finished. By the beginning of 1896 the town's post office was closed. Meanwhile, the growing town of Eddy was becoming prosperous. C. B. Eddy hosted a tour by Standard oil millionaires, but much of their discussion was of irrigation projects and the cattle business,[31] and it would be years before anyone realized the extent of oil and gas reserves under the Halagueño Ranch.

The optimism of the times was palpable. Newspapers declared an agricultural miracle was in progress as a result of irrigation. Corn grew fifteen feet high. Alfalfa, sugar beets, and orchards of every description stretched as far as the eye could see. Phonographs were popular in 1892, and recorded music could be heard at all hours. By 1893, some people had gas stoves. The Westinghouse electric plant came into operation in November 1892, and by 1894, most of the town had electricity. In the spring of 1895, an ice plant was built to provide the wherewithal to ship the valley's agricultural produce.[32]

Like all great dreams, though, the bubble of the Pecos Valley would burst. In late July 1893, the Clayton Wells headquarters of the Eddy Ranch burned to the ground, and then it began to rain. The Pecos River built up behind the dams. Canals and floodgates built so carefully in the preceding years began to crack and break. The Avalon and Texas dams were destroyed, and there was heavy damage at the McMillan Dam.

The Pecos Valley flooded from riverbank to mountaintop. The river was eight miles wide south of Eddy. Even the Peñasco River was a mile wide. Among the first to realize the dams would fail, C.B. Eddy telephoned a warning to those downstream, but telephones were soon knocked out by the flood.[33]

After the flood, Eddy wrote a letter to the people of the Pecos Valley telling them not to give up. He and his brother did not have the resources to rebuild, but asking J.J. Hagerman in Colorado Springs for help meant relinquishing control. Hagerman was not in a mood for bad news. Foreign markets had begun to drop silver as the basis of their currencies. The repeal of the Sherman law depressed the silver market further; the Mollie Gibson, Hagerman's immensely profitable silver mine, flooded, and now the Pecos projects had been destroyed. Even so, C.B. Eddy was determined to rebuild. The working relationship the men had developed over the years evaporated, and they bickered so badly an angry Hagerman wrote Eddy, "If you will quit lying about me, I will quit telling the truth about you."[34]

Even with all the bad news, however, the newspapers reported the grass was the best in years. The VVNs began one of their last roundups, and cowboys worked day and night rounding up 6,000 head of cattle. Undoubtedly, Martin Mrose was busy throughout that fall, but by the next spring, everyone knew the dream was over. *The Eddy Argus* reported on April 25, 1894, that C.B. Eddy had relinquished control of the Pecos Valley projects to Hagerman. Not long afterward, the Halagueño Ranch was sold, though it continued under new owners as the VVN Cattle Company.

Rebuilding the dams was a temporary reprieve for Eddy and Phenix, though. Among the first to give up were Ed Lyell and his wife Ellen. "[T]wenty men and about sixteen women left for Globe [Arizona] in three six-mule-team wagons, each with a second wagon hitched on behind. [...] Lon Bass was captain of the outfit. Perched high on one of the big loads was violinist Dan Kinkle, playing a spirited rendition of Bonaparte's retreat for the entertainment of the spectators."[35]

As other businesses faded, however, Martin Mrose applied for 320 acres under the Desert Land Act. Prominent men helped him in this enterprise. It was a nine-hour, one-way stage ride from Eddy to Roswell,[36] yet C.B. Eddy, Bart Nymeyer, Jeff Chism, and other prominent men made the journey as witnesses on affidavits granting Mrose rights in the Northern Canal.

The key to a desert land application was at least one-eighth of the land had to be cultivated. Differing from a homestead filing or a preemption grant, which both required residence on the property, a desert grant had to be plowed, planted, irrigated, and harvested. Witnesses had to support claims of irrigation and cultivation. Mrose, not known as a farmer, contracted the cultivation. For a crop he chose Egyptian corn, a variety of sorghum. He irrigated—but probably not enough. Nothing came of the crop, yet he was granted the patent anyway. Mrose was a cattleman; he probably didn't want the land for farming, but he went through the motions, and he got the land. Even so, this failure worried him.[37] To the south of Eddy, farmers were making a fortune growing alfalfa and sugar beets.[38] Mrose's land and water rights meant nothing without the husbandry of an attentive, dirt-poor farmer.

The secret to an investment like this was water. Water was the miracle of

Pecos Valley agriculture; it was the instrument of the Eddys leaving that part of the state; and it contributed to the failure of Martin Mrose's cultivation. It's hard to remember, now, but when Eddy County was settled, there was plenty of water. Moaned one old-timer, "I recall vividly those days of water in abundance and mourn—with many others—the present period of man's continued pillaging of our planet."[39]

The Pecos had always been full. Grass had grown deep along the Pecos Valley, and for cattlemen in the 1870s and '80s, it had been a paradise, but by the mid-1890s, ranchers, developers, and farmers had ruined it. Less than a generation after being settled, the Pecos country turned from short grass prairie to mesquite-choked drainages and high yucca desert. It was an ecological disaster on an unprecedented scale. Thanks almost entirely to J.J. Hagerman, the town of Eddy would survive. The dams along the Pecos survived; the irrigation projects survived too. Farms along the river survived, but step ten feet off irrigated land today, and the brutal desert intrudes.

The Eddy brothers left the Pecos valley forever. They would go on to develop central New Mexico, including the town of Alamogordo. Of their later ventures, it's been said that "Apparently [C. B.] Eddy learned […] that absolute prohibition was not a solution to the social evil of the saloon."[40] There would be no more Phenix, Seven Rivers, or Eddy in the Eddy brothers' future.

PART THREE
The Gunfighter

"Tell wes to be a good man And Keep out of trouble."

—Sheriff Tom Bell, Hill County, Texas,
April 14, 1894

6
THE CELEBRITY
1877

"By shooting even one man-jack,
You made sure your demise.
You later got yours in the back,
Or right between the eyes."[1]

Picture any contemporary criminal exiting a court. Escorted by police and surrounded by media and the curious, the killers, bound in locks and chains, make shuffling walks out of the courthouses and disappear from history. There was once, however, a killer who made this very walk out of a courthouse and down the steps into the law-abiding sunshine, but he has never really vanished. His influence is still felt in Texas today, though he has been dead a hundred years.

He was a man considered so dangerous in his time that when he was arrested in Pensacola, Florida, on August 23, 1877, it took twenty-five men to do it,[2] and even then, after he was beaten unconscious, restrained with shackles, chains, and leg irons, the lawmen still feared him. The man had been in the same situation before and had managed to kill his captors. On top of that, having acted without proper warrants or extradition papers, the lawmen had to go through last-minute legal maneuvering to get their prisoner to Texas. When the papers arrived, the suspect, surrounded by six armed lawmen, set off by express train to stand trial for the murder of Deputy Sheriff Charlie Webb in Comanche, Texas. He was also suspected of the shooting of State Policeman Speights[3] and the murders of Officer Jim Smoley, two men in Peoria, a man each in Trinity, Comanche, and Wilson counties, plus assaults in Smith County and Navasota.[4]

It was a strange and awful comeuppance for this young man, but it was well deserved. He was called "the terror of the Mexican border,"[5] and, though things had gone against him now, of one thing we can be sure: he began to plot an escape.

There was no direct route over the swamps of Louisiana and the mighty

Mississippi River, so the party headed north by train, then west to Texas. Along the way, depots were crowded with curious spectators. In Austin there were so many onlookers the prisoner couldn't be brought to jail; he had to be carried bodily over the heads of the crowd. Food, flowers, letters, and gifts were sent to him, and one man claimed the cell was "the busiest place in Austin, even busier than the governor's office."[6] He would remain in this cell for three weeks, and during that time, he would lack nothing in the way of comforts.

On September 19, 1877, Comanche County Sheriff Frank Wilson and his deputies took the prisoner and escorted him to Comanche County for trial. Two thousand people gathered outside the jail to witness the transfer as a company of Texas Rangers escorted the heavily shackled prisoner, chained to a seat in the middle of an open wagon. Twenty armed men rode in front, behind, and on both sides of the wagon, each heavily armed with rifles, pistols, and an occasional shotgun.

The trip took several days, and en route, one of the most curious spectacles of the Old West occurred. The prisoner was given a gun to show off his skills. The gun was unloaded, of course, but what these lawmen wanted to see was the man's extraordinary talent manipulating a weapon. One Texas Ranger marveled, "He can take two six-shooters and turn them like wheels in his hands and fire a shot from each at every revolution."[7]

Today, every western movie features gunplay such as this. Pistols are whipped out of holsters, spun like tops, fired repeatedly by fanning the hammer with the left hand, then passed from hand to hand like it was a common thing a hundred years ago. In point of fact, however, there was only one man who did it, the original, and he could do it drunk or sober, while under fire from an angry posse, in dark and crowded barrooms, on a racing horse in heavy brush, or while "surrendering" meekly, then rolling the guns around faster than the eye could blink to get the better of anyone stupid enough to confront him. He could do it with a remarkable assortment of guns, too, some big, some small, some in what the old-timers called "scabbards," some in pockets, and some dangling from a cord around his neck. He was so good he could make the cheapest gun hit its mark and the strongest man bark like a dog.

In short, he was the greatest gunfighter of all time. We don't really know how many people he killed during his short, violent career; we only know how many he admitted killing. His final tally may have been between forty and sixty.[8] What's worse, he felt he could justify each of his murders.

These were not Hollywood shootings with guns that never needed reloading. They were, for the most part, buckle-to-buckle bar fights with guns that were inaccurate, poorly maintained, and notoriously unreliable. These were not fights where one shooter gets splattered all over the wallpaper, while the other gets only a scratch. No, the old-time gunfighters knew the risks: even the winner of such a fight might die or be maimed. The trick was, that in the roar and smoke, the winner would have been the one with the presence of mind to aim. Rex Beach, who knew a number of bad men in boom towns from Alaska to Central America, observed, "It is commonly believed that Western bad men were quick on the draw and deadly marksmen, but the truth seems to be that the quicker they drew, the wilder they shot."[9]

Because of this, much of the true gunfighting of the Old West revolved around the "dance" the men did to get psyched up. It was common to send messages to the intended victim that he was to be killed. One old-timer said, "You may think that was part of some code. I think it was [.... A]fter they'd send you word like that, they would as likely as not lie in wait, and shoot you in the back without giving you a chance." [10]

This dangerous prisoner did live by a code. He never had a gang. He never killed a woman, though he threatened one once. He never shot the witnesses, though one newspaper reported after the murder of Charlie Webb he "commenced an indiscriminate slaughter of men, women and children. This led to a general engagement [...] which was finally put down [...] but not until many lives had been sacrificed."[11] Though accused of every dastardly deed in Texas in the Frontier Era,[12] in truth, he never robbed a bank or a stage or a train. He demanded just one thing: respect. When Wild Bill Hickok acknowledged him, it made his day—and he was barely eighteen years old at the time. Even so, Hickok did not back down from the brash gunman. He quietly walked away, biding his time, for Hickok knew the young man would never shoot him in the back. That was against the code.

One newspaper commented, "Nearly everybody got out of his way when he was in an ugly mood, and this led him to believe he was cock of the walk and bore a charmed life."[13] He was "as typical a Texas desperado of the earliest type as was ever portrayed in the dime novel. He was of medium weight, nearly six feet tall, straight as an arrow and light complexioned, with an eye as keen as a hawk. [... I]t was almost sure death for anyone who was in front of his gun."[14]

As dangerous as he was, among the ironies of his life is the fact that, though he was shot and arrested several times, he would be taken only three times, all within a period of three weeks, once by a man maintaining order in a saloon district, once by a woman barely in her twenties, and once by an old man who walked with a cane.

But now, shackled and humbled, the humiliated prisoner finally arrived in Comanche, Texas. Backers and detractors, witnesses and partisans packed the courtroom. The saloons did a roaring business. The courthouse square was full of horses and wagons at all hours of the day and night. In the end, the killer was sentenced to twenty-five years of hard labor. For many, this sentence for second-degree murder was not harsh enough, but for others, the long sentence was a disappointment. He was not a bad boy, some said. He's only bad when he's drinking. His father's a minister of the gospel. The young man's misunderstood—

Misunderstood or not, the message was clear once he walked outside the courthouse to be transported back to Austin pending an appeal. As he stood there on the steps surrounded by twenty heavily armed lawmen cradling Winchesters and shotguns, there was a cheer from the crowd. It was probably hard for the young killer to distinguish whether he was being cheered or the long prison sentence, but shackled and restrained as he was, he acknowledged the crowd as well as he could. In his own mind, he must have realized then for the first time in his life that he was special. He was the most dangerous man alive, yet he had become something of a hero, a celebrity in a field that didn't encourage careers. From the most isolated farms to the customarily crowded barrooms, he was the subject of every conversation in Texas.[15] Everyone knew of him and feared him. Everyone had a story about him, true or not. He was what today would be called a "superstar." He was at the summit, the top of his form, but he was to be locked up until he would be too old to go wrong again.[16] Texas could breathe a sigh of relief. The greatest gunfighter of all was going to prison and might die there.

Just the mention of his name could freeze small children in their tracks, and his fame teased whole generations of future pistoleer wanna-bes into twirling guns like acrobats.

His name was John Wesley Hardin.

7
THE DANGEROUS CHILD
1853-1874

"[N[ever tell this to mortal man. I don't believe
you."[1]

Much has been written about Hardin over the years, yet he remains as elusive now as he was then. Two biographies, *The Last Gunfighter* by Dr. Richard Marohn, and *John Wesley Hardin* by Leon Metz, are available. Marohn, a psychiatrist, wrote a detailed analysis outlining Hardin's "narcissistic behavior disorder;" and, as a result, his biography is dark and complex. Unfortunately, Marohn died shortly after publication, and those of us with questions are left holding them in our hands, along with our hats.

Metz, a popular El Paso lecturer and writer, wanted to capitalize on the centennial of Hardin's death by producing a quick, readable biography, but it didn't turn out that way. Like Marohn, Metz was affected by the work. He wrote, "The [...] biography was an emotionally devastating book to research and write. [... W]riting about Hardin was like slogging through a dark swamp ...."[2] For Metz, Hardin had proven too evil for words.

The epitome of violence in Texas, Hardin never wanted to die; he wanted to live forever, and to that end, he wrote an autobiography. He was one of few in the Old West to leave such a legacy, but it can't be trusted for even a page. Certain elements are undoubtedly true. Named for the founder of Methodism, John Wesley Hardin was born on May 26, 1853 near Bonham in Fannin County about a mile from the border with Grayson County.[3] His family was from a proud line of pioneers that had fought in the American Revolution and settled Tennessee. Hardin's paternal grandparents had been early settlers in the Republic of Texas. An uncle had fought in the Texas Revolution.

Hardin's father, James G. Hardin, was a Methodist minister. For a time, he was a circuit rider in north Texas, and this is where he met Elizabeth Dixon, whom he married May 19, 1847. Their second son, John Wesley, or "Wes," grew up in Fannin County. His neighbors were Roger and Ada McCown, whose daughter Minerva would marry another neighbor, John Jacob Helm, a man who would figure large in Hardin's later life.

Wes' father, a frail man afflicted with poor health, had chosen to preach, but he had minimal ability to do so. A family account said his coughing was aggravated whenever he led prayers.[4] Because of this, the elder Hardin studied for the bar and tried his hand at farming, though he was best at teaching. He helped establish a school at Sumpter, Texas, and when the school was sold and moved to Round Rock, Wes may have attended there for a time.[5]

Hardin's father voted against secession, but as Texas prepared for war, he accepted election as a captain of Confederate volunteers. Due to his health, however, he was persuaded to remain at home. Curiously, he promptly moved his family to a different county. The reason may have been the divided feelings of north Texas. Methodists were suspected of fomenting rebellion among slaves; they were assumed to harbor dangerous Unionist tendencies.[6] Though Hardin's father may have wavered in his loyalties to the South, he did buy a slave in 1863.[7] The Hardins lived south of the Wild Cat Thicket where so-called "brushmen" survived in a semi-guerilla fashion throughout the war.[8] Nevertheless, the elder Hardin espoused secession, and he was hurt by the defeat of the Confederacy in 1865.

About a year later, Texas was placed in a special military district; Union troops occupied Austin. Some troops were black; in addition, the new Freedmen's Bureau forced drastic changes, and a requirement that states could only be readmitted to the Union after they ratified the Fourteenth Amendment poured salt on the defeat. When federal troops were withdrawn in 1868, many Texans resisted the changes forced upon them. Even law-abiding citizens opposed the stringent laws; it was not considered disobedience, it was obedience to Southern heritage.

John Wesley Hardin grew up in this climate of disobedience. He witnessed assaults on blacks and Unionists; he heard his parents rail against the tyranny of the North and uppity former slaves. Soon, Hardin began to look for trouble on his own. In November 1868, he visited his uncle, Barnett Hardin, in Livingston, Texas. His cousin[9] Barnett Jones matched Hardin and himself in a wrestling match with a former slave named Mage. The two boys threw the man to the ground.

Hardin recalled, "Negro like, he got mad and said he could whip me and would do it. [...] He said he would kill me, [...] 'that no white boy could draw his blood and live....'"

Next day, Hardin encountered Mage again. "[H]e came at me with his big stick. He struck me, and as he did it I pulled out a Colt's .44 six-shooter and told him to get back. By this time he had my horse by the bridle, but I shot him loose."[10]

One can't help but wonder why Mage would attack a hotheaded teenager on a deserted trail. Hardin showed no particular skill in killing him. It was a melee, worsened by a bucking horse trying to get free of a stranger gripping its bridle. In the hands of an expert, the 1860 Colt can be devastating, but in the hands of a teenager, the gun was cumbersome. Though shot five times at close range, Mage took days to die. Wes Hardin was fifteen years old.

In the eyes of his family, Hardin was a rebel, not a criminal. It's appropriate here to contrast the reactions of another father, also religious and Southern, with a similarly dangerous son. Campbell Longley, father of William Preston "Bill" Longley, was faced with a teenager embarked on the outlaw trail.[11] Bill Longley claimed, "I have always known that I was doing wrong, but I got started when I was just a fool boy, led off by bolder heads, and taught that it was right to kill sassy Negroes and then to resist military law."[12]

For his father, however, religious convictions were paramount. Campbell Longley brooded over his son's dark choices and rejected them. Despite the heartache this caused, he ostracized his son and never supported his criminal career. Not so with James G. Hardin. Weak-willed and vacillating, he swallowed his son's lies, believed his excuses, and supported his choices. Both fathers were broken by their sons, but Campbell Longley could hold his head up. James G. Hardin could not.

John Wesley Hardin never reflected on the damage he did to his family. He never had the time. Soon after Mage's death—if his autobiography is to be believed—he ambushed three soldiers looking for him. After that, he claimed to have hunted down a black bully. "I [...] told him to say his prayers. [...I]t had the desired effect, for it reformed him completely. That Negro afterwards became one of the best citizens of that county...."[13]

This shocking image of himself as a hero would sustain him for years. At the time, there were plenty of Texans who viewed his crimes in a favorable light, and yet, for each story of Hardin as hero, there are dozens of tales as killer. An example is: "Black man. Talked bad about Hardin. Hardin's friends told him and Hardin came in and told the black man to stick out his tongue. When he did, Hardin shot it off."[14] Another is that Hardin "became so inured to taking lives that on one occasion he bet his cousin a bottle of whiskey he could shoot out a man's eye. By the time Hardin composed his life story, he could no longer be certain, but 'supposed' he had won the bet."[15] Still another, "He kills men just to see them kick, and on one occasion charged Cuero alone with a yell 'Rats to your holes!' and such a shutting up of shops has not been seen since...."[16]

Hardin and his cousin, Simp Dixon, each killed a soldier in a running fight soon afterward. For sixteen-year-old Hardin, the killing marked his fifth man.[17] Perhaps to regain control of this dangerous teenager, his parents moved to Navarro County. "I had been receiving letters from my father and mother urging me to quit my wild habits and turn to better ways."[18]

Instead Hardin got into a card game with men who robbed him of pistol, boots, and cash, but Hardin borrowed a gun and killed the ringleader. After that, he may have tried to settle down on his uncle's farm at Brenham, but life there was too tame. He rode to town at every opportunity to gamble and carouse. He claimed to have met desperadoes like Phil Coe, Bill Longley, and Ben Hinds. In January 1871, he was arrested in Longview by the State Police, who planned to transport him to Waco to stand trial. In those days, prisoners were not patted down, and Hardin bought a pistol and hung it around his neck on a cord under his shirt. He later retrieved the gun and killed policeman Jim Smolley.[19]

Wes was now an accomplished killer, but after each murder, he ran home and confessed. His father, he wrote, listened to his excuses and agreed the victims deserved to die. James G. Hardin did not counsel him to surrender, but his attitude changed. In his autobiography, Wes Hardin makes the astounding admission, "I told my father what I had done. [...] He said, [...] I don't believe you, but go to Mexico, and go at once."[20]

But Hardin did not. He was invited by his cousins, the Clementses, to go on a cattle drive. "Of course, in this kind of a life I soon learned how to play poker...."[21] In one of these games he shot a Mexican and assaulted two others, but he concluded, "The best people of the vicinity said I did a good thing."[22]

Hardin's vision of a cowboy's life was hardly normal. In his autobiography, he never mentioned the dust, drudgery, or danger, yet he professed to be one of the best drovers in an era when, to be a cowboy was the ideal. He also claimed he was paid $150 a month, nearly four times the going rate.

Droving was a specialized trade that required not only good horsemanship, but roping skills and experience. Not many amateurs rode up the trail; they stayed at home learning to herd and brand. Only real cowboys were chosen for the arduous trek north, yet Hardin says he set off for Abilene with a trail herd of 1,200 cattle. Hardin claimed to be entrusted with herds on the drive to Kansas, but this is another of his lies. There is no doubt Hardin was a horseman, but he was no cowboy.

Hardin's most famous killing occurred in Kansas.[23] Another herd crowded too closely on the trail. In an altercation over keeping the herds apart, Hardin met the Mexican drovers in classic style: as the men rode at each other, Hardin stuffed his reins in his teeth and shot the Mexican trail boss through the heart. In the melee that followed, Hardin killed four more Mexicans. He was now a legend along the Chisholm Trail, and he was soon to meet another legend, Wild Bill Hickok.

In Abilene, two smarter Texans, Phil Coe and Ben Thompson, co-owned a notorious saloon called the Bull's Head—and the name had nothing to do with the part of a bull's anatomy that had horns. Tall, long-haired, thirty-two-year-old Wild Bill Hickok was provoked by an explicit painting over the saloon; he had the sign repainted and the offending member excised. As town marshal, akin to today's Chief of Police, his prime directive in running Abilene was no one could wear a gun in town. Hardin, of course, broke the ordinance out of spite. Hickok walked up to him. Tens of thousands of words have been written about this encounter. Did Hardin force Hickok to back down? Did he pull his slick trick, the "border roll" and catch Hickok off guard?

There are those who say the encounter never happened; that it happened the way Hardin recalled twenty-five years later is doubtful. It's likely the deadly Hickok would have fired when the teenager began his spin, so what probably happened—if it happened at all—was a grudging admiration between the men. Hickok could have killed Hardin but chose not to, and he walked him into a saloon to have drinks. It was exactly the right thing to do. The older man stoked the teenager's ego, but it impressed the brash young man with his seriousness.

For Hardin, it wasn't enough. It's possible he shot a man through the mouth; soon thereafter, he rode back to camp to await Wild Bill's reaction. Here, he learned a supposed friend had been killed by a Mexican named Bideño, so Hardin tracked the Mexican down. On June 28, 1871, near today's Sumner, Kansas, Hardin killed Bideño. Newspaper accounts indicate he gave the Mexican no chance, shooting him through the forehead while he was eating dinner.

Hardin rode back to Abilene, much like he had ridden to his father each time he'd killed in Texas, but this time his "confessor" was Hickok. The good will evaporated between the two men. During the night of August 6, 1871, Hardin was annoyed by a man snoring in an adjacent hotel room. He shot through the wall to stop him. Details about the incident are contradictory[24] but the tale of killing a man for snoring circulated in 1878 and is apocryphal now. Whatever happened, Hardin didn't wait for Hickok's reaction. Knowing he faced a confrontation with the lawman, Hardin fled Abilene so fast he left his pants behind, settling for all time who was the most fearsome gunman: Hickok.

After Hardin returned to Texas, the death toll rose. In his autobiography, he claimed killing four more black policemen,[25] one or two Mexicans,[26] "some fellows,"[27] State Policeman Speights,[28] Phil Sublett,[29] two policemen,[30] J. B. Morgan,[31] and possibly a man named Jake Christman.[32]

But times were changing. Governor Davis' State Police were a deadly force commanded by four captains, and one of these was Jack Helms. Born about 1840, Helms was big for the time, about five feet nine inches tall and quite heavy. Helms had had a short, violent career in the Confederate Army. By 1869, he was elected DeWitt County Sheriff; in July 1870, he was commissioned a captain in the State Police. He and his men were known as Regulators.

Hardin was a candidate for arrest. Two black policemen ran into him in a store in southern Gonzales County on October 19, 1871. One, Green Paramore, ordered Hardin to hand over his pistols; Hardin handed the guns butt-first toward the unsuspecting policeman, then rolled a pistol over in his hand and shot the man through the head. He chased the other policeman, John Lackey, into a lake, where the man hid by submerging everything but his nose.

Hardin was a hero again, a role he relished. He called himself protector of the poor. Gonzales County was a good base for him, for his cousins and other relatives lived here.

One day, [...] Mrs. O.M. Christian[33] and a Mrs. Cooksey [...] were walking down the street in front of Boothe and Lewis' store. [...] Standing on the sidewalk were 2 Black soldiers. Mrs. Christian and Mrs. Cooksey asked to be allowed to pass. The soldiers replied that they didn't have to move just for 'two white women.' Mrs. Christian disagreed and was again refused passage. As was the custom of the time, [she] carried with her a parasol. [...] Using her parasol as a weapon, [she] jabbed one of the soldiers in the stomach with the sharp end of the post, then, as he bent over in pain, she whacked him on the head.

Later, on the way home, they had to cross Kerr's Creek Bridge. As they drove their buggy up on the bridge, the two soldiers [...] appeared and held the horses. The soldiers [...] had some very unsavory plans for both ladies. [...] At this time a young man [...] appeared. The soldiers did not take him as a threat, but before they were even aware it had happened they were both shot dead. This young man's name was John Wesley Hardin. [34]

Another story from this period is, "Out at the old Billings store [Brown] Bowen, Wes Hardin and others would toss $20 gold pieces in the air. Every so often Wes Hardin would hit one; the others couldn't. They'd throw a flour barrel top in the air. Wes could hit it with both pistols simultaneously."[35] What may sound like good-natured fun was actually practice. In a gunfight, targets were moving. It is significant that "every so often" Wes would hit a coin in the air. Someone with no familiarity with pistols might claim he hit a coin every time.

In September 1871, Gip Clements married the daughter of George

Tennille. Eighteen-year-old Hardin took his sweetheart, fifteen-year-old Jane Bowen, to the celebration. The marriage had a deleterious effect on the couple, and on February 29, 1872, Hardin married Jane at Riddlesville, in Gonzales County.[36] For a normal man, the marriage would have had a gentling effect. Hardin could have settled down, but patient Jane Hardin was another enabler in his life. She put up with his excuses, encouraged him in all he did, and in return, he made her life a living hell. Two months after the wedding, he was on the trail again, this time to south Texas on a mysterious errand.[37]

Along the way, he may have killed another Mexican. In Hemphill, he shot and wounded a state policeman. In September, two lawmen nearly caught him, but in a gunfight, Hardin killed at least one with a shotgun. Hit in the thigh and unable to ride, he realized the time had come to surrender, so he sent for Cherokee County Sheriff Richard B. Reagan to arrest him.[38] Hardin was taken to Rusk with four bullet holes in him. He was jailed in Austin, then transported to Gonzales County, from whence he escaped on November 19, 1872.

About this time, "Hardin was having some hammer trouble with a .44 Colt Army cap and ball [. … He] contracted with [a] blacksmith to repair the Colt. About two days later he returned for his revolver and asked permission to test it out. The blacksmith supplied a […] wooden shingle […] to use as a target. [He] paced off about 30 feet and started to tap the wooden shingle into the ground with his hammer. [Hardin] then said, 'Instead of facing me, hammer it in so that the edge can be the target.' Hardin took a casual aim and appeared to score at least five hits on this narrow target, splintering it completely."[39]

Such ability with a gun was useful. Texas' most famous clash was underway, the Sutton-Taylor Feud, and Jack Helms was solidly on the side of the Suttons. Hardin's cousins were on the side of the Taylors, so Hardin's loyalties were decided for him. On May 17, 1873 in Albuquerque, Texas, Wes Hardin and his compañero, Jim Taylor, ran into Helms at a blacksmith shop. Helms armed himself with a knife. Hardin held off townsmen while Taylor killed Helms.

Things were getting hot now, but his brother, Joe, had a comfortable life in Comanche County, and Hardin's parents had recently moved there too. Wes Hardin was persuaded to move his wife and daughter to the safety the rest of the family enjoyed. He was in and out of the county for the next several months as he raced horses and gathered cattle, but he returned in time for his twenty-first birthday, May 26, 1874. He celebrated with a win at the races, and he and his friends cruised the saloons. In town that day was Deputy Sheriff Charlie Webb from Brown County.

Twenty-six-year-old Webb found twenty-one-year-old Hardin inebriated. Webb may have pulled his gun first, but in an exchange of fire, Hardin killed the lawman. The shooting was the most flagrant murder yet. Townsmen poured into the streets, shooting as they came. Hardin claimed he wanted to shoot it out, but more sober heads prevailed, and he was hustled out of town.[40]

He was on the run for the last time. He had killed a deputy this time, and as he had done after all of his murders, he wanted to get home. It was a pattern he had followed over and over in his violent career, but this time, things were different. Rather than his loved ones being in Gonzales County where he was headed, he had to leave them behind in Comanche, where they were terrorized by vengeful mobs. His brother, Joe, his cousins, and his friends were lynched by vigilantes. Even those who should have been safe—friends "Scrap" Taylor, "Kute" Tuggle, and James White, arrested and transported two hundred miles away to DeWitt County— would be caught up in the hysteria after the murders of the Swift Tragedy.[41] They were hanged in a tree near a graveyard, one Hardin ally, Doc Bockius, escaping through intervention of a relative.

Hardin's father, a support during dangerous times, was living in fear; his mother was frightened nearly to death; his remaining friends were on the run or dead; and his wife cowered in terror.[42] John Wesley Hardin had escaped, but the cost was very dear.

Photograph about the time of Helen's marriage to Steve Jennings. Helen, standing, top left, was about sixteen. The regularity of her features and her poise promise the great beauty so often remarked upon later. Courtesy Thomas and Wilda Fay Jennings.

Front Row:
Bill Williams, Edgar & Ann
Eliza Williams

Back Row L. to R.
Helen Williams, William W.
& Kate Williams

Uncle Bill Williams
and family

The back of the Bill Williams' family photograph. Bill was 50. Helen's mother, Ann Eliza, was 43. Kate Williams was 8. Willie 7, and Edgar nearly 5. Courtesy of Thomas and Wilda Fay Jennings.

Bill Williams, Helen's father, late in life, holding his family bible. Courtesy Glenn Wilkins.

Close-up of Helen Williams prior to her marriage to Steve Jennings. Author's collection.

Marriage license between Steve Jennings and Helen Williams.

Glenn Wilkins with the Bill Williams Family Bible, which records Helen's birth, children, marriage to Steve Jennings, and her death. Author's collection.

Brands registered by Martin Mrose at the Eddy County Courthouse, evidence he was not a rustler. Rustlers don't register brands. Author's collection.

The greatest gunfighter in his prime. Courtesy Robert G. McCubbin.

8
THE HELLHOLE OF TEXAS
1877-1894

"Stranger, what asylum are you from?"[1]

After the killing of Deputy Sheriff Charlie Webb, John Wesley Hardin knew he'd gone too far, but this time, he didn't contend with "impudent Negroes" or the hated State Police. Now it wasn't rewards offered for his capture or warrants of under-gunned sheriffs. No, this time, Hardin faced the wrath of Texas.

In Gonzales County, he had only enough friends to hide him for a short time, for he faced a new and deadly threat: a recently organized police called the Texas Rangers. There weren't many, but they were a formidable force using investigation, trickery, and terrible, concentrated power. Not a one was a match for him, but working together, they would hound him from every hideout, drive his friends before them like doves before a storm, and coerce his closest allies into giving him up.

In Comanche, Hardin's father was paralyzed into inactivity. He and his wife were worried sick. Furious townspeople read his mail looking for clues to the whereabouts of his son, searched his home for evidence, and strangled him out of active life in the community. Living in a hornet's nest, he could do nothing to help his errant son now.

Stepping in to replace him, however, was his brother Robert Echison "Uncle Bob" Hardin, who was farming near Brenham in Washington County. It was he who brought John Wesley Hardin from Gonzales County and hid him for several weeks. Two of Uncle Bob's granddaughters would also play pivotal roles in Hardin's life, the first being fifteen-year-old Lora Edney.[2] No one suspected this teenager of knowing Wes Hardin, so she was the perfect "front" to send and receive messages from him. It was a letter from Lora Edney, for example, that brought Hardin the devastating news his father had died, and Hardin's greatest support in his outlawry was gone. Not only that, but on December 25, 1875, his buddy and partner in crime, Jim Taylor, was shot to death in Clinton, Texas.[3]

John Wesley Hardin would have to run far this time. He would have to leave Texas and hide like a rat to survive. There was no going north; he was known along the cattle trails. Going west was not an option either, but going east offered hope. His wife's family was originally from the area north of Pensacola, Florida.

Of course, he couldn't use his own name. Within the family was a constable in Brenham who was willing to get involved. His name was Harry Swain and his wife was Jennie Hardin Swain, a cousin of Hardin's. John H. Swain, a kinsman of Harry Swain's in Smith County to the north, had been born in January 1853 and was almost exactly the same age as Hardin. There may have been a physical resemblance too, so, while a fugitive, Hardin adopted his name, John H. Swain.[4]

Harry and Jennie Swain accompanied Jane Hardin and her baby to New Orleans. Wes Hardin and his wife then continued on to Gainesville, Florida, where Hardin bought a saloon. Sweeping floors, setting up glasses, and inventorying beer kegs were not part of his plan, however, and he soon got into trouble.[5]

Hardin next traveled to Pollard, Alabama, where he met up with his wife again. Domesticity was boring, and before long, Hardin left his family to travel back and forth to the gambling dens of Mobile. Trouble continued to plague him.[6]

About this time, Hardin's brother-in-law, Brown Bowen, wrote a letter that was intercepted by the Rangers. Hardin was located, and his arrest effected. According to Hardin, the arresting officer exulted, "John Wesley Hardin, you are the worst man in the country, but we have got you at last."

He was returned to Texas, convicted, and waited in the Austin jail pending an appeal. During this time the jail housed a rogue's gallery of Texas' worst troublemakers: George Gladden, John Ringo ... and now Brown Bowen, the man responsible for Hardin's being arrested by the Rangers.

Meanwhile, Hardin's family lived in fear. Hardin commented, "It drove my father to an early grave; it almost distracted my mother; it killed my brother [...] it left my brother's widow with two helpless babes [...] to say nothing of the grief of countless others."[7] Hardin, however, didn't mention his pregnant wife's predicament and what his incarceration meant for her.

John Wesley Hardin's prison sentence was confirmed, and he was transported to the hellhole of Texas, Huntsville Prison. Arriving on October 5, 1878, he was given prisoner number 7109. Described in the prison ledger as twenty-six years old, five feet, nine inches tall, about 160 pounds, with scars all over his body[8] he was assigned work in the wheelwright shop. Immediately, he began to plan an escape,[9] believing "in jail even a coward was a brave man."[10]

To Hardin's surprise, he was betrayed by other prisoners, and as soon as he was released from solitary, he planned another escape. His cellmate, Hardin believed, betrayed this plot, too, and Hardin was flogged. "My sides and back were beaten into a jelly, and, still quivering and bleeding, they made me walk in the snow across to another building...."[11]

Though Hardin was "clean-shaven and boyish in appearance,"[12] he showed signs of being seriously unbalanced. He became a malingerer and hypochondriac. He lost weight, suffered depression, was thin-skinned, and humorless. He couldn't understand why others feared him. At the same time, he fed off the idealized comfort of his mother and wife, and he gave lip service to the glorified image of male figures in his life. He became a religious zealot and taught Sunday school classes. He wrote preachy letters full of criticism but couldn't take his own advice. He grumped about other prisoners, jail conditions, guards, and food.

The truth is Hardin was not a model prisoner. He made trouble as often as he could. He planned escapes; again and again, he was punished. From 1879 through 1883, his life was confrontations and punishments. He was flogged, confined in solitary, had his writing privileges revoked—though he secretly corresponded through the services of a guard, appropriately named J. C. Outlaw— and he was restrained by a ball and chain. Still he refused to work; he threw food; he was deliberately lazy.

His letters were full of excuses. He convinced himself if he promised he would bear no ill will toward the citizens of Comanche, the "facts" of the killing of Charlie Webb would come out, and he could be released from prison. He railed against the "cruel and inhuman" conditions in Huntsville. He characterized his trial as "illegal and unjust," and he called the people of Comanche a "cowardly mob;" he designated Huntsville "a dungeon of obscurity;" he crowed he had singlehandedly defeated the State Police and the Freedmen's Bureau.

A peculiarity of Hardin's letters from prison is the cool tone he takes with his wife. In contrast to his lack of understanding for her plight, is the compassionate way he mentions a prostitute, Sallie Campbell. The likely candidate for this woman was eighteen years old, a servant living in the household of Neil Campbell, related to Hardin through his in-laws, the Bowens. What makes this woman interesting is she was black, and if she were the prostitute mentioned so favorably in Hardin's letters, it adds a new layer to Hardin's ambivalent feelings toward black people in Reconstruction Texas.[13]

In prison, Hardin desperately needed support. He asked his mother and wife to visit him, a difficult journey of 300 miles in deep winter. This unreasonable request showed Hardin's self-absorption. His wife wasn't much help either. Jane Hardin has always received sympathy. None of her letters to him survive, but an examination of dates of surviving letters he sent to her—and which she dutifully saved—shows she was not a prolific writer herself. Hardin was on his own.

He claimed to have backed out of an escape plan in 1883, but evidence is he was involved right up to the last minute. He was sick most of 1884 with an abscessed wound, which was lanced three times, and his weight dropped to 135 pounds. From 1886 to 1893, he was an average convict, but then in May 1893, he was again punished for resisting authority, inciting a riot, gambling, and impudence.[14]

Even so, prison gave him what he needed: discipline. For a fragmented personality subject to fits of rage, jail reduced him to the elementals. He rose, slept, and ate at the direction of the prison schedule. His only contacts were limited to guards and other prisoners. Eventually, he came to have affection for them, once even writing, "I am getting along splendid and of late have no trouble and believe that the keepers of this place are above [sic] treating a man confined to their care with anything else than with humanity and kindness."[15]

Feeling better physically, Hardin settled down. He began to study law. He was not, however, the only inmate who tried this. The *El Paso Herald* of November 13, 1895 reported the arrival of "Lawyer McIntyre, who served with Hardin in the tailor shop at Huntsville." Even though Hardin's law studies were not particularly unique, he soon became the most famous "jailhouse lawyer" of the time.

Hardin was taken from prison to stand trial for the murder of J.B. Morgan in Cuero, Texas, on January 3, 1891. His wife sat beside him at the trial, her first contact with him in years. Found guilty of manslaughter and sentenced to two years to run concurrently with his previous conviction for murder, Hardin was described as "reading law, and to judge from the remarks he made to this court and jury ... he has been quite a student and may yet make his mark." [16]

Two major events now affected Hardin's future. The first was the death of Jane Hardin on November 6, 1892.[17] In poor health, she had been staying at the home of her sister-in-law, Sissie Cobb, at Sedan, in Gonzales County. Though Hardin was anything but close to her, her death weighed on him. Loyal, patient as a saint, and consistently supportive, Jane had provided his most stable anchor. Though she was the mother of his children, Hardin had spent little time with her during their marriage, and he went years without communicating with her; nevertheless, he was shaken by her death.[18]

A second event affecting Hardin was a new climate of forgiveness for Texas' Confederate veterans, many of whom had been discriminated against during Reconstruction. A generation had passed since the end of the Civil War, and the veterans were old men. Texas began to review their petitions for pensions on a county-by-county basis. Pardons, paroles, and pensions were handed out freely. Helen Jennings' father, Bill Williams, for example, was one who benefited, being approved for a Confederate pension in Williamson County. Hardin was seen by as a kind of rebel, too, though his experience was resisting federal authority during Reconstruction.

So, beginning about 1891, Hardin gathered supporters,[19] and on February 17, 1894 he was released, having served 15 years, 135 days. It was big news all over the country. Gushed one newspaper, "John Wesley Hardin, whose victims number between 20 and 50, not counting Mexicans and Negroes, has been released from Huntsville after serving over 50 [sic] years in the pen."[20]

About a month after his release, Hardin was granted full restitution of his rights. A Certificate of Prison Conduct issued on March 15, 1894 at the instigation of Governor J.S. Hogg noted Hardin had committed offenses in prison, including "mutinous conduct, conspiring to incite impudence, throwing food on floor, laziness, [and] gambling." Nevertheless, Hardin's supporters believed he was a reformed man.

On July 21, 1894, shortly after returning to his old stomping grounds in Gonzales County, Hardin passed the Texas State Bar exam. He tried to assert his authority over three adult children who didn't remember him, and he renewed friendships.

John Lackey, a mulatto blacksmith, had been a State Policeman in 1871. He and another policeman, Green Parramore had encountered Hardin in a store in southern Gonzales County. Hardin killed Parramore outright [. ...] Mr. Lackey had lost his teeth to Hardin's gunfire and headed for a lake where he remained with his nose out of the water until Hardin had left. Twenty-three years later [...] Hardin [...] again met up with John Lackey [....] With Hardin's usual sense of humor, he mentioned the lake incident to Mr. Lackey, who told how he had 'really mixed it' with Wes Hardin.

'Have you seen Hardin since that day[?]' Wes asked.

John replied, 'No, never laid eyes on him since.'

Then Wes said, 'Well, you're looking right square at him now.'

Mr. Lackey's terror of the situation subsided quickly when Wes Hardin assured him that all was past and forgiven—and that they were friends.[21]

Though Hardin had given lip-service to the raising of his children, he didn't know what to do with them now that he was back in Gonzales County. "Mollie, John Jr., and Jennie were glad to see their father and get to know him after so many years, but they were about grown, and they soon missed their friends and their real home, the Sedan area. Mollie was especially restless, since she and Charles Billings had been waiting to get married for nearly a year, and her father had talked her into putting it off for awhile."[22] His youngest daughter, Jennie, had never really been part of the family, for she had been born after her father's incarceration and had been raised by Hardin's sister, Aunt Matt Smith, in Red River County, three hundred miles north. She yearned to return to those she knew best. Young Wes, a gentle boy who favored his mother, accepted his new role dutifully.

Hardin's control over his children, his preachiness, and his messing with their lives probably led to conflicts. Another possibility, however, is that he didn't spend much time with them. Inexorably, saloons were calling him back; his old friends hadn't amounted to much over the years, and they gave him a siren call he must have found hard to resist.

> Some of [Hardin's] friends [...] asked him to show how fast he could shoot, promising not to tell anyone about it.
>
> He agreed. They then chose the target, a knot on a tree about 60-70 feet away, approximately eye level, and about as big as a saucer.
>
> Taking a gun in each holster, Hardin stood with his back to the tree. Someone yelled, 'Look out!' He whirled and by the time he had turned, both guns were out and shooting. He fired 8 shots and holstered his guns.
>
> 'Sorry, boys,' he said, 'but I don't empty my guns for anybody.'
>
> The group then checked the target. There were eight bullet holes in the knot and the whole incident had not lasted longer than 2 1/2 seconds.[23]

In the fall of 1894, confident of his position in Gonzales County, Hardin decided to get involved in the campaigning for sheriff. William E. Jones, the Democratic nominee, had been sheriff in 1872 when Hardin had escaped from jail. Jones's opponent was Robert Coleman, the Populist nominee. Wrote Hardin, "Bill Jones by his treacherous conduct toward me has forced me to oppose him for the office of Sheriff and to favor RR Coalman. [sic] Now he has forced me to oppose him by trying to turn John Lackey against me. [...] He expects to be elected by the negro vote—but I think he is badly beaten."[24]

Hardin solicited affidavits from kinsmen and friends alleging Jones' involvement in his escape in 1872. He also published letters calling Jones "Judas Iscariot" and "Benedict Arnold," but when the votes were counted, Jones narrowly defeated Coleman, a humiliation Hardin could ill afford.

He began drinking again. His new status as a celebrity brought him as many free drinks as he could hold. In those days, there were no laws preventing ex-cons from having a gun—though in truth, Hardin was pardoned, and his civil rights had been restored—but it's obvious he now had plenty of guns. His incredible skill handling a weapon had not diminished in prison, but even so, he began practicing day and night after his release. Due to his drinking, his shooting, and his hopeless friends, Hardin could not have been much of a father.

At the same time, he was infected with a sense of hopeless drift. His wife was dead, but he'd never spent much time with her. His children didn't know him and didn't warm up to him after his release. He didn't live anywhere; he just stayed with friends. He was lost and alone. His single-minded goal for years had been to get out of prison, but having achieved that, he wandered from event to event without plan or control.

He had failed in the saloon, horse-trading, and lumber businesses in Alabama and Florida; he'd failed as a butcher and cattleman, too, and time after time, he was drawn to the easier money of gambling. He was someone who could capitalize on others' weaknesses. That is why gambling appealed to him, and the practice of law did not.

So, summoned to visit his younger brothers and cousins in faraway Kimble County, Hardin packed up his grip on November 12, 1894[25] and moved on. Since his release from prison until his departure from his adult children, he had known them only eight months, and it was a tiresome experience for them as well as for him. About a month later, his daughter Mollie married Charles Billings. Hardin did not attend the wedding and may not have even been invited.[26]

9
THE FLIRT
NOVEMBER 1894–JANUARY 1895

"[S]he is full of Hell. We have kept her at home, but
the Devil is in [her]...."[1]

There is only thing more dangerous than an aging ex-gunfighter with no prospects: a teenager with everything to gain. John Wesley Hardin was ripe for the picking. He had fame but no fortune. He had a plan but no drive. In the late 1870s, after the violence of the Sutton-Taylor Feud and the lynchings of Comanche, Hardin's surviving cousins, the Clementses, settled in Kimble County, Texas. Barbed wire fences were less controversial here; there was less history to the waterholes and cattle trails, so the Clementses bought land, strung wire, began to improve their stock, and do their own haying. Jeff and Gip Hardin, Wes's younger brothers, joined the Clements and Denson families in the summer of 1894. They settled easily into the rhythms of the modern cattle industry, and they were on their way to being middling ranchers.

Kimble County had opportunities for a newcomer. The county seat of Junction City had a lot of promise. Rather than being a little fish in a crowded pond in Gonzales, there was a chance to be a big fish in a new pond in Kimble County.[2] The Clementses wrote Hardin of the possibilities, and he walked away from the controversial elections of Gonzales County to start anew. About the end of November 1894, he journeyed to Kimble County. As an up-and-coming attorney, he could make a reputation in a criminal case, and with his name-recognition built in, get elected county attorney or judge and live a comfortable life in a drafty Victorian home surrounded by pecan trees. When he died, he could have a ten-foot marble headstone and a hundred Masons walking bareheaded in a procession accompanying his hearse to the cemetery. None of this was out of reach. Hardin could achieve goodness, as other 1870s hardcases were doing in the 1890s.

But Hardin could not. He lacked direction. His only cronies barflies,

Hardin reacted to events rather than controlled them. He was welcomed to the Kimble County Bar as an attorney, but he spent his time in bars. He was indiscriminate. He drank beer; he drank wine; he drank whiskey; he drank what anyone else was paying for. Hero worship was his only reassurance; the glory of the past comforted his listless soul.

The reality of John Wesley Hardin in November 1894 must have been shocking to the Clements family, who had known him in better days. He had once been so devil-may-care, so fun, so flamboyant, but now he was adrift. For cowboys like the Clementses, Hardin's appearance seemed unnatural. Though he had acquired horses in Gonzales County as payment of legal fees, and though he made inquiries about dealing in horses in Polk County,[3] one of Hardin's physical complaints now was hemorrhoids, and sitting a saddle was uncomfortable. He had no interest in cattle and cowboying either, for they symbolized work to him, and he had spent the last fifteen years proving how lazy he could be. How odd, the Clements family must have thought; how pathetic they are, he must have believed.

And so, the Clements family decided to reform him. The first thing he needed was a stable feminine hand to take charge, to guide and counsel him, to give direction, to add sparkle and zest to an otherwise hollow and gray man.

Hardin was always charming, intelligent, and entertaining. He could hold babies in his lap by the hour, and he was a favorite of old people. In Texas of the past, the chief entertainment in the evenings was sitting on verandahs spending time together. Families were closer then. They knew each other's stories and weaknesses; they forgave more, and they enjoyed each other more. Hardin was raised as part of this, and he was full of stories. He loved barbecues and Fourth of July picnics. He was great at funerals and church socials. And he must have liked to dance.

Another person who liked to dance lived twenty miles away.[4] Her name was Carolyn, or "Callie," Lewis. She was the daughter of Bettie and Londin Lemuel Lewis. Lem Lewis, born in 1838 in Springfield, Illinois, had been in the Union Army in the Civil War, came to Texas in the mid-1870s, and bought a half section of land in the northeast corner of Kimble County. Like many men of his day, he was a horse trader with an interest in race horses.

Lem had married Betty Boyce Anderson, born in 1857 in Burnet County,

Texas. They had four sons: Seth, Vann, Jack, and Damon, and two daughters, Carolyn and Annie. A slender man with an erect posture, Lem Lewis staked out 40 lots for a city center and donated a block of land for a square, hoping the area would grow into a government center; several years later, he promoted a plan to petition the Legislature to form a new county from parts of Kimble, Mason, and Menard counties, similar to a plan in northeastern Mason County to form Mineral County. Land surveys were expensive, however, and nothing came of either plan.

In 1895, the Lewises lived in London, Texas.[5] Lem Lewis was postmaster, justice of the peace, hotel keeper, and ran a wagon yard and stable. As his dream of developing his holdings into a new county seat faded, Lewis would move his investments. He bought and operated a hotel in Mason for a while; later, he and his wife homesteaded near Terry, Montana.[6]

Callie Lewis was an attractive, spirited teenager. She loved to laugh and flirt. She was popular with the boys. She could ride well. Her parents indulged her more than most parents did. For a flirtatious fifteen-year-old,[7] they allowed her a lot of freedom.

In December 1894, someone hosted a dance. In the way of such things then, families came from miles around. Horses, mules, and wagons filled the yard; we can imagine the menfolk smoking and drinking. Since it was about Christmas, treats and good, solid food strained the tables. Knowing Texas, there was probably a calf turning on a spit over a mesquite fire. Smoked hams, perhaps some venison, poultry, and *cabrito* were also laid out for the hungry guests. There was shooting at targets out in the trees; horses were shown off and probably raced. There was a preacher, and doctors and lawyers. Cotton farmers and stockmen rubbed elbows with cowboys. Children played everywhere. Babies were passed from hand to hand. Most people were dressed in their finest. This was the kind of crowd in which Hardin excelled. He and his cousins, the Clements and Denson boys, circulated among the crowd. Hardin was the most celebrated guest. The host and hostess probably introduced him proudly, and Hardin lorded over the gathering.

He was firmly in his element. We can picture him kissing babies, shaking hands, and taking a drink. Perhaps he shot at targets to impress the boys. He may have talked outlawry but probably not jail. He talked religion; he demonstrated his mastery of law. He may have solicited clients and passed out business cards. We can suppose he showed an interest in the horses, and he met and impressed Lem Lewis. Not long after this, Hardin began to dance. He probably danced with fat ladies and thin; he took a turn with the grandmas too, but sometime at this party, he met the long-haired, vivacious Callie Lewis. Sparks flew.

Callie enticed Hardin from the beginning. Her parents approved, but so did Hardin's relatives. A cousin, Green Denson, knew Callie. Callie's supporters believed she was what Hardin needed; Hardin was what Callie and her parents wanted. He seemed a good match; he was charming, a lawyer, famous, and a big talker. He claimed to be writing a book and looked serious and settled. He was also knowledgeable about horses, and that was good with Callie's father.

If the above scene is correct in most respects—and it is likely—an interesting scenario must have happened. Callie and Hardin may have gone outside for a breath of air. The starry Texas skies, the heat of the dancing, perhaps a sip or two of Old Tanglefoot, and the two had a moment. We don't know what was said. What is apparent is plans were made.

On December 30, 1894, Callie wrote, "Mr. Hardin, I guess you will be a little bit surprised to receive a note from me. Either that or think me cheeky to address you first but you told me if I wanted to see you to let you know so I will tell you I will expect you [N]ew [Y]ear's."

Callie was quite forward in this short letter to Hardin. On January 1, 1895, he replied,

> I [...] am highly pleased at your effort to inform me that you again desire to see one who wishes and hopes to be more to you than a friend nominally speaking. I will, on the account of bruises received in a runaway the evening I left you, have to forego seeing you now but assure you that I will come at a more convenient day. In the mean time, be sure of my sincerity of purpose. You know my proposition, so please let me hear from you at your earliest and direct [mail to] me.

From the above, it's apparent Callie and Hardin had talked marriage the last week of December. In her next letter she seems abashed at her flirtatiousness. She was more secretive, too, which Hardin must have insisted upon. On January 2, 1895, she wrote:

> I received your note and was sorry that you could not come New Year. I went to a dance last night. Miss Nora Ivy is with me. They are going to have that party Friday night at Uncle Boyce's aunt Palestine(?) Tolds me to be sure and write you to come. She is going to look for you and I will be disappointed if you don't come. Be sure and come.
>
> P.S. Don't let any one see this.[8]

It was a teenage conspiracy. Nora Ivy wanted to see Hardin, but Callie would merely be disappointed if Hardin didn't show. Hardin is addressed as Mr. Rogers, and Callie signs herself as his "cousin." Her first letter had been too forthcoming; this time out, she was withdrawn. Callie was playing Hardin like a fish, and she must have felt the joy of an angler when the bobber goes down. As her letter went out for the day, Hardin's next letter arrived. Later on January second—though still misidentifying the year as 1894—she replied,

> You spoke in your Letter about the Proposition you made. I will say That I don't like to answer such question by letter. I had rather see you yourself To answer such question. I think papa would like to see you so come as soon as you can.[9]

Things moved quickly after that. We can suppose Hardin went to the dance at Aunt Palestine's. Flattered by the girl's attention and accepted by her parents, he was encouraged by his relatives. Callie was egged on by her parents. She may have found it hard to believe the greatest celebrity in Texas was interested in her. There's no evidence either Hardin or Callie wondered at how easy it all was, how smoothly things fell into place.

A week after Callie's third letter, John Wesley Hardin and Callie Lewis were married by Justice of the Peace F. Wahmund.[10]

It was probably a raucous wedding. Hardin's relatives were there: Green

Denson, the Clementses, Hardin's brothers Jeff and Gip, and the Taylors. Callie's proud parents probably threw a shindig. Gip Hardin emptied a woodshed for the honeymoon suite.[11] This being Texas, there was a shivaree, a mock serenade, and as soon as the lamp went out in the woodshed, pots and pans were banged and guns shot into the air to interrupt the happy couple. Hardin was dragged off, all bashful and embarrassed to have a few snorts with the boys; a laughing Callie was feted by her female relatives. The woodshed probably never got used that night.

In the Hardin Collection today, there is an envelope postmarked London, Texas, suggesting a letter, now missing, dated January 11, 1895. It was probably a congratulatory message to the newlyweds. No one stopped to think that a forty-one year-old ex-con had married a fifteen-year-old virgin.[12] With Lem and Bettie Lewis accompanying them, Mr. and Mrs. John Wesley Hardin traveled to nearby Kerrville, Texas. There are rumors the Hardins traveled on to a honeymoon in Mexico. A postmaster notified Hardin he was holding his mail in Kerrville,[13] and then the Lewises wrote a long letter to the happy couple January 23, 1895:

> Tell Callie to send me an order for her mail. There is a letter in the office for her from her auntie, Mrs. Susie Westerman, that's my sister, and I will read it and send it on, if she says so. Also tell her to tell Mr. Brewer [the postmaster?] to turn Callie's letter box over to me. [...] Tell us how you are pleased with the trip.[14]

This letter is the most significant the Lewises wrote. There are stories the marriage didn't last an hour, or survived just one night. For example, "Some old-timers declare he left her at the altar. Others say he took her to Mexico on a short honeymoon, brought her back and then left her."[15] Another is, "About the only time I ever heard it mentioned by her was once [when] one of the ladies from the church snapped at her that she'd only been married one day to this Hardin fella, and [Callie] came back, 'One month.' And she never spoke to that lady again."[16]

Among the legends, there are stories Jeff Hardin destroyed any chance of the couple's happiness when he joked his older brother was robbing the cradle. There are unfounded speculations of failure—Hardin's as a man, perhaps impotent with a virginal teenager, perhaps too rough after fifteen years in prison;

and Callie's failure as an immature, grasping flirt. Both of them would be stung to the bone the rest of their lives by what was to happen between them, but the truth may be more complex. Rather than being a failure on someone's part, the end of the marriage may have been a simple recognition on Callie's side. She may have understood, in the end, she did not know the man she had married.

It may have had origins in the small talk of newlyweds over dinner. Hardin didn't have much to chat about. He had started an autobiography, and she may have seen his first draft or listened in horror as she realized she had surrendered her virginity to the most sociopathic killer of the Old West.

The real John Wesley Hardin was not the charming fellow bouncing babies on his knee at an ice cream social. The real Hardin was probably revealed in a Mexican hotel one night. It may be hard to picture people of a hundred years ago having sex, but imagine this anyway: Hardin is nude, standing beside the bed in flickering lamplight. His eyes, remarked upon by all who would remember him, were snaky. He was pale, more so than the average man, for he had just spent fifteen years in Huntsville, the Hellhole of Texas.

"He had scar wounds on his right knee, left thigh, right side, hip, elbow, shoulder, and back."[17] The wounds were from pistols, knives, whips, and shotguns. He had a slightly crooked left arm from a fall off a horse.[18] This was not a man who could be the gentle lover of a fifteen-year-old girl. The myths of cattle drives, escapes from posses, and a brave young man resisting authority wilted hollowly away in the face of reality. The romance was gone forever. The end of the marriage was not Callie's failure, nor Hardin's. The truth is Callie Lewis Hardin grew up on her honeymoon, and she didn't want this marriage any longer.

Even so, neither seemed to know what to do. Callie was a good girl, with respectable parents. Divorce was out of the question; an annulment was not possible.

The second week of February, Hardin returned Callie to her parents' home. Callie wouldn't talk about what had happened; Hardin was vague, but he offered the Lewises hope things would work out. And then he did the manly thing: he left town, his options open, his future uncertain. In the coming months, he and Callie kept up appearances. She was a married woman; Hardin had responsibilities, but he had no idea how long they would last. In the Hardin Collection is another empty envelope, postmarked February 7, 1895, from D. Doole, Mason, Texas, to Kerrville, then forwarded to Austin, where Hardin was again trying to elicit interest in his life story. It was the classic business-trip gambit. Callie's husband was "away on business," and she was still respectable. Her life could go on.

Even so, Lem and Bettie Lewis were perplexed. They didn't know what had happened. Neither Hardin nor Callie was talking, so the anxious parents assumed Callie was merely having second thoughts. On March 4, 1895, Bettie Lewis wrote Hardin:

> Callie seems to be downhearted. I can't tell whether she has changed any or not. I let her go to one dance with Green Denson, but she did not dance any. That is the only time that she has ever gone with anyone. She stays home with me all the time. [...] She is so young and so much like a baby that I think maybe if you send her money or clothing that she would see and think that you were the best friend that she has got. [... S]he seems like she is wild. All of the young people are mad with me because I won't let Callie go to dance like she did before she was married. I always tell them she is a married woman and at home with her mama is the place for her while her husband is gone. I will do everything for you that I can. You may rest assured that I am a true friend to you, and that Callie will not have anything to do with any other men more than just being polite. [...S]omeday in the near future, I may see you and Callie living happily with each other.[19]

The same day, Lem Lewis, promoting himself to "major" on the return address on the envelope, wrote:

> Callie is just as you left her. She is full of Hell. We have kept her at home, but the Devil is in her. What and how she will come out is more than I can tell. I would like to see you. [...] I suppose Green Denson can tell you more news than I can, as he has been around more than I.[20]

Still there was no change. The Lewises did not press their recalcitrant daughter, but as they gradually lost hope, Lem Lewis wrote Hardin again on March 23, 1895:

> I received a letter some time ago, but waiting to see if there was any change in Callie. I see no change in her. She seems just as you left her. You said in your letter you wanted me to be plain in the matter. I don't think she will become satisfied with you, although she may change any day. Green Denson has not been since he came back from Pecos. Green can tell you more and can do more with Callie than all of us put together. I hope she will become satisfied and make you a first-class wife, but I am at my wit's end. If Green Denson can't fix the matter between you and her, we might as well let the matter sleep awhile.[21]

The same day, Callie's mother wrote Hardin, "I can't tell any change in her. She wants to see Green Denson. Since he came back from [Pecos, Texas] I think that Green could get her to go to you. She has more confidence in him than anybody. I never knew what was the cause of your and Callie's first trouble, but it seems to be something that she can not get over. Sometimes I think that Callie will get alright, but if you want to get a divorce I would not object. [...] I believe that if you had not met your brother and sister when you started off that you and Callie would have been living together now, but of course, you know more about that than I do...."[22]

And that's how it ended. Callie kept the name and maintained appearances. The *Mason County News*, May 31, 1895, reported "Mrs. John Wesley Hardin spent Tuesday in town on her return from Burnet to her home at London, Kimble County."

Hardin, who could hardly support himself, let alone a young wife, left her under the control of her parents. His cousin, Green Denson—not the best man to have acting for his interests since he was just a card shark—tried to intercede, but after a short time, he gave up. The separation was complete.

10
THE TROUBLE IN PECOS
JANUARY–APRIL 1895

> "Come at once by Sunset Route. [W]ill meet you at
> Sierra Blanca."[1]

Bud Frazer shot Jim Miller on two occasions. To understand this, it is necessary to appreciate the fact that in Pecos, Texas, Jim Miller was not a snake. There were rumors about him, to be sure, but he was a small town nobody on the verge of greatness. He was dangerous, but not yet fearsome.

Born October 25, 1861 in Van Buren, Arkansas, Miller, together with brothers Andrew and William and sister Georgia, was brought by his parents to Coryell County, Texas. When his father died is uncertain, but in the 1880 census, Miller was being raised by his widowed mother Cynthia and possibly his grandparents.[2] Shortly afterward, Miller's sister married John T. Coop, a farmer who lived nearby. Though the motive is unknown, on July 30, 1884, Jim Miller murdered his brother-in-law with a shotgun. In what was to be a pattern, he claimed innocence, blamed others (including a brother), and confused the legal process with a brilliant defense team. He was convicted, sentenced to life in prison, won a retrial on appeal,[3] and was acquitted.

Dee Harkey, unreliable as he is, claimed Miller then ran into trouble in San Saba County, Texas. A number of Millers lived north of the Jennings' homestead, near Fredonia. It was the Miller family who had lent a horse to Helen Jennings to flee her marriage to Steve Jennings. Though their relationship is uncertain, it's probable Jim Miller was connected to these Millers.

"Jim Miller was tall and somewhat raw-boned. He had ears that stood quite a way [sic] out from his head, and behind them he had bony lumps like half an egg. One of the Pecos women called them 'murder bumps.' Apparently amateur phrenologists thought they meant a killer temperament."[4]

By 1886 Miller was a friend and employee of Mannen Clements in McCulloch County. Once as wild as his notorious cousin, John Wesley Hardin,

Clements had settled down, married, and had livestock in Ballinger. On the afternoon of March 29, 1887, "Deputy Sheriff Joe Townsend, Sheriff Formwalt[5] and Manning [sic] Clements were in the Alamo Saloon. The two latter were drinking, and Formwalt had fired off his pistol in Hamilton and Conner's Saloon a short while before. [...] Formwalt was drawing his pistol, and Townsend had seized it, when Clements with a oath ordered him to stop, and was leveling a pistol which he had in the meantime drawn, on Townsend. Retaining his hold upon Formwalt's pistol, Townsend instantly fired, the ball entering about an inch above Clement's eye, ranging backward and upward."[6] Clements, one of Hardin's closest relatives and benefactor of Jane Hardin and her three children during the early years of Hardin's incarceration, died violently like many connected to Hardin.

Jim Miller took offense at Clements' death. On November 11, 1887, Joe Townsend was shotgunned in his restaurant in Ballinger. He survived with the loss of an arm. The man who shot him was Miller. A shotgun was Miller's weapon of choice, and shooting from ambush his favorite style, and therein lies the problem with Jim Miller. Every bit as complicated as John Wesley Hardin, Miller deserves a major psychological biography, but so far, no one has stepped forward to do it. We are left with a dark rumor that deserves research: he may have murdered his grandparents when he was eight years old.

On February 15, 1888, shortly after ambushing Townsend, Miller married Mannen Clements' daughter, Sarah Jane "Sallie" Clements, Hardin's first cousin, once removed. Not long afterward, the newlyweds moved to Pecos, Texas, where they operated a hotel and ran a few cows.

G.A. "Bud" Frazer, born April 18, 1864 in Fort Stockton, Texas, was a solid citizen of Pecos. His father was the district judge. Frazer was a former Texas Ranger, and it was perhaps inevitable he run for and be elected sheriff of Reeves County in November 1890, reelected November 8, 1892, and served until November 6, 1894. He seems to have been a fairly good sheriff for that sparsely populated district, but he was a terrible judge of character.[7] Shortly after his election, Frazer hired Jim Miller as a deputy. It was the first of five times he underestimated Miller.

Several hard cases arrived in Pecos about this time. Best known was

Barney Riggs, a man who could brag he had gone to prison for killing one man and released for killing another. After his release, Riggs relocated to Pecos, where he married Frazer's sister, Annie.[8]

Bud Frazer was a tiny man with a chip on his shoulder. With a hothead for a deputy and an ex-con for a brother-in-law, Frazer was immersed in the culture of the gun. The first to use it, however, was Miller. Though the date is uncertain, Miller killed a Mexican prisoner he was escorting to Fort Stockton to stand trial. Miller claimed the prisoner was trying to escape, but Frazer didn't believe it. The incident was a watershed in relations between the two men. Though Frazer was ineffective in his dealings with Miller, his intentions were good. Unable to prove anything, he fired Miller, but his troubles were only beginning. Miller had ingratiated himself with some of the best citizens of Reeves County. He attended church regularly—indeed it was at this time he earned the nickname "Deacon" Jim Miller. He began to wear a long black frock coat. Though he played cards, he didn't drink and never cursed or used tobacco. Furthermore, he had ambitions.

In 1892, Jim Miller ran for sheriff against Bud Frazer. Prominent citizens supported him in the election, and relations between the two men were acrimonious. Nevertheless, Frazer was reelected. Shortly afterwards, the Pecos City government appointed Miller as town marshal. That month, in an unrelated development, but one that would impact events later, William Earhart moved to Eddy, New Mexico, from Las Cruces. He would soon be joined by a friend, John Denson, a cousin of Jim Miller's wife. Both men had nasty reputations as drinkers, rapists, and brawlers.

Tensions between Frazer and Miller grew worse. In May 1893, while escorting prisoners to Huntsville, Frazer received a message Miller was going to assassinate him upon his return to Pecos. A drunk named Con Gibson told his brother, Reeves County Clerk J.B. Gibson, of a plot hatched by Miller and Martin Q. Hardin, distantly related to Miller's wife through the Tennessee branch of the Hardin family. Brothers John and Billy Ware tried to talk Con Gibson into participating, but Gibson refused to join the scheme.

The plot had several intrigues. Said Frazer, "Miller wanted to get me to a Mexican *baile* to kill me. Was also told by Con Gibson of a plan to kill me at the bridge. John Ware also told me and Manning Clemmons [sic] in the presence of Mr. Lakey, that Miller wanted to pay him to kill me. A Mexican named Juan Rubio also told me that a Mexican named Guiterez told him that Miller tried to get him (Guiterez) to kill me."[9] Another plan was that as Frazer was disembarking from a train, two accomplices would stage a disagreement, and Frazer would be killed by a "stray" bullet.

Frazer anticipated the plots by riding straight through to El Paso and organizing his supporters, including the Texas Rangers. Miller and Mart Hardin were indicted for conspiring to kill Frazer, but tensions did not lessen. The Rangers returned to Pecos in August, but even so, rumors swept the little community that Frazer had been killed. On November 10, 1893, the men accused of conspiracy to murder Frazer were acquitted.

With tensions at a fever pitch, there was only one way to end the suspense. On April 12, 1894, Bud Frazer shot Jim Miller. Up to that point—and ever afterward in most historians' minds—Bud Frazer was the underdog. It was a classic preemptive strike, an under-gunned lawman faced with a formidable foe better with a gun than he. Other lawmen would use the same tactic in the West and get off on self-defense, hung juries, or legal delays. The shooting of Jim Miller, however, was different.

Bud Frazer was no chicken. When he "threw down" on Miller, he went right to shooting. For a moment, it seemed a typical Texas gunfight. Smoke obliterated the scene; the noise was deafening as the .45s roared, but in one of the most surreal gunfights of the Old West, Jim Miller did not go down. Hit in the right arm, he swung his gun over to his left hand and commenced firing back. Hit at least once dead center in the chest, he continued firing, and he was still firing as Frazer ran away. Said the *Eddy Argus* prophetically, "This shooting, in all probability, is but the beginning of the feud."[10]

Frazer testified, "[A]s I was passing, Miller [...] reached for his pistol [....] I was quicker than him and fired one or two shots before he got his gun out. I may possibly have fired three. He backed away from me and was trying to get in an alley and before I fired my fourth shot, he had reached the corner of the building and was aiming at me. I aimed with both hands and fired, hitting the corner of the house. [...] I had shot at him with a pistol and [...] I wished I had a shot gun."[11]

As noted in Chapter 5, about a month after the shooting, Con Gibson, who had informed Frazer about the plot to kill him, was shot to death in Phenix, New Mexico, by John Denson.[12]

Miller disappeared, reportedly to a hotel in Lordsburg, New Mexico, owned and operated by Mart Hardin. For a time, Frazer controlled the roost in Pecos, but even so, the tide was against him. Unpopular now, he ran against Daniel Murphy for reelection as sheriff and lost. Frazer had worn out his welcome in Pecos with the talk and feuding.

The *Eddy Argus* of December 21, 1894 announced Frazer had given up and moved to Eddy to set up a stable and livery business. Even so, it may have been a ruse, for three days later, Frazer had a second shootout with Jim Miller on the streets of Pecos. Like the first, Frazer had to run after emptying his pistol, and Miller was left standing though hit several times. Frazer must have been spooked; he couldn't kill Miller. Miller also seems to have been scared; he couldn't shake Frazer. For a second time, Miller secreted himself at Mart Hardin's hotel in Lordsburg.

Miller had Frazer charged with assault to kill. Not trusting the legal system, however, he surrounded himself with supporters and called in big guns, so to speak. One of these was attorney John Wesley Hardin, Miller's wife's cousin, who was down-and-out in Junction, Texas. Wrote Miller from Lordsburg, "I guess you know that I have had so much trouble that I am eternally broke but considering all of that I have got lots of friends in Pecos. The best citizens of Pecos said they would make up a reasonable fee for you if you would come and prosecute [Frazer.]"

Writing on February 22, 1895, the El Paso District Attorney wrote Hardin in Pecos, "I will be pleased to have your assistance in the preparation and trial of the Fraser [sic] case."[13]

So, John Wesley Hardin traveled to Pecos. There was a smell of gunpowder in the air. Pecos was alive with conspiracies. Jim Miller and his wife probably danced from foot to foot they were so excited. Hardin was in his element at last. A celebrity lawyer asked to help prosecute the case, a well-dressed, handsome man in his prime, he accepted the role naturally. Miller decided to show him off, taking him to a girl's sixth birthday party. "Hardin was a very handsome man. Miller was quiet. Sat back and let the others do the talking. They had an ice vream [sic] freezer going ever since morning. In those days, it wasn't so easy to get ice cream. Miller and Hardin came after most everybody else was gone."[14]

With Hardin in town, Frazer made himself scarce. Though the case was named, "State of Texas vs. George Frazer," the newspapers referred to it as the Miller-Frazer case, and it was moved to El Paso on a change of venue. While he was in Pecos, however, Hardin made himself useful. It was only one hour, fifty minutes by train to Eddy, New Mexico. Frazer was up there, and so was John Denson, who was in trouble for assaulting Phenix City Marshal Lon Bass.

W.H. Smith, an Eddy County constable and Denson's cousin, wrote Hardin on February 28, 1895, "John Denson is still in jail—have been trying to get him bond but have failed. Vick Queen is willing to go on it for all he is worth but he is the only one that I can get that is acceptable. Queen says that he knows you. Or did know you when he was a boy, and would be glad to see you. [Also] Kemp and Bass [....] They are keeping still about John of late and if we can get him bond I believe we will get the trouble settled. I haven't heard if Frazer is going to Pecos or not." [15]

The Queen reference is significant. Victor Queen[16] was the first cousin of John Wesley Hardin's wife, and again, as so often happened in Hardin's life, he gave lip service to family. Hardin also called W.H. Smith a cousin, but the relationship is tenuous—a cousin's cousin.[17] With Denson, Smith, and Queen only ninety miles away, it was natural Hardin make a quick trip north.

Those who've studied Hardin in the past have assumed this trip to New Mexico was a combined pleasure and business trip to look into the legal troubles of John Denson and indulge in what had become the Las Vegas of the Old West, the saloon district of Phenix. There was gambling, drinking, and whoring aplenty along Phenix's streets, and it can be assumed Hardin indulged his tastes in all three. He may have renewed his acquaintance with his kinsmen Victor Queen and John Denson; he also met one of Eddy's prominent citizens, Martin Mrose and his beautiful new wife Helen Mrose. It was the second time Helen had seen Hardin, and this time, it made an impression on him.[18]

This may not, however, have been Hardin's only interest in Phenix. Hardin may have been gathering evidence for the prosecution, but a second motive was his own. In 1887, Hardin had tried to escape from Huntsville Prison. The plan failed, and the reason was Hardin had been ratted out. He says, "[M]y fellow convicts always gave me away and generally got some privilege for doing so."[19]

One of these former convicts was now living in Eddy. Imprisoned at Huntsville when Hardin was there and serving a similar twenty-five-year sentence for murder, this convict had cooperated with authorities and was released and pardoned in 1887. He became a cowboy in Hamilton, Erath, Nolan, and Fisher counties in Texas, then pulled up stakes and, in 1888, moved to Eddy County, New Mexico. He was a man with friends but potent enemies, too. He carried a gun and was not afraid to use it. He was a business owner and a strong man with ambitions.

Who was this mysterious ex-convict, this informer on his fellow prisoners? His name was Dave Kemp, the ex-sheriff of Eddy County and best friend of Martin Mrose.[20] If Hardin desired revenge for what had gone wrong in prison, the object of his anger was surely Dave Kemp.

Surprisingly, Kemp wasn't concerned. Writing on stationery from Sheriff J.D. Walker's office on March 6, 1895, he addressed Hardin with a familiar, "Friend John," then offered his analysis of John Denson's chances in court, "I think that Dinson [sic] has a very hard case, in fact I don't think there is any show for him to beat it." He concluded, "I will be up in Pecos in side [sic] of 4 or 5 days and I can explain things to you better in person than I can write. I would be glad to have you come up and stop with me a week or two...."[21]

Prison buddies getting together? Would they have reminisced about old times on the cellblock? Somehow, the whole thing smacks of danger. Kemp understood he was playing with a snake; as long as he had it in sight, he was safe.

This makes the W.H. Smith letter especially interesting. Smith said, "Queen [...] would be glad to see you. [Also] Kemp and Bass [....]" Kemp and Hardin's relationship must be described as having a dangerous undercurrent, but Lon Bass was the man Denson had assaulted and the reason he was in jail. A competent gunman in his own right, Bass may have wanted to see Hardin to meet—and kill—the greatest celebrity of the Old West.

On March 8, 1895, Hardin, described by the *Eddy Current* as a "reformed desperado and practicing attorney of Texas," arrived in Eddy to look into the case of John Denson. On March 13th, the paper described Hardin as "probably one of the best known men in the west." It went on to declare "Hardin is a young appearing man, weighing about 200, without a gray hair on his head or mustache, which latter is much lighter than his hair, which is quite dark. Hardin [...] now has more legal business than he can attend to. He is a cousin of John Denson, and by simply giving his word that Denson should be on hand at the next term of court, he obtained sufficient bond among people here, who no doubt would not otherwise have signed the bond."

Who did John Wesley Hardin convince to put up bond for Denson? None other than Martin Mrose was listed as one of the sureties. John Denson was liberated on Monday, March 11, 1895 and was reported to have left town March 12th with his uncle, Jim Clements, for Junction City, Texas.

Shortly afterward, John Wesley Hardin, Jim Miller, Mannie Clements, John Denson, Jim Clements and other hangers-on traveled by train to El Paso to prepare for the Frazer assault case, which had been moved there on a change of venue.

> Mayor [R.F.] Johnson met [Hardin] at the railroad station and advised him to step carefully and leave all the local killing to [John] Selman or else [.... W]hether the mayor met Hardin or not, the chief of police [Jeff Milton] did. He followed the distinguished visitor and a group of his hip-heavy relatives to McClain's saloon. There, identifying the gunman by the fact that he was making more noise than anybody else, he stepped forward and introduced himself.
>
> 'Our laws don't permit people to wear pistols on the streets,' he said quietly. 'So you will have to put your six-shooters and rifles in the care of the bartender.'
>
> Hardin was miffed but he also seems to have been puzzled. 'Do you know who I am?' he asked without raising his voice.[22] Unfortunately for Hardin, Milton knew who he was—and didn't care. Hardin and friends were disarmed.

Hardin had family in El Paso. His first cousins (once removed) were Roberta Whitmore, wife of El Paso city alderman and prominent contractor, James L. Whitmore, and Jennie Louise Powers, wife of Frank Powers, a businessman. These young women were the daughters of Hardin's cousin John Dixon Hardin, a son of "Uncle Bob," Robert Echeson Hardin, who had aided Hardin's flight to Florida years before and financed his defense in Comanche in the Webb murder trial. Roberta was the second of Uncle Bob's granddaughters to become involved in Hardin's affairs. It's likely Hardin stayed with the Whitmores or Powerses for a week or two, but El Paso was a fast town, and Hardin probably found it advantageous to take lodging elsewhere.

On April 10, 1895, the examination of witnesses began, among them Eddy County ex-sheriff Dave Kemp,[23] who had talked to Frazer at the Pecos depot the morning of the shooting. On April 14, the jury in the case was split 8-4 for conviction. With a hung jury, the case was rescheduled. Frazer asked for a change of venue and a second trial was set for Colorado City in Mitchell County. Bud Frazer and his father, according to El Paso papers, were in and out of El Paso at least through June 1895. Jim Miller, still plotting and conspiring, wrote Hardin, who had chosen to stay in El Paso, "I write you in regard to the Red Fox. I wish you would find out when he is coming down, then arrange and let me know when he takes the train, and in case he intends to stay on at El Paso or not."[24]

The "Red Fox," of course, was Frazer, but whether Hardin participated any further in Miller's machinations is not known. By this time, he had become intimate with a woman and seemed well fixed. He leased an office, had business cards printed, and solicited business. El Paso was his kind of place. A fast town with an active red light district, bustling saloons, and gambling that even Jeff Milton, in a short career as Chief of Police, had been unable to suppress, El Paso appealed to Hardin's vices, not his ambitions. He decided to stay, have some fun, and work on his autobiography.

And Miller was left to stew.

PART FOUR
El Paso

"Whereupon he promised with an oath to give her
whatsoever she would ask. And she […] said,
"Give me […] John [the] Baptist's head […], and
the king was sorry; nevertheless for the oath's
sake, and them which sat with him at meat, he
commanded it to be given her. And he sent, and
beheaded John …. And his head was brought […]
and given to the damsel."

—Matthew 14:7-11

11
THE DESPERADOES
MARCH 1895

"Martin Marose's little girl sends it to you."[1]

T he windy spring of 1895 was an unstable one in Eddy, a time of omens and portents. On March 9th, Dave Kemp tore down a gallows on which he'd hanged murderer James Barrett in September 1894. The gruesome gallows had brooded over the town for months. There was a blood-red eclipse of the moon on March tenth, not a cloud in the sky, and residents of Eddy got a perfect view.[2] Finally, Dee Harkey was elected a constable in January 1895 and appointed a Deputy U.S. Marshal in the spring of 1895.

Harkey considered Martin Mrose the greatest rustler of the age. Years later, he claimed Mrose had offered him a thousand calves a year, plus cash amounting to his annual salary as a cattle inspector to turn a blind eye to rustling operations.[3] At this time, just after the Panic of 1893, the floods of the same year, the closeout of VVN operations, the national economic crisis, and the Eddy brothers selling their interests in the Pecos Valley, there were probably not a thousand calves in Eddy County, let alone calves under the control of one rustler.

The range was overgrazed; water resources after the flood of 1893 were uncertain. From 1893–1895, ranching was difficult. "Most of the herds were in poor condition, the range having long ago been eaten out and trampled until the grass is dead."[4]

It's appropriate here to bring this absurd claim into focus. If rustlers could afford such a bribe for one officer, their total operation would have had to have been ten times that number, amounting to thirty or more cattle stolen every day. Legitimate ranchers would have been wiped out. And what would Harkey have done with so many calves with other men's brands on them? Put his own brand on the cattle? It is a fact Harkey did not have a ranch nor a brand of his own until years after the alleged rustling was over. Besides that, in November 1894, an Eddy County grand jury concluded its session by bringing in only one indictment against a rustler, finding no other cases to indict.[5] Even worse, Harkey wasn't appointed a cattle inspector until April 1895, and by then the alleged rustlers were gone. On top of that, it wasn't until October 1897 someone was tried and convicted of cattle theft—in this case, for stealing one calf![6]

Even so, Harkey made this preposterous claim in his book, *Mean as Hell*, and it's been quoted carelessly ever since. Most of the people Harkey wrote about were dead by the time the book was published, but one oldtimer, Cis Stewart, former sheriff and a neighbor of Harkey, was still alive and so incensed by the book he said, "He's just no good, and if he's got ten friends in Eddy County I don't know who they are except his own family. [… H]e's wrong, the fella's wrong, that's all [….] He lied."[7]

A friend of Dave Kemp said, "I wrote to the man that wrote that book, and I told him […] he had better not write any more, because I would take this book and see that he was persecuted [sic], taken to trial. That's exactly what I told him. If it had taken everything I had!"[8] Harkey was sued twice; he spent his last years living with a daughter.[9] Upon his death, she took a pile of unpublished chapters outside and set them on fire. The copyright to the book was thrown into the public domain by the courts.[10]

So, if Harkey was wrong, what is the truth? The truth is Martin Mrose and William McClendon were indicted for receiving stolen goods on November 17, 1894.[11] Despite the accusations since, the warrant was more a misunderstanding than anything else over a stove and cooking utensils worth ten dollars, plus 1,500 pounds of Egyptian corn valued at $11.25 and dishes costing three dollars that had belonged to a man named C. F. Bassett. The incident leading to this warrant dated from April 1, 1894, about the time Mrose was plowing, planting the Egyptian corn, and irrigating a portion of his land in neighboring Chaves County.[12] The crop came to naught, Mrose admitting that same month his agricultural production consisted "of grass only. 80 acres plowed and cultivated [but…] no crop yet raised…."[13]

Mrose was served with the warrant by his friend Sheriff Dave Kemp the day it was issued by the grand jury. Mrose went to the courthouse and pleaded not guilty; he was ordered to appear for trial at the February term of the court. The case against Mrose was dismissed on April 14, 1895.

Different than an indictment was a complaint, and these were usually filed through a justice of the peace. S.I. Roberts, JP in Precinct 1, reported for the quarter ending June 30, 1895 that Victor Queen was charged with defacing brands and larceny, and Martin Mrose with unlawful brands, defacing a brand, horse stealing, and rustling. None of these charges resulted in a warrant or an indictment by a grand jury. The *El Paso Daily Herald* declared, "He was accused of receiving about $25 worth of stolen household goods and having them in his possession. However, he had ample proof to show he purchased the goods. This is the only case filed against Mrose."[14]

With a charge—even a minor one—hanging over him, however, Mrose must have felt concerned. The legal climate was changing. Kemp, his friend, was no longer sheriff, though he still worked as a deputy for the new sheriff, J.D. Walker. Squirrelly little Dee Harkey had wrangled himself an appointment as a constable, and Les Dow was tearing up the plains as another. More than any of these, however, the witchhunt of the Edmunds Act lay like an angry storm on the horizon.[15] Without a doubt, Helen Mrose felt threatened. If she and Mrose were investigated, the unfinished mess she'd left back in Fredonia, Texas, was sure to be discovered. If anyone in Eddy County was guilty of an Edmunds Act violation—in this case bigamy—it was she.

Another consideration was the erratic court schedule. It was hard to get anything settled. Continuances and delays, as well as uncertain court dates plagued every legal action. One resident complained, "I do not know when court convenes. The clerk did not know when I was there. You know they do not hold the court until they get the money, but it will be sometime this fall."[16]

As a precaution, Mrose began to sell out. His ranch, cattle, and his Seven Ladders cattle brand—often called the "Golden" Ladder—and his horse brand, the Fiddlecase, were sold to the Witt family.[17] Mrose then sold most of his remaining cattle to Todd Barber and William McClendon. As a matter of course, the bill of sale was routinely recorded at the courthouse. A witness to the transaction was Barber, Mrose's friend and a kinsman of Helen's.[18]

An indirect look at accusations against Mrose reveals that someone made a complaint Mrose had stolen one cow. This resulted in two requisitions from the office of William T. Thornton, Governor of the Territory of New Mexico. The actual complaint of this theft has never been found, and that leaves only one other documented source accusing Mrose of anything: a civil suit in 1892.[19] Ivy Cass, the complainant, alleged Cornelius A. Collier and his wife, Ivy's sister, had taken charge of her 75 horses and sold most of them to Mrose for $12.50 a head.

Cornelius Collier admitted in court documents Ivy did own a half interest in the horses, which she and her sister had inherited from their father. Collier stated that as soon as Ivy came of age in June 1892, he arranged the sale in order to settle accounts with her, minus expenses. Mrose and his fellow defendants were represented by two of the ablest attorneys in the territory, Albert Bacon Fall and W. A. Hawkins, the Eddy brothers' personal attorneys, but the suit never made it to trial, being dismissed upon the death of Collier. Mrose wasn't accused of any wrongdoing, merely with buying the stock against the young woman's desires.

The best evidence against whether Mrose rustled cattle is in the Eddy County Record of Marks and Brands. A huge outfit like the Eddy-Bissell Cattle Company registered three brands. Martin Mrose registered sixteen different brands. Without a doubt, this is an indication he made a business of buying out smaller cattlemen, absorbing their brands as his own, and lawfully registering them at the courthouse. Rather than being proof of stealing, it is evidence of a legitimate enterprise.[20] Mrose had "bought and turned herds loose."[21] That comment, and others, is supported by the records. At the same time, the county assessor increased Mrose's taxes based on an inventory of his valuation. A rustler would certainly not want an inventory of his cattle for tax purposes.[22] Still another telling detail is that in 1894, Bart Nymeyer and the great promoter C.B. Eddy traveled through blizzards to Roswell to transfer water rights and appear as witnesses for Mrose's Desert Land Application. They wouldn't have done this if there were any hint of scandal attached to him.

With a threat of legal nuisances increasing, Mrose, by all accounts, departed Eddy County alone on horseback.[23] That his decision was sudden is hinted at by the appearance bond solicited by John Wesley Hardin just three days before on behalf of John Denson. Martin Mrose and Thomas E. Jones had put up bond of one hundred dollars.[24] On March 16, 1895, two days after posting bond, Mrose took leave of Eddy County. Shortly afterward, Helen Mrose and her daughter Laura Jennings caught a train to Pecos.

Despite the rumors of Mrose's departure and warnings to watch out for him, a touching incident during Mrose's trip showed the true mettle of the man. One morning, he rode in to the William Edwin Bass Ranch, near a lake twenty miles north of Eddy.[25] Bass's wife, Susan, was the sister of Jeff Chism, Martin Mrose's friend and the foreman of the Eddy ranch. Mrose was in a hurry, and he needed two good saddle horses. For trade, he had driven in a small herd of his stock. William Bass owned a thoroughbred stallion and other fine horses, and he brought them for Mrose to look over.

As the men dickered, Bass's little daughter, Eva, born in 1890 and about the same age as Laura Jennings, played in the dirt outside the family's tent. Poor, isolated, out-of-touch, the little girl had no toys, and she had learned to make figurines out of clay, hanging them in the mesquite bushes to dry. A few days afterward, her brother, Holland, drove up to the Bass Ranch bearing a package for Eva, a gift from one little girl to another.

She recalled, "When I run out to meet him I see a small baby sitting next to him on the wagon seat. [...] And Holland bursts out laughing because it's not a baby beside him on the wagon seat, it is the largest doll I have ever seen. 'Martin Marose's [sic] little girl sends it to you,' he says."[26] It was a beautiful "Sleepy Doll," her very first doll.[27] Eva would remember this generous gesture the rest of her life. Undoubtedly, Mrose had noticed Eva's miserable clay toys and mentioned them to Helen and Laura. It's possible they bought a doll and had it sent to her, but it's more likely the doll was one of Laura Jennings's own toys, not needed now that they were on the go.[28]

So, which way did Mrose go? It's long been known he went to Midland, Texas, but knowing the exact route would reveal much about the man. In the 1890s, southeastern New Mexico was overgrazed, and dwindling water resources were changing the land to what we know today. The terrain is harsh desert, scraggly brush land, and rugged mountains. To the south of Eddy, the landscape is pebbly and covered with spiny agave, cow's tongue cactus, creosote bush, yucca, and screwbean mesquite. East of the Pecos, the country is dust and sand covered with half the thorned plant varieties of North America: Palo Verde, catclaw, ocotillo, and wait-a-minute bush. There was little grazing here except within a twenty-mile swath near the Pecos River. Every water hole, well, and windmill was known and visited regularly. A knowledgeable cowboy checking his stock would circle a tank first to read in the dust the register of visitors the night before.

East of Eddy, the high plains were more accessible. Windswept and dotted with cactus and Spanish Swords, the plains were the land Mrose knew best, the range land of the VVNs. Every cowboy, settler, and freighter knew him here. There was nowhere to hide.

Which way did Mrose choose to go? The answer comes from one of Martin Mrose's friends, Stem Daugherty[29] who ranched northwest of Midland, Texas. He had a ranch 75 miles east, on Monument Draw. Martin Mrose rode in to the Daugherty Ranch in March 1895. He came "with [a] pack horse and another saddle horse and said if I'd give him a horse I had, he said he'd leave his horses. Was going to Midland to meet this woman who [sic] he had married. He went down with me in [a] buggy, and just left all his horses. When we got there, he gave me a bill to all his stuff. Then she came down by train from Eddy, stayed there awhile, and came on to El Paso. He had $6000 and said [he] was going to El Paso and on to Mex[ico to] buy a ranch. Had more than [he] wanted to carry and left $2500 with me. I gave him [a] receipt for it."[30]

So, Martin Mrose had ridden northeast of Eddy, to Monument Springs and the safety of the Daugherty Ranch. From here, he and his friend made an unhurried buggy ride to Midland. Mrose took few precautions, though it's apparent he was careful whom he trusted. He rode the most predictable route, through country he knew best, and he carried with him what was—at that time—a vast amount of cash. His ride to Midland was not a serious evasion of the law.

Mrose's destination was so predictable one of his bondsman, newspaperman W.H. Mullane, anticipated him and convinced Midland County Sheriff W. D. Allison to look for him for skipping out on a bond. Allison found his quarry camped beside a water hole a short ride northwest of Midland. Mrose and Daugherty were cooperative and agreeable. They followed the sheriff into town to face the music. While there, they got a hotel room, then took time to go to the courthouse, where Mrose sold Daugherty his remaining horses and cattle.[31] Helen Mrose and her daughter Laura Jennings joined Mrose in Midland. They must have thought they'd left their troubles behind, but all hell was about to break loose.

After being arrested twenty miles from Midland, [...] Mrose gave the officers and W.H. Mullane, his bondsman, a promise to come to Eddy without a requisition, and they released him. When, near train time, they called at the room occupied by himself [sic] and the woman who traveled with him, Mrose had disappeared.[32]

Another account says, "Mrose agreed to waive his right to a requisition if the sheriff at Midland would accompany him home, being then under arrest and in charge of the sheriff. On going to supper the sheriff left Mrose [...], he being then in his room at the hotel, but on going to his room after supper, it was found Mrose had escaped through some back way. Mrose probably procured a horse and left for Mexico, where he may some day be found."[33]

No one can say what happened exactly, but it seems clear Mrose got wind of dangerous news sometime between his arrest and scheduled departure. Dee Harkey hints at it in his book, but there are few details anywhere else. Unfortunately, Midland newspapers from this time do not survive. What appears likely is that the cattleman's association offered a reward for Mrose.[34] Who gave him the news is not known, but a friend, J.M. McKenzie rushed into Midland and gave him cash and horses.[35] Besides McKenzie's money, Mrose was known to be carrying thousands of dollars he'd brought from New Mexico.

With perhaps a thousand more offered as a reward, he was suddenly the most targeted man in North America. It's probably safe to estimate Mrose's "worth" to a lucky captor as somewhere around $10,000. Leaving $2,500 with Stem Daugherty was a wise precaution. McKenzie's handout in Midland—claimed to be evidence of Mrose's complicity in "rustling," of which McKenzie was sometimes suspected—is just as likely a sign of good faith and friendship towards a granddaughter of the Ellisons, longtime friends of the McKenzie family in Caldwell County, Texas. For this reason, ten thousand dollars on the hoof seems a plausible, conservative estimate of what pursuers could expect.

For sure, lawmen George Curry, Charles Perry, J. D. Walker, Doña Aña County Sheriff Pat Garrett, plus Brand Inspector and Cattleman's representative Les Dow, newly-appointed Deputy U.S. Marshal Dee Harkey, not to mention

Sheriff W. D. Allison of Midland County, Texas, Deputy U.S. Marshal George Scarborough and Texas Ranger Frank McMahan, plus assorted border guards, customs officers, city police, El Paso Constable John Selman, Sr., Customs Inspector Johnny Behan, Eddy resident and semi-retired Col. G. W. Baylor, El Paso Chief of Police Jeff Milton, plus an assortment of banditos and barflies[36] were suddenly interested in Martin Mrose. For that reason, Mrose, Helen, and Laura Jennings were in great danger, perhaps as great as anyone ever faced on the frontier. Taking a train out of the danger zone was not an option. Everyone would be watching for a big man, a beautiful woman, and a little girl. An alert porter on a train platform and a telegraph would be all that would be required to catch them. Up and down the Pecos and Rio Grande valleys the word spread like wildfire. Anyone with a badge could make a fortune by bagging this suspected rustler encumbered with a helpless woman and a four-year-old girl.

How could they get away? It was three hundred miles to the safety of Mexico, and the desert was swarming with lawmen. For at least part of this journey, Helen and her daughter accompanied Mrose by horse, but at the first whistle stop out of Midland, Martin and Helen Mrose may have come up with a stratagem to get them to safety. "We divided what money we had," Helen revealed. "I took $2,000, and he took a check for $2,500. [...] I arrived in Juarez the latter part of March."[37]

And Laura? Remember, a little girl and a pretty woman would stand out rather obviously for those looking for them. "You know, the story's told that the woman cut the little girl's hair and carried her to Mexico."[38]

Helen traveled under the name Beulah Mrose. There is not a single documented use of this alias before this time, yet it is the name Helen Elizabeth Williams Jennings Mrose is best known under today, and there are hundreds of references to Beulah, Helen Beulah, or Helen Beulah Mrose after this time. Undoubtedly, the alias was a defiant answer to the witch hunt of the Edmunds Act in Eddy County, for Beulah is a Hebrew word meaning "married."

And so, shortly down the line from Midland, the three parted ways. Helen and Laura caught a train to El Paso and quietly crossed over to Juarez, Mexico. But what of Martin Mrose? What was his escape route across the howling desert? Incredibly, he rode back to Eddy to face his accusers and settle his debts. W.H.

Mullane, editor of the *Eddy Current*, who had put up his bond, never spoke badly about Martin Mrose again. Did Mrose pay him back? It's probable, and if he did, he also took care of his close friend Todd Barber, who had also put up bond.

The *El Paso Daily Herald* of May 7, 1895 says, "He kept his promise to [return] to Eddy while the officers supposed him far away. It seems that he spent one or two nights in Eddy or vicinity; that he took supper in town and stood on the courthouse square for two hours, after dark, talking to one citizen in a few rods of the jail he did not wish to occupy. After consulting with several friends, the fugitive concluded to skip to Mexico."[39] Without a doubt, two of the friends Mrose consulted were Dave Kemp and Tom Fennessey.

"Martin Mrose came back to Eddy, you know," Helen Bond Melton, a longtime Carlsbad resident, librarian, and amateur historian, told the author in 1997. "Yes, Mrose came back to Eddy from Midland and dared anyone who had a grudge or a claim against him to step forward. He stood out there on the courthouse square for two hours, and quite a crowd gathered, but no one had anything against him, so's [sic] he mounted up and said, 'If any of you ever say my name again or speak of my wife, I'll come back here and kill every one of you.'"[40]

Another man recalled, "My grandfather worked for Sheriff Walker. When Martin Mrose rode back into town, everyone was surprised and scared. The sheriff ordered supper be cooked for him [i.e. the sheriff], and he ate it. Mrose stood out there on the southwest corner of the courthouse hollering. Quite a lot of people come [sic] to see him. Everyone liked him, and they come [sic] to give him money and help. After a couple hours, Mrose rode out. Walker then finished his supper and appeared and wondered what all the fuss was about? [sic]"[41]

But why go back to Eddy? This might best be answered by an obvious question: where is the safest place out in an open desert swarming with lawmen? Behind them, of course.

Now, having been spotted in Eddy, with telegraphs singing and telephones ringing ahead of and behind him, posses on his trail south of Roswell, south and east of Eddy, southwest of Midland, and north of Pecos, with bounty hunters, Texas Rangers, lawmen, cowboys, settlers, and everyone in between alerted, Martin Mrose made his flight across the desert. There was not a water hole in two hundred miles he could safely visit, not a shanty for shelter, not a corral, or a fresh horse not known to his pursuers. One-armed Eddy City Marshal Jesse J. Rascoe came the closest to getting Mrose. "It appears that out at the Guadalupe mountains, the fugitive was hidden in a cabin when Marshal Rascoe stopped and took dinner while pursuing two horse thieves, though Rascoe never suspected how close he was to making an unexpected capture."[42]

It's possible Rascoe, a friend of his, knew he was there and turned a blind eye, thereby allowing him to slip away, but all the other pursuers put their best desert sense to use and missed him completely, another indication Martin Mrose may have been one of the best cowboys and horsemen of his day. For that reason, it's easy to picture him wahooing in triumph as he escaped into Mexico, shooting into the air as he splashed across the Rio Grande River somewhere east of El Paso, Texas.

12
BEAUREGARD LEE
APRIL 1895

> "I saw in an upper window of a lodging house [...]
> the wife and daughter of the fugitive."[1]

On April 6, 1895, a furious windstorm swept across the desert. Dust and grit swirled everywhere in the streets of Eddy and El Paso; roofs were torn off, windows were broken. Many of the irrigation ditches so laboriously dug by hand near Eddy were buried by drifting sand. The west wind was hot and angry. It would be an eventful day. Martin Mrose would be apprehended in Mexico.

The arrest of Mrose was the result of investigative police work by a Santa Fe Railroad detective named Beauregard Lee. Born in August 1868[2] in Virginia, Beauregard Lee was part of the proud Lee family of Virginia. His father, a cousin of General Robert E. Lee, was James Garnett Lee, who had been born in Bedford County, Virginia, in 1817. He married Susan A. Moorman in 1841, and together they had eight children. The family was burned out in the Civil War while James Lee and his brother, Garnett, were off fighting; by 1870, the Lees grazed sheep between the Apishapa River and the Pickett Wire of Las Animas County, Colorado.[3]

In 1879, the Lees crossed into New Mexico. James Lee and his sons homesteaded along Tinaja Creek in Colfax County, which had little land available for homesteading, for the Maxwell Land Grant occupied most of the land. The Tinaja Creek homesteads were strategically located to control grazing and water access southeast of Eagle Tail Mesa. In 1890, two years after "proving" their homesteads, the Lees sold their properties and moved into the town of Raton.[4] The Santa Fe Trail passed through Raton on its way from Missouri to New Mexico. The Atchison, Topeka and Santa Fe Railroad partially followed the trail through Raton Pass in 1879, and the town of Raton was founded in 1880. Here, James and Susan Lee built a house at 630 S. 2nd Street.[5] Beauregard, their son, made his home in the Buena Vista District, a honky-tonk area paralleling the railroad yards near the Crystal Palace Hotel.

By 1895, Beauregard Lee was a railway detective. This says a lot about the young man. In 1894, partly as a result of the Panic of 1893, the Pullman Company, the railroads, and the labor unions were locked in a tense standoff. In Raton, the strike became confrontational. Crowds of stranded passengers, hundreds of soldiers, dozens of federal marshalls, and others descended on the town. Martial law was declared, and troops stayed in Raton for two months guarding railroad property. That Beauregard Lee was employed by the railroad after the strike, and, furthermore, was in a trusted position as a railway detective, not only says a lot about his trustworthiness, but his competency as a lawman.

Lee must have been impressive. His mother-in-law said when she arrived in Raton from Chicago, she was accosted by a whiskey-filled miner. Beauregard Lee picked the man up like a sack of potatoes and threw him across the tracks.[6] Lee was big and darkly handsome.[7] Family tradition hints he was fluent in Spanish.

When no law officer could locate Martin Mrose, Beauregard Lee traveled to Juarez to try his luck.

> The ever watchful eye of Beauregard Lee was directed to a suspicious female in Juarez last Saturday. He at once engaged the services of Señor Francisco Haro, the valuable, tried and trusted commandante (or chief of police) of Juarez. The eagle eyes of the two vigilant officers of the law followed her alternately until she prepared her departure for Magdalena, Mex., via the Mexican Central train. Then both boarded the train and as unseen companions accompanied her on her journey to meet the object of her love and the object of their search, Mr. Martin Mrose. Magdalena was reached, her pretended destination, while in fact subsequent arrangements made with the conductor shows that her real destination was the City of Mexico, both baggage and boodie. At this point, both officers alighted on opposite sides of the train to await developments.

> The train had hardly stopped when a large, fine-looking man entered the car and was in the tender embrace of his faithful companion.

'Hold up your hands,' was the order of the hour, and in a moment more Mr. Mrose was in the embrace of a pair of patent hand cuffs, relieved of his pistol, a prisoner. Wife or woman as the case may be, as yet had not been heard from. Daring law and layman, she delved into robes around her for a woman's weapon in the shape of a .38 calibre revolver, but the wary watchmen, too well trained in trifles, relieved her of the pistol and $1,880 concealed in her pedal garments.[8]

The Mexican Central Railroad had advertised a special fare to Mexico City, $20 round trip, good for thirty days. The railroad was an extension of the Santa Fe railroad south of El Paso. It was owned and controlled by the same men who owned the Santa Fe; many engineers and technical people were the same, too. Lee, a Santa Fe railroad detective, had passes on both lines and operated with impunity deep into Mexican territory.

Another account of this sensational arrest said:

> Beauregard Lee, a detective for the Santa Fe company [...] was the first officer to shove a six-shooter under Martin Mrose's nose and corral him. This occurred the day of the terrific gale in April. [...] Mr. Lee knew of the reward for Mrose and naturally did not see why he should not have a hand in the capture if he could. He went over to Juarez, and saw in an upper room of a lodging house there a woman and a child who subsequently proved to be the wife and daughter of the fugitive. He also saw New Mexico officers going up, and suspected something. Lee had a Mexican go into the passenger station later and ascertained the woman had purchased a ticket for Magdalena. Then he and Chief Haro of Juarez followed on the train and set [sic] where they could see Mrs. Mrose. At Magdalena station Lee got off from the off side from the depot while Haro disembarked on the station side to watch. The Santa Fe officer presently saw a large, red-faced man mount the car where the woman was, and enter. He followed him, and convinced the man was the much wanted cattle thief, quickly brushed by him as the fellow laid one hand on the woman in the way of welcome,

and shoving a big sixshooter up under [...] Mrose's chin, called on him to throw up his hands or be blown in two, as he had a warrant for his arrest. Mrose did not comply, when suddenly, ere the officer carried out his threat, Chief Haro rushed up behind Mrose and grabbed his arms [,] shoved them up into the air exclaiming, 'Don't shoot! For God's sake, don't shoot!' Mrose was handcuffed ere he could do anything; but as soon as the woman caught on to what was going on, she made a dive into her bosom for a gun, which, however, was immediately snatched from her by a passenger and Mr. Lee, although some force was necessary. The captured and captors then returned to Juarez on the next north-bound train. Mr. Lee, who is a fearless officer, says that but for the quick action of Chief Haro, he would have killed Mrose then and there—would have had to have done it, because he knew of him as a most desperate character, a man with whom he would take no chances whatever. [9]

Another account reported, "A very important arrest was made at Magdalena, Mexico, a few days ago when Beauregard Lee of Raton, arrested Martin Mrose. The officer's attention was called to the suspicious actions of a woman at the Mexican Central depot in Juarez. He boarded the same train which she took south and at Magdalena had the satisfaction of seeing her met by the redoubtable Mrose. The woman attempted to draw a gun but was disarmed and $1,880 taken from her. The prisoner with the woman, also under arrest, was brought north and lodged in the Juarez jail."[10]

These accounts of the arrest are fairly straightforward, but questions remain. First, where was Laura Jennings in all this commotion? The answer may be rather simple. A Mexican Central time table lists departure from Juarez at 6:35 P.M. with arrival in Chihuahua, 240 miles south, at 7 in the morning.[11] This would make the time of the arrest about midnight, so, in the way of children, Laura was probably asleep in the seat. This may explain the "robes" on the seat mentioned in the *The Eddy Current* report. When awakened, she probably did what any four-year-old child would do: she cried in terror and confusion, and after Mrose was handcuffed and her mother disarmed, Laura probably required much of Helen's attention.[12] It's possible Helen Beulah was jailed temporarily in

Juarez; what became of her daughter during this time is unknown.

As Martin Mrose was being handcuffed, Helen didn't meekly surrender. Instead, she pulled a .38 revolver from her bosom[13] in an attempt to save the day. Helen Beulah was no delicate spring flower. She was a daughter of the Texas frontier. Her father and grandfather would have been proud of her. A family tradition of the outlaws A.J. Williams, Jeff Ake, and a host of others flowed through her veins, and she did not hesitate. She had learned to shoot as a child and was good at it. A measure of her competence with firearms was she didn't have a .45, which would have been difficult to conceal; instead, she pulled a .38, a more manageable "ladies" gun.

A second question is who were the mysterious New Mexico officers who found Helen in Juarez and what did they want from her? Beauregard Lee did not name them, but he knew them. It points out the fact that following the woman was so obvious a plan it occurred to others trying to capture Mrose, but instead of patient police work like Lee used, they tried to cut a deal. They probably offered Helen a portion of the reward money; certainly, they threatened her, but she didn't give in. Frightened, alone in a foreign country, with a four-year-old daughter to worry about, she stood up to the officers and made her plans to flee in secret.

It's possible Les Dow and Sheriff J.D. Walker of Eddy County, New Mexico, approached her. Other "New Mexico officers" who might have taken an interest were Pat Garrett and Charles Perry. The only officer known to have been in Juarez, however, was Dee Harkey. Squirrelly in manner and deed, dangerous and devious as well as deceitful, Harkey appealed to Mrose's wife as a perfect ploy.

> Harkey boasted, "I struck the trail of [Mrose's] horses. I followed them to Juarez, Mexico, and found the horses tied in front of a saloon. I went up to the chief political headquarters and told the chief about Martin [Mrose...] and what I was following them for. He sent a couple men down and arrested them and had them put in jail in Juarez. He took the horses and saddles. I told him there was a $500 reward for these fellows, if he would deliver them back to me in Texas. He told me to get my governor to give me an order for the men and horses, and he would deliver them across the river to me."[14]

This account may be accurate up to a point,[15] for it seems Harkey did make an appearance to gain the extradition of Victor Queen, captured on March 29, 1895[16] on the request of Jeff Milton, El Paso Chief of Police. Queen, "a man of fine physique, being fully six feet tall and fine build with raven black hair, eyes, and mustache"[17] was also in the Juarez *juzgado*.[18]

When Mrose was brought back to Juarez, he joined Queen in jail. Mexican jails are still notorious, but a hundred years ago they were worse. Even so, it is likely Mrose was treated well. He was bigger and more dangerous than other prisoners, he probably spoke Spanish, and his legal status was uncertain. Either returned to the U.S. under an extradition request or released and allowed to reclaim his $1,880, there was big money involved. Victor Queen, already a friend of his in New Mexico, attached himself to Mrose as an ally. Though their situations were different, they were united by common interests, and Mrose's fate became Queen's and vice versa.

Another question about the arrest, however, is where was Mrose arrested? Magdalena is the simple answer, but as is so often the case in this story, it is not the truth. There are several Magdalenas in Mexico.

"The first I heard of Mrose was at Magdalena, and I went there to see him," Helen said in an interview.[19] Magdalena was reached on the Mexican Central Railroad from Juarez, Mexico. The town was—according to Beauregard Lee—a regular stop, where a northbound train could be caught. No extant train schedules list Magdalena, so to understand where Magdalena lay, one must use Mexican records, which are, in fact, more specific than American newspaper accounts. The Mexican case file of Mrose specifically names the site of the arrest as "Villa Ahumada," and, five miles south, just a couple of hundred yards east of the Mexican Central Railway is a village named Magdalena. One can imagine the train leaving Villa Ahumada and building up steam. As the clackety-clack of wheels on rails increased, Martin Mrose felt he was safe, and he rose from his seat, walked up the aisle, and greeted his wife. The distance traveled by train would have been about five miles.

An obvious question then arises. No one was going to stop a train at a place that wasn't a whistle-stop. They must have traveled on to the city of Chihuahua for the return journey. Here we must recall another arrest, years before, under similar circumstances. This arrest also occurred on a train, also without a warrant or extradition papers, and involved a railroad man and a lawman outside their jurisdictions. The arrest happened in faraway Florida in 1877. The outlaw, John Wesley Hardin, was similarly surprised on a train, violently arrested and handcuffed, then whisked away and returned to Texas to face the wheel of justice. The arrest was technically illegal, but no one grieved the process, and he was convicted and sent to prison.

Now, Mrose faced the same peril in this curiously parallel arrest. While they were on railroad property, Beauregard Lee could claim jurisdiction, though he worked for another railroad company. And Commandante Francisco Haro, who was out of his jurisdiction too, carried weight in the state of Chihuahua, for his father was the military garrison commander in Juarez. The two officers rushed Mrose north, getting him out of the city of Chihuahua and the range of the governor and Mexican law. In this case, the arrest was semi-legal, and it provided a basis for Mrose to petition for release, which he did.[20]

An even bigger mystery, however, is what happened to Mrose's money?[21] Helen said they split their money in Midland, and she took half. When arrested on the train, she had $1,880 left.[22] She had probably bought clothes, luggage, and trinkets in Juarez, plus lodging and meals for her daughter and herself, amounting to a few hundred dollars. That would make it appear Mrose had kept $2,500 or more with him, and this was after he had left a similar amount back in Texas with his friend Stem Daugherty.

Mrose wasn't reported to be carrying money on him at the arrest. This may have been routine, but it was probably because the amount was unremarkable. What this suggests is Mrose had disposed of it somehow, perhaps in a Mexican bank account or in a land transaction near Magdalena.[23]

Helen's share of the money–a veritable treasure in those days–was seized by the Mexicans after her arrest. A receipt for the money was issued by Felipe Leijas on April 6, 1895.

> By order of [the Political Headquarters of the District of Bravos],
> the sum of one thousand eight hundred and eighty [dollars] is deposited

with Messrs. Ketelsen and Degetan, said amount includes a fifty [dollar Confederate] bill. It is agreed that said sum is equivalent to the amount of U.S. currency received from Mrs. Bula Mrose, who is accompanying the American Martin Mrose. And as proof thereof for Mrs. Mrose, the present document has been issued. [24]

Without protection and faced with crossing into Texas alone, where her status was uncertain, especially as it related to Mrose's case in Juarez, but also in regards to her status as the run-away wife of Steve Jennings, Helen Mrose continued her crafty subterfuge. "My mother cut my hair and dressed me as a little boy," Laura would recall later.[25]

Just as Martin Mrose had entered the history books by crossing the Rio Grande into Mexico, Helen Mrose did it by crossing the Rio Grande back into Texas to search for a lawyer. She may have contacted Mrose's friends in Eddy County, and days later, Tom Fennessey arrived in Juarez, leaving his wife behind in Eddy. A foreclosure filed in April 1895 complained Fennessey had departed the county, but his wife was still a resident. Fennessey's loyalty to Mrose would cost him everything he had.[26]

For one man, however, the arrest of Mrose was a welcome event. On April 25, 1895, Beauregard Lee married Rae Wilmarth, a pretty young woman from Chicago. The wedding took place less than three weeks after Lee's stunning arrest of Martin Mrose, but it may have been in the works for some time, for Beauregard's sister, Mrs. Ida Tinsley of Lancaster, Kentucky, was in town for the wedding. The timing of the marriage, however, seems to have been tied to the arrest of Mrose and the hope of a large reward. Unfortunately, it's doubtful Lee ever received a reward, in which case the arrest of Martin Mrose may have been for naught.

13
THE HOOSEGOW
APRIL–JUNE 1895

"We come to you in [search] of protection...."[1]

Martin Mrose and fellow New Mexican, Victor Queen, were jailed together pending extradition. For the next two months varying progress was made on the extradition request, but then the desperadoes were released, having applied for Mexican citizenship. This is how it was reported in the newspapers;[2] this is how it's been written about since, but it isn't the truth.

For one thing, Mrose and Queen were never in danger of extradition. Most likely, they were involved in a shake-down scheme, an extortion attempt on Mrose's money by the political boss of Juarez, District Judge Jesus Najera. They were housed in the Juarez *juzgado*. Helen was allowed conjugal visits. "[T]he wife of Mrose brided [sic] the officer of the guard with $250 in American money, and her gold watch and chain to let her enter the prison at times to see her husband ...."[3] Mrose and Queen may have received catered meals and segregation from other prisoners.

Modern bureaucracy does not work any faster today than in the 1890s. New Mexico was a federal territory headed by an appointed governor. A formal extradition request would have had to go through the Eddy County sheriff and the Fifth District Court, to the governor. From there, it would have to travel to Washington, then be routed from the State Department to either the embassy in Mexico City, the Consul General in Nuevo Laredo, or the Consulate in Paso del Norte, as Juarez was called by American officials.[4] The American ambassador or the consul would present the extradition request to his opposite number in the Mexican government, and it would then find its way to the state capital of Chihuahua and the town of Juarez. Even so, there is not one document in the collected papers of the U.S. Consul at Juarez or at the Consul General's office in Nuevo Laredo related to either Mrose or Queen.[5]

An example of the dreadfully slow process a request might take was the case of Prisoner Bothwell, an American jailed, tried, and acquitted of murder in 1891, yet still incarcerated nine and a half months later! Said A.J. Sampson, the consul in charge, "[T]o an American, [the case] progressed very slowly."[6] In the end, through Sampson's intercession, "Mr. Bothwell was sent out of the jail [...] to go on some errand. He has not yet returned to jail to report, having found it to his taste to cross to the United States side of the Rio Grande."[7]

The Bothwell correspondence contains a lurid description of the Juarez juzgado: "As to being put in a room of filth and vermin, without ventilation, [Bothwell] says he was with thirteen other prisoners, so he must have been receiving the same kind of treatment as Mexican prisoners [....] Standing by an iron post in the hot sun, cleaning up the [latrine], put in a box in front of the [latrine], in close confinement, etc., were all things done under the pleas of discipline for violation of prison rules."[8]

There was no heat or ventilation. For food, the prisoners ate tacos.[9] Coffee was provided in the morning. Cells in a similar jail were described as "without seat, bed, or blanket, in a dark place six feet square, with plastered walls and cement floor."[10]

At the time Mrose and Queen were jailed, there were more important affairs going on. The outgoing consul, Charles E. Wesche, was relinquishing his office to Louis M. Buford, the newly appointed consul. Inventories of the consulate were made, correspondence was closed out, and papers were shuffled. At the same time, a serious trade dispute broke out between Mexico and the United States. Porfirio Diaz, the president of Mexico, decreed new rules governing the importation of foreign goods into the country. This action was in retaliation for a Joint Resolution of the U.S. Congress, referred to as "Number Twenty," regarding trade with Mexico. Diaz' decree directed all imports be shipped to three Free Zones, all seaports, to the detriment of American railroads. American products shipped to Mexico now faced increased duties. The effects were immediate and serious, and for a period of months, the climate of cooperation between Washington and Mexico City was frosty, at best. An extradition request arriving during this period was apt to be delayed for months, or even years.[11]

Because of this, the requisition may have been informal. The border states had, for over twenty years, an unofficial arrangement to extradite accused foreign nationals across the border. This seemed to have worked best in Arizona. It was illegal, of course, since only the federal government could deal with a foreign power, but even so, the arrangement worked fairly well. Such an extradition request would have had to travel from Eddy County to the governor's office in Santa Fe, thence to the governor of Chihuahua, and back to the comandante of Juarez, a fairly extensive paper trail.

On April 20, 1895, such an extradition request was made by New Mexico Governor William T. "Poker Bill" Thornton for Martin Mrose on a charge of stealing one cow.[12] A similar requisition was made on April 27 for both Mrose and Queen, and Sheriff J.D. Walker of Eddy, who had already departed for Juarez on April 18th in anticipation of the documents being approved, was named as agent to receive the prisoners.

Unfortunately, copies of the requisition documentation are missing from New Mexican territorial records. What the two requisitions might reveal, however, is suggested by the case of "Big Red," alias Sam Lockwood, arrested in Ojinaga, Chihuahua, Mexico, whose extradition requisition was made July 7, 1896. The "Big Red" requisition, issued for the murder of Levi Herzstein in Guadalupe County, New Mexico, included an application for requisition and extradition from Governor Thornton's office, a certified copy of the original complaint on file in New Mexico, a copy of the original warrant, and affidavits from two complainants or witnesses. Other documents name as agent of the Territory of New Mexico, John R. Hughes, to receive the prisoner.

A theft of one cow was a common charge in court records at the time. Such a charge was often beaten, either by being dismissed due to lack of evidence or absence of witnesses. Even in the few instances on record when a defendant lost his case, punishment consisted of a small fine. Mrose and Queen ran little risk if sent back to New Mexico, yet they fought extradition tooth and claw.

"The process of extraditing wanted men from Mexico ranged from very difficult to impossible throughout the territorial era, depending upon the status of relations between the two republics."[13]

For this reason, the extradition effort was doomed from the start. Mrose's arrest and incarceration may have been designed to relieve him of some or all of his cash. In this case, did it work? El Paso newspapers—and historians using those sources—reported Mrose and Queen were released from jail, and they had "applied for Mexican citizenship."

On April 18, 1895 Sheriff Walker departed for Ciudad Juarez. In June he traveled again to El Paso to look into the case;[14] there he met Captain Haro and other Mexican officials, but nothing came of his trips. In late June, Deputy U.S. Marshal George Scarborough wired Eddy County for a reward for Mrose's arrest, but whom he consulted is not known. The only people interested in Mrose's extradition by then were the Southeastern New Mexico Cattleman's Association, probably the very ones who had made a complaint in the first place.

What it all suggests, however, is that Mrose wasn't worth much. His cash may have been spent on a ranch deep inside Mexico or on fees, fines, or "mordida" during the extradition negotiations. He and Queen may have been living on the good graces of friends. One of these was J.M. McKenzie, of Midland, Texas, who was reported to have come to contribute thousands of dollars.

Mrose did, however, need competent legal assistance to not only fight extradition but to regain control of the cash and $50 Confederate bill seized from his wife at the time of their arrest.[15] For this reason, Helen Beulah Mrose crossed the Rio Grande River and looked for an American lawyer.

There is reason to believe Mrose's and Helen's common interest in recovering the money seized from her was their only shared legal maneuver. From this time on, Mrose's fate was tied not to his wife but to Victor Queen, and the two men adopted a strategy that had little to do with the legal wrangling across the border. Mrose retained Mexican legal talent[16] and Helen sought American expertise.

By this time, mid-April 1895, one lawyer in particular needed clients. John Wesley Hardin was in town, talking about making his residence there. He had taken an office during the Frazer trial, and he was making the rounds of the saloons … to drum up business, of course. Everyone seemed to know Hardin was trouble, but he was popular, and men vied to buy him drinks. He began to shoot holes in playing cards and hand them out for favors. Crowds were astonished by his skill with a pistol, but not everyone was awed. The newspapers often called him a "stranger in town."[17]

Even so, Hardin was a fascination for many. One, a young boy named

Edgar Fewel, encountered Hardin on San Antonio Street. "Mr. Hardin, how many men have you killed?" the brave youngster asked.

"Well, son, upwards of a good many," Hardin replied.[18]

But there were other dangerous men. El Paso claimed several notable gunmen as law officers. Chief among these was Deputy U.S. Marshal George Scarborough, the very man who had killed Helen Mrose's uncle, A.J. Williams, in the Road to Ruin Saloon eight years before. Another was Constable Mannie Clements, Hardin's cousin, who killed Jim Cooksey in Pecos when he resisted arrest in February 1893. There was also Jeff Milton, former Chief of Police, who had been too strict enforcing restrictions on gambling and was replaced in May 1895. Dee Harkey, who did not second-guess these men's activities, said, "There were some shooting sheriffs, good and bad. George Scarborough and Jeff Milton were two of these...."[19]

One of the "shooting sheriffs" visiting El Paso at this time was Chaves County Sheriff Charles Perry. Dee Harkey claimed he accompanied Perry to El Paso to kill Hardin. "I tried to persuade Perry to forget a thing like that, but he paid no attention. [... Perry] told Hardin that he was posing as a bad man and a killer, and that he had come some distance to make a finish of him. Hardin declared he was unarmed; Perry told him he knew he was lying, but to show him that he could shoot square with him and didn't want to take advantage of him, he would place two six-shooters on the bar and they would step back six feet and make a run for the pistols and the best man would win. [...] Hardin told him he was three kinds of a damn fool to think he was that easy, and he walked out on Perry."[20]

Harkey didn't recall events correctly. When Perry met Hardin at the Wigwam, with "a pistol in each hand,"[21] Hardin was visiting with HooDoo War gunman (and lucky survivor), George Gladden.[22] Hardin declined to be provoked by Perry, whereupon Perry transferred his attention to Gladden. He laid two pistols on the bar and slapped Gladden's face. Gladden filed assault charges against Perry, who was arrested by Constable John Selman, Sr. Perry was charged with displaying a pistol and assault and battery; he was fined five dollars and costs.[23] Hardin acted as Gladden's attorney. Ominously, *The El Paso Daily Herald* commented, "There may be more behind the gunplay of Sheriff Perry than has come to the surface. He has been here for some time on business over which there has been a gunplay before. [...] The M'Rose-Queen matter is likely at the bottom of the gunplay at the Wigwam. Someone will lose their life over that matter yet."[24]

Another version of the confrontation comes from an anonymous report, "I was in El Paso [...] when Perry came here looking for John Wesley Hardin. He announced on the streets that he was hunting Hardin for a fight. I did not tremble for Hardin, because I knew Perry had no idea of facing him. However, he went further than I expected him to go. He tanked up on whisky [sic] and allowed John Selman to persuade him to go to the Wigwam [....] If Hardin had showed up that morning he would not have lasted two minutes, but he would probably have killed Perry. When Perry called for Hardin at the bar that morning, John Selman was standing on the stairs with his gun in his hand. After taking a nap, Perry realized he had run a bad risk, so he sent word to Hardin that he would be around to apologize to him in a few minutes, and I heard him make the apology."[25]

A volatile Charles Perry was but one lawman running around half-cocked. Other dangerous officers worked in or near El Paso. Among the Texas Rangers often in town was Frank McMahan, George Scarborough's brother-in-law,[26] and finally—and certainly not the least among these dangerous men—was "Uncle" John Selman, Sr., who had enhanced his reputation in a shooting behind Tilly Howard's pleasuring house on April 5, 1894. A Texas Ranger named Baz Outlaw[27] had drunkenly begun shooting and killed fellow Texas Ranger Joe McKidrick. He then threw down on Selman, who had rushed through Howard's parlor to confront him on the back porch. Half-blinded by gunpowder from Outlaw's gun and shot in the hip and leg, even so, Selman managed to put a bullet in Outlaw that resulted in his death a short time later.

Said one newspaper, "Constable Sellman [sic] is an old officer and has a record as a killer of smugglers and thieves. Some years ago he fought a band of cattle thieves in Dona Aña County, N.M., and killed two and captured the rest, four in all. He killed Bass Outlaw a deputy United States marshal, [who] had come to Texas in such a hurry he neglected to bring his right name along, and in an emergency picked up the one he sailed under in Western Texas."[28]

Selman may have been one of the deadliest gunfighters of all. Close-mouthed about his past, he had fought in the Civil War as one of Moseby's Rangers, then established a nasty reputation for murder and rapine all over Texas and New Mexico. He married and had children. For a number of years, he lived in Mexico. He was a staunch Catholic and a good family man. Constable of Justice Precinct One under Judge W. D. Howe, Selman was left-handed, "and held the pistol in his left hand and fanned with the right." He was five feet ten inches tall and weighed about 160 pounds. His outstanding feature was pockmarks covering his face from smallpox.[29] He was known to be charitable to those in need and supportive of his church, but he thought nothing of shaking down the prostitutes of El Paso for his cut. He was a favorite of street urchins and was fondly called "Uncle John" by most of them, but his eyes were pale, deep-set, and chilling to look into. There was a rumor he was well-endowed, and the prostitutes seemed to know him intimately. In short, he was a most reptilian man.

All these dangerous men, all these loaded guns and badges, all these saloons packed into the bustling downtown section of El Paso were bound to lead to trouble. That is not to suggest, however, that accidents could not happen too. In a curious example of how men who lived with guns were amazingly careless, on June 16, 1895, W.D. Allison, Sheriff of Midland County, wrote Hardin about another charge, this in Midland, against John Denson. After recommending Hardin send money to have someone stand in for Denson and plead guilty to the charge, Allison added, "Manning [Mannie] Clements is at my home this evening, wounded in right hip. 'Flesh Wound' from an accidental discharge of his pistol, While it is painful, yet it is not dangerous, and he shall have good care and attention. He sat down on a cott [sic] and pitched his pistol on a palate [sic] on the floor, and the hammer being on a cartridge, it was discharged."[30]

Just three days later, Mart Hardin accidentally shot himself too. Reported *The Arizona Daily Citizen*, "His pistol fell from the scabbard and striking a rock exploded, the ball entering the body near the kidneys, ranged upward and is supposed to be lodged under the right shoulder blade. He was taken to El Paso for treatment."[31]

Two Hardin relatives, experienced gunmen both, accidentally shoot themselves within days of each other? The coincidence is startling, but the significance reaches beyond that. Mart Hardin's appearance in El Paso has been portrayed as part of a buildup of support during the Frazer trial. With him shot, he couldn't have been much support at all.

Meanwhile Victor Queen and Martin Mrose languished in prison. Queen, arrested on March 29th, was detained without formal charges. When Mrose joined him April 6, 1895, Mexican authorities considered their cases—and fates—joined. District Judge Jesus Najera suspended their rights on the premise men facing extradition did not have the same guarantees as Mexican citizens. Someone, however, gave the jailed men good advice. They hired a middling translator named Sebastian Vargas and wrote a letter to the president of Mexico.

Vic Queen and Martin Mrose before you respectively [say...] the Political Chief [of Juarez] reduced us to prison at the request of the government of the United States which was asking for our extradition, for which reason we come to you in [search] of protection [... against the] order [of] formal prison without the guarantee [of due process] that [... the Mexican] Constitution grants, but we have known that [...] President [Porfirio Diaz] has had to [redirect] our extradition [... for] the protection as [our] initial object to restore [things] to the state which they had before the violation ....[32]

It was a smart move. Rather than waiting months or years for action in their cases, things began to move quickly for the two men. Their plea to President Diaz removed jurisdiction from the civil authorities in Juarez and elevated it to the federal level immediately. Their letter was based on the premise their arrest and detainment were illegal under Article 19 of the Mexican Constitution of 1857.[33] They argued they were being held by the chief political officer in Juarez[34] and were in danger of illegal extradition and perhaps death.

While this was happening, Jesus Najera, the District Judge of Juarez, wrote an opinion saying that since New Mexico was notified by telegram of discrepancies in the requisitions and then by a follow-up letter on April 20th, there should have been plenty of time to resolve the issue of evidence. "Taking into consideration that the case in question doesn't require an immediate resolution [...] the crime has not been proven."[35]

Mrose and Queen's plea for protection did not fall on deaf ears. On May 24th, literally within days of receipt of their letter, the Mexican federal government began to consider their cases. Fourteen federal judges perused their extradition requisitions from New Mexico. Questions were raised. First, the New Mexican requisitions were made in the absence of Governor Thornton. There was, therefore, doubt the requisitions had gone through proper channels, and, though New Mexican authorities asked that Mrose and Queen continue to be detained and promised to submit proper papers, it was too late. The documents were reviewed on their own merits in Mexico City, and discrepancies were adding up. Said the Mexican Secretary of State in a strongly worded letter on June 6, 1895, "In a telegram of [April] 19th [...] the Political Chief of Bravos informed the Governor of Chihuahua that up to that date he had not been presented the documents for the extradition of Mrose and his accomplice, V. Queen...."[36]

The Mexicans noticed Queen was accused of stealing one horse and a bull, but they also observed the horse theft was witnessed by only one man and the bull had only disappeared for a short time—not an unusual thing on the plains.[37] Mrose was accused of a horse theft by a man who said "he left the stolen horse at his house, but that when he sent for him, [Mrose] didn't turn it over to him because there was a police order for him not to do it."[38] As far as the theft of a cow, the complaint included a curious statement from "a butcher [who] declares to have purchased [it] from Mrose with the brand of [a cow] said to be stolen [, but] the one writing [...] this does not believe that the crimes are sufficiently proven to warrant extradition."[39] It's unlikely the complaining man was Eddy butcher Walker Bush, half-brother of Sheriff Dave Kemp, but then that leaves the only other butcher, Dee Harkey, an acknowledged enemy.

In both Queen's and Mrose's cases, the Mexicans returned parts of the extradition requisitions to ... Texas, rather than New Mexico, reason unknown.[40] Reluctantly declaring the American claims unsupported, Judge Najera sent 23 pages of the remaining files to the Mexican Supreme Court on May 24, 1895.

Decreed the Mexican Secretary of State afterward, "[T]his Secretariat answered that, Queen and Mrose [having] requested protection, the Judge would resolve the matter of detention, having suspended the competence of the Governor [of Chihuahua] to dispose [of] the prisoners."[41]

Meanwhile, attorney John Wesley Hardin was wavering in his support of Mrose. Ostensibly hired to help him, by mid-April El Paso newspapers reported him as working to get Mrose extradited back across the Rio Grande River. Before long, Mrose's friends were declaring Hardin would never get Mrose extradited. On Sunday, April 21, 1895, Hardin met with these men, who, he said, "tried to bulldoze him and grew quite saucy in their talk when they saw he did not want to have a row. Mr. Hardin is a spirited man and quick tempered, consequently this little Sabbath day collision did not sit well on his good natured stomach."[42]

Reading between the lines, it's easy to see Mrose's friends were not awed by Hardin's reputation. Faced by at least five hard-nosed cowboys, Hardin thought better of making a move, but next day, on Monday, accompanied by two unnamed friends[43] he met former police chief Jeff Milton in Juarez.

Together, "the four adjourned to a private room [...] to order refreshments. On entering the room they found themselves in the presence of five of Mrose's friends in consultation with Mrs. Mrose. To have backed out of the room would have looked like a retreat, so the four friends entered, saluted and took seats. The conversation soon became general, Mrose's case was brought up and hot words passed between Hardin and Fennessey. Both men sprang to their feet. In an instant Mr. Hardin had slapped Fennessey's face and had his gun at his breast. In another instant Mr. Fennessey would have been a dead man, but quick as thought Chief Milton grasped the pistol and was struggling with Mr. Hardin. In the meantime the two gentlemen who accompanied Chief Milton and Mr. Hardin had the Mrose party covered. At the request of the chief Mr. Hardin returned his pistol to his pocket, but his blood was up and remembering the occurrence of Sunday night, he walked up to Lightfoot and gave him a slap in the face that could be heard a block. Chief Milton, as cool as if he had just stepped out of a bath, placed his back to the door of the room and stated it was best to settle the little trouble right there and then if it was to have a continuance in the future. The first occupants of the room, though game themselves, saw that they had four cool, brave men to deal with and quickly agreed the matter should be dropped."[44]

Mexican police poured into the room, but Milton took charge and explained the incident as a misunderstanding. No one was hurt; no one was arrested, but tensions in Juarez increased. This sensational confrontation was an indication of shifting alliances. Helen Beulah's relationship with Hardin and her desire to get her husband out of jail were seesawing back and forth. In financial trouble since the loss of his job[45] Jeff Milton is clearly acting in support of Hardin, and Hardin himself is revealed as not nearly as tough or fearless as he was in his younger days. Strangely, Hardin continued in Mrose's employ, and by June 6th, he was quoted as saying Mrose would never be extradited back to the United States.[46]

Helen Beulah said later that Mrose's "friends [...] became a burden on my hands and fearing that I would be left penniless and having a child of my own to raise, I told Mrose that I would have to stop spending so much money [....] This enraged him and he threatened and abused me. His friends also abused me. When this occurred I notified Mrose that I could stand it no longer and told him I was going to quit him. I then moved [to El Paso.]"[47]

On June 6, 1895, the Mexican Supreme Court delivered a unanimous opinion written by Magistrate Mariscal that no further proof had been offered in the interim against the two men. "[T]he crimes were not proved sufficiently [...] in accordance with the treaty in force with the United States ...."

After thoroughly reviewing the papers, each of the fourteen justices initialed the documents, and then the court ruled, "[T]he detained, finding themselves under the jurisdiction of the federal tribunals because of the [violation of Constitutional Article 19 by the Political Chief of Paso del Norte] protection proceedings instigated by them, [the Mexican] government can do nothing for now, but that if [the proceedings are] finished, [...] Queen and Mrose, [who] were placed at your disposal, you should set them free."[48]

Responding on June 7th, Judge Najera complied, promising his "attentive consideration,"[49] and then, on June 8th, the Secretary of State of Mexico telegraphed, "[Y]ou may certainly decree liberty." Permanent orders from the Mexican Supreme Court granting Queen and Mrose's petition for protection under Article 19 were signed and telegraphed to Juarez June 12, 1895.[50]

Martin Mrose and Victor Queen walked out of jail on June 8, 1895, apparently without much help from Mrose's wife.[51] They had gained their freedom not by applying for Mexican citizenship as the American newspapers reported, but by appealing for protection from the President of Mexico—as anyone could. Rather than having their cases drag on for months, the two men had achieved justice in weeks, an amazing accomplishment even today.[52]

More importantly, they had, through the careful deliberations of the Mexican Supreme Court and the diligent inquiry of numerous pedantic justices, proven what some have long since forgotten: the claims of rustling and horse theft were baseless and groundless, unsupported by evidence, illegal in execution, and flawed in concept. Martin Mrose and Victor Queen were innocent of these crimes and should not have been subject to arrest or detainment. The implication of this, however, is the two men—and the Mexican government—knew the people wanting them on the American side of the border did not intend they see justice, but, instead, planned violence against them. By winning their freedom, the two men were sure they had proven a point, and their innocence was irrevocably established.

Unfortunately, hard eyes glared at them from across the Rio Grande. Former Eddy County Clerk Tom Fennessey, Sam Kaufman, James Lightfoot, and nearly two dozen other friends[53] linked arms with Martin Mrose and Victor Queen in Juarez to show their support.[54] None of them was a match for the gun talent they faced to the north, but right was right, and the nervous men now gathering in Juarez hoped for justice and common sense to prevail.

14
THE WOMAN AND THE GUNFIGHTER
APRIL–JUNE 1895

"[T]hat was a wide-open town." [1]

The stage was now set. Guns and alcohol, money and sex; they were about to come together with Helen Beulah Mrose and her little four-year-old daughter, Laura Jennings, living in El Paso. The combustibles were there; Helen was the incendiary match. Not only was she loaded with cash, she was stunningly beautiful.[2]

In contemporary descriptions, Helen was described as "a vivid blonde [....] As women of her amiability were rated socially in our town in those days, she was one who would decorate the establishment of any man who could afford her. John Wesley Hardin fell for the idea that he could do so, and he made the experiment. He brought the lovely creature across the [border], installed her in gaudy lodgings, [and] bestowed upon her informally the honorary title of Mrs. Hardin...."[3]

Years later, John Selman, Jr., who had a notable encounter with Helen Beulah, recalled wistfully, "Never had we [...] gazed upon such a beautifully charming creature. She was a pretty arm number, all night,[4] and as I look back on those days I can't get away from the idea that mighty near every male in El Paso was a little jealous of John Wesley. She was something that queens are made from—no doubting that. She turned the whole town's head. A carriage was at her disposal day and night and she spent money recklessly."[5] Selman also called her "the blonde Venus," and he effused, "She was a natural blonde with blue eyes and a shape that was the envy of all the women. She wasn't skinny like most of the women of today. She had a pair of hips. But of course, hips were stylish in those days."[6]

Another man remembered, "When [Mrose] came to Juarez, he had a very attractive blond, with big baby blue eyes." Eugene Cunningham, acquainted with a number of people who had known Helen, called her "a dashing blonde lady of statuesque beauty;" J. Evetts Haley, a friend and biographer of Jeff Milton, described her as "a voluptuous blonde with big, baby-blue eyes;" another writer called her "a luscious blonde," and C.L. Sonnichsen called her "a handsome blonde woman."[7] "A queen," another said.[8]

Still another account says Hardin "showed up one night and proudly put on exhibition a flashing and alluring blonde. None of us knew her, and, of course, all who wanted to know started asking, 'Who is she and where did he get her?'"[9]

Not only that, but Helen dressed fashionably. In a famous photograph of her and her shorn daughter Laura, Helen is wearing a tailored jacket with puffy sleeves. "A number of El Paso ladies," commented one newspaper, "not content with ordinarily large sleeves, must needs endeavor to further increase the same by inserting wires. This does the business, and sleeves in consequence are now making the biggest county fair pumpkins shrivel up with envy."[10]

Robert J. Casey said Helen, a "luscious blonde in the costume of Diamond Lil entered a saloon for a drink. 'Do you know,' [Hardin] is quoted as having said, 'that you are very beautiful?' 'Sure,' replied the lady. 'And what of it?'"[11]

Probably within a week of Helen's arrival in El Paso, she and Hardin were an item. A fine-looking man in his own right, Hardin was remembered by John Selman, Jr., for "the brisk and alert manner in which [he] carried himself. He seemed to be a human dynamo of action. He dressed in black, soft black Stetson hat and black bow tie. He was quite heavily built and a little under six feet in height [sic]. At a short distance, he gave one the impression that he was smiling, but at closer range, his face showed a certain hardness. One had only to look into his keen brown eyes[12] to see that Wes Hardin was a bad man with whom to fool. Another thing I noted was that he carried one of his arms slightly raised. Apparently the arm was from an old wound."[13]

While Helen and Hardin worked to retrieve the money seized from her during the arrest in Mexico, she also began to collaborate with Hardin on his autobiography. Hardin was entering his darker moments. He wrote, "While I write this, I say from the deepest depths of my heart that my desire for revenge is not satisfied, and if I live another year, I promise my friends and my God to make another of my brother's murderers bite the dust."[14] With romance blooming and progress made on the autobiography, it wasn't long before Laura was an encumbrance.

Fortunately, Helen's parents, Bill and Ann Eliza Williams, lived at Cartwright, Arizona, a small farming community northwest of Phoenix. In the day that electric fans were first put to widespread use, making the intense desert heat of Arizona tolerable, Cartwright was in the midst of an agricultural miracle: irrigated desert lands were producing astounding crops. In Tucson, an ostrich farm was in operation, mostly producing feathers for women's hats. Today, similar farms produce ostrich meat, eggs, and hides for expensive cowboy boots.

Baled alfalfa was selling for the phenomenal price of ten dollars a ton. Much of the alfalfa was used by dairymen, and the Phoenix area was becoming known as a dairy center. Cream was sent by daily train to Prescott; the Phoenix Dairy and Produce Company made cheese and butter. Hogs were grazed on the alfalfa fields, and their weight gain was hard to believe. Locally produced ham, bacon, pork ribs, kettle-rendered lard, and pigs' feet were advertised in the papers. One farmer declared, "I have two five-acre fields of alfalfa, so that I can pasture my hogs in one while the other rested and was being irrigated. One year I raised 385 head on ten acres of alfalfa pasture, and, at fattening time, [...] they weighed from 150 to 300 pounds, dressed weight."[15]

Oranges, peaches, apricots, almonds, grapes, watermelons, and nuts were grown around Phoenix as well as blueberries, flowers, and vegetables of every sort. In 1895, "Strawberry Williams" was selling berries profitably all over Phoenix.

Bill Williams, Helen's father, and Lon Williams, her brother, got into this agricultural boom early. They had a dairy in Cartwright and developed several parcels north and south of that town. Their main investments, however, were at Gila Bend, where Bill Williams was promoting a dam and irrigation venture. Unfortunately, W.H. Horton, "the promoter of the Bill Williams Fork irrigation enterprise,"[16] died in New York. There were other problems, too, and Bill Williams was soon over-extended. Water rights, construction difficulties, and legal expenses drained his finances. His land in Williamson County, Texas, and his holdings at Fredonia, just south of the Jennings homestead were gradually squandered in Arizona.

Nevertheless, in the spring and early summer of 1895, Bill Williams anticipated success,[17] and, in an ebullient mood, acceded to his daughter's request to mind Laura for a time. To this end, in mid-May 1895, he traveled to El Paso to pick up the girl.[18] It was at this time he met John Wesley Hardin. Within Williams and Jennings family descendants today, there is no collective memory of Martin Mrose, so it's probable Helen neglected to tell her father of her bigamous marriage to a desperado locked up in a Juarez jail. Instead, Bill Williams came away from El Paso with a romantic version of Helen's developing relationship with one of the West's biggest celebrities. Williams invited the happy couple to Cartwright to meet the family.

This had just become possible and relatively easy. The Southern Pacific's Sunset Route had undergone a schedule change. Both eastbound and westbound passenger trains met in Tucson at 7 A.M., where the passengers could disembark and eat breakfast. The Santa Fe, Prescott, and Phoenix Railroad ran north and south from Tucson, construction of which finally reached Phoenix on March 9, 1895. The night Sunset Route express, leaving El Paso about 6 P.M., arrived in Tucson at seven the next morning, plenty of time to connect with the train north. On the return journey, a pleasant layover at one of Tucson's hotels was required to meet the morning Sunset express back to El Paso. Hotel arrivals were routinely reported in Tucson papers, and, sure enough, on page one of the *Arizona Daily Star* of June 15, 1895, the Hotel Orndorff reported the arrival of "John Wesley Hardin and wife." The same paper, on August 22nd, recalled Hardin and Helen in Tucson in mid-June. Perhaps they spent a day or two in Tucson, for the paper called Hardin "a well-known Arizona character."

It was perhaps the happiest they would ever be. Make no mistake about it: when Helen met Hardin, it was love. It was probably the third time she had seen him, once as a small child at Berry Creek, once in Phenix, and now here, in El Paso. Hardin represented all that was exciting about Texas. One of the greatest celebrities of the day, he was known to everyone, no matter how poorly informed. His name was a household word. He was romance personified. She looked on him, and all that was good within her family rose to the surface: the sacrifice undertaken to fight for the Confederacy, the devastating loss of the Civil War, the resistance of state and federal authority during Reconstruction, the romance and excitement of the cattle drives, the heart-pounding adventure of brave young men fleeing posses. So, when twenty-one-year-old Helen Beulah Mrose got together with forty-one-year-old John Wesley Hardin in El Paso, he was all she could ever fantasize about.

On the other hand, when he saw her-breathless, bosomy, and loaded with cash-he realized every man's middle-aged dream, and even worse, he saw an outstanding opportunity. Her feelings for him—though immature, thoughtless, and hasty—were genuine. His feelings, on the other hand, were those of a man in reckless conflict. He was a widower, a failure at all he'd set his hand to, an ex-convict, an undistinguished lawyer, a run-away husband of an under-age teenager, a so-called family man with no loyalty to those who loved him. Helen was wide-eyed and hot; he was desperate and hurt. He was her fantasy, her savior, and her hope. She was his mealticket.

15
THE SALOONS
APRIL–JUNE 1895

"The Road to Ruin"[1]

The people of the 1890s were members of another culture. Food tended to be fresh or stale; the only alternative was canned and expensive. The fancier hotels and gathering places had ceiling fans; in private homes, electric Singer sewing machines and various models of refrigerators were becoming popular luxuries.[2] Though products common today were advertised then—Lea & Perrins Steak Sauce, Hires Root Beer, Aunt Jemima pancakes, Schlitz beer, and Grape Nuts—there was, of course, no television or radio. Newspapers were moralizing. Lights after dark were becoming more common, but people tended to go to bed early and rise with the sun. Houses were not warm in winter, or cool in summer. Fuel and energy were constant problems.

Arthritis and agues were normal, but people tended to be stalwart and uncomplaining. Blindness and deafness were common, as were disabilities and disfigurements of all sorts. People died from apoplexy, Bright's disease, or dropsy, or the tuberculosis infections of consumption, Pott's Disease, and scrofula, or puerperal exhaustion, variola, or Lagrippe.[3] Few had perfect teeth or good hygiene. Childhood diseases were major scourges. Pneumonia could kill, as could infections, a broken leg, or an abscessed tooth.

There were not a lot of old people. Thoughtlessness, rudeness, rashness, risk-taking, and, yes, even the violence of the Old West are attributable to the immaturity of society.

Though we think of the 1890s as purer than today—pure sexually since it was the Victorian era; purer in intake for there were fewer chemical additives in food and fewer pesticides or herbicides in use; purer in environment with pristine water and uninterrupted vistas—in fact it was a harsh world. Death was common.

A good part of the average nutrition was alcohol. There were few "mixed drinks." There were no rules against drinking on the job, and an on-duty policeman armed with a loaded pistol might rub elbows at a bar with a dynamite tamper drinking whiskey on his lunch break. For this reason, the biggest complaints of the growing temperance movement were the loss in wages, rise in accidents, and unproductivity among blue-collar workers.

Saloons tended to be narrow and cramped, ceilings high, and chairs comfortable. The bars normally ran the length of the room. On the American side of the border, the draws were alcohol, conversation, and gambling. In Mexico, entertainment was as big a draw as the alcohol. Traveling *mariachis*, cockfighting, and wrestling or boxing matches were featured.

The bars were chest-high. On the patrons' side were brass rails and spittoons. On the bartenders' side was revealed the reason the bars were so high: to accommodate kegs of beer standing on end, with spigots to draw liquid refreshment. There was also space for glasses, baseball bats, and shotguns. Some bars were equipped with zinc-lined sinks and vats to contain beer kegs in crushed ice—which was being manufactured in quantities by then.

For a celebrity like Hardin, saloons were a natural place to revel in the adulation he felt he deserved. Men vied to buy him a drink and listen to his stories. Remembered John Selman, Jr., "He was a sort of 'cock-of-the-gun-fighting-walk' and seemed to know it. Crowds gathered and begged for the honor of paying for his whiskey. He took all this hero worship as a matter of course, as the expected thing, and when he began to feel pretty good would condescend to josh with his admirers. He started in at once to breeze along, touching only the high spots. Gambling and drinking all night, he [...] had tapped an inexhaustible money supply."[4]

An inexhaustible money supply? All the drinks he could hold? Hardin was back in his lowlife routine. In April, he accused a dealer at the Acme Saloon of cheating, and he pulled a gun and recovered his money. Then, in the early morning hours of May 2nd, he robbed a gaming table at the Gem Saloon.

> Said Hardin, "[A]fter I had lost a considerable sum, I was grossly insulted by the dealer in a hurrah manner, hence I told him he could not win my money and hurrah me too, and that as he had undertook [sic] to hurrah me he could deliver me the money I had played and you bet

he did it. And when he had counted out $95 I said that is all I want, just my money and no more. He said all right Mr. Hardin, and when I left the room and had gotten half way down the stairs I returned, hearing words of condemnation of my play. I said to everyone in the house and connected with the play, I understand from the reflective remarks that some of you disapprove [of] my play. Now if this be so, be men and get in line and show your manhood, to which no one made any reply, but others nodded that I was right, and that they approved my play. Now someone has asked for my pedigree. Well he is too gross too [sic] notice, but I wish to say right here, once and for all, that I admire pluck, push, and virtue wherever found. Yet I contempt [sic] and despise a coward and assassin of character, whether he be a reporter, a journalist, or a gambler. And while I came to El Paso to prosecute Bud Frazier [sic] and did do it on as high a plane as possible, I am here now to stay."[5]

Another version of the Gem holdup said, "Last night ... [l]uck was against [Hardin] and he lost several hundred dollars. He grew tired of the game and said to the dealer, 'You seem to be pretty damned cute, so you may just hand me back the money I paid for chips.' The dealer, Phil Baker, was going to protest but Hardin cocked his revolver. Baker replied, 'Certainly sir, you can have anything you want,' and Hardin walked off with the money."[6]

The holdup at the Gem was big news, which the dealer, Phil Baker, was not happy about for it brought unwanted attention to the fact he had resumed gambling before a new city administration took over. Almost overlooked in the hullabaloo was a simple business notice, "Mr. J.W. Hardin has purchased a half interest in the Wigwam Saloon from Mr. M.W. Collins."[7] For someone so easily corrupted by saloons, it was a poor decision.

Meanwhile, John Wesley Hardin and Jeff Milton had issues to settle between them. Milton was on record as irritated he had been maneuvered by Hardin into providing a second gun when Hardin confronted Mrose's friends in the saloon in Juarez. Another issue had to do with gambling, and Hardin's purchase of an interest in a saloon added fuel to the fire.

Hardin told Milton he was going to open up the Wigwam Gambling House on Monday morning [May 6], and he said there would be no interference by the law. [...]

Milton told him, 'That is where you are mistaken. You will be under arrest an hour after you do it.'

He said, 'If I am, I know how to protect myself,' and said, 'I won't need any law and courts to do it.'

[...] As a matter of fact, Hardin did open the gambling house that morning and was under arrest before noon that day and did not carry out any threats.[8]

On May 6th, "Hardin was arrested [...] by Sheriff Simmons on an indictment by the grand jury for carrying a gun."[9] The same day, Milton's creditors garnished his roll-top desk at police headquarters, hoping to find in it something of value. Three days later, Milton was replaced as chief of police by incoming mayor Robert Campbell. From this point on, Milton's financial troubles were a matter of public record.[10]

On May 16th, Hardin was tried on the gun-carrying charge. During testimony, a witness, Charles Jones, "testified he saw Hardin show his gun, and when asked if he was gambling at the table himself, said, 'No, I was broke.'"

The prosecutor pressed him, "Did you get broke there?" and Jones answered, "No, I have been broke ever since Cleveland has been president of the United States. I was there only watching the game. I went up to the club rooms with the [crowd.]"

An attorney asked for clarification, "What was the [crowd]?" and Jones provided the surprising information, "Oh it was Justice Howe and the other fellows."[11]

Hardin was found guilty and fined twenty-five dollars. On July 1st, he pleaded guilty to a gambling charge and was fined ten dollars and costs. He was also arrested for robbery, but the case never came to trial. Phil Baker, the dealer at the Gem, was tried for gambling; he was fined $25 and spent ten days in jail. Grumped George Look, co-owner of the Gem, "So far I have not had a word to say about these cases, but it does look a little tough when the court discharges the man who holds up another and fines the man who was held up $25 and sends him to jail for ten days."[12]

Hardin must have realized things were not working out as he had hoped. At the end of June, the *Times* announced he, "has sold his interest in the Wigwam saloon, and will devote himself to the task of writing his own biography. It will no doubt be an interesting book."[13] The *Herald* concurred, saying, "Mr. Hardin is to be congratulated on this righteous resolve."[14] Nevertheless, Hardin must have been moody and depressed.

As a boy, Carl [Longemare] was a messenger for Western Union. … [I]t was with fear and trepidation that he set out to deliver the telegram to Hardin at the Wigwam Saloon …

Hardin was in the back room gambling when Longemare handed him the telegram. It must have contained bad news because he turned to the boy and said, "Son, don't you ever bring me a telegram like this again." Longemare ran from the saloon without even waiting for a tip. Shortly after that another telegram arrived for Hardin […] and Carl was the only one available to deliver it. As can be imagined, the boy didn't want the job. But he marched to the Wigwam and into the back room, where he suddenly lost his nerve. He hung around, fearing to approach Hardin, when finally the gunman caught sight of him.

"What's the matter, boy?" he asked. Longemare managed to blurt out that he had another telegram for Hardin. "Bless you, boy, what's the matter with that?"

"B-b-but sir, you told me the last time not to bring you another telegram like that other one," Carl stammered. Remembrance flooded Hardin's face and he gave the boy a big bear hug. "Son," he said, "I was only foolin'. I didn't mean anything. Now let's have the telegram." Needless to say, Carl got a fat tip this time.[15]

To be fair, Hardin was not the only one to have troubles as a result of the time he spent in saloons. George Scarborough, though not a habitué of saloons like some lawmen, was not popular in El Paso. One newspaper reported, "If [a certain gentleman] had known what was going on about town [...] he must have heard of Scarborough's severely beating Si Ryan's cousin over the head with a 6-shooter in the Palace Saloon; he must have heard of Scarborough's drawing his gun on a railroad man at a Gem ball; he must have heard of Scarborough making a gun play at Dutch Charley in the Bank Saloon, when the latter disarmed him; he must have heard of Scarborough's making a bluff at a well known ex-county officer in a gambling house, and when the latter knocked him down he arose with gun in hand and was disarmed by bystanders; he must have heard of Scarborough taking a poker pot away from John Selman while holding his 6-shooter in the old man's face [.... I]f the gentleman [...] had inquired [...] he would have learned that Scarborough has long been the terror of every gambling room in town."[16]

Even so, everyone was afraid of Hardin. Part of Hardin's problem was that when drinking, he tended to shoot off his mouth. The night of August 6th, very drunk and emotionally distraught over his passionate affair with Helen, Hardin made the mistake of verbally attacking George Scarborough. This was a dangerous development, and Scarborough confronted him when Hardin was sober. Hardin agreed to retract his statement. He wrote a short announcement for the newspapers,

> I have been informed that on the night of the 6th, while under the influence of liquor, I made a talk against George Scarborough [....] I do not recollect making any such statement and if I did, the statement was absolutely false, and it was superinduced by drink and frenzy.[17]

Due to his drinking, Hardin was now out of control. R.M. Glover, a friend partly responsible for getting him out of prison, wrote from Gonzales after the Gem holdup, "[Y]our many friends here that know you and are acquainted with your honorable aim in life very mutch [sic] regret that you have found it necessary to again return to your old gaming life as they think it will throw temptations in your way which could be avoided in the quiet practice of your chosen profession."[18]

For those who still believed in John Wesley Hardin, it must have been depressing watching him slide downhill, but the fact is Hardin would always have trouble in saloons....

16
THE NOTE TO ALBERT
JUNE 1895

"[T]he wish of the woman that loves the most in the world."[1]

Among Hardin's papers is a legal instrument dated May 27, 1895, a writ of injunction in the divorce and custody proceedings between Augustin Terrassas and his wife Eulalia. On January 16, 1892,[2] Eulalia Saldaña had married William H. Smith in Eddy, New Mexico; in 1895, she made plans to bring her daughters to join her and Smith in Eddy. With the help of attorney John Wesley Hardin,[3] Augustin Terrassas filed an injunction to keep his "ex-wife" from taking his ten-year-old daughter out of El Paso, claiming his wife was kidnapping her.[4] The case eerily parallels another situation, this one four hundred miles away between Steve Jennings and his wife. The irony was surely not lost on Helen Beulah Mrose.

In this case, the husband won custody as well as a divorce, but then William Smith and Eulalia Terrassas asked the presiding judge to marry them, and he did so in the very courtroom where he had granted the divorce.[5] A witness to the marriage was Smith's kinsman, John Wesley Hardin, and possibly, Hardin's paramour, Helen Beulah.[6]

The Terrassas Injunction is remarkable, however, for other reasons. First, it is one of the astonishingly few legal papers Hardin kept. Hardin purchased a set of law books during the summer of 1894. After receiving his license to practice law, he may have handled one or two criminal cases and a host of civil ones. He assisted District Attorney McGowan in the attempted murder case against Bud Frazer. He had business cards and paid an occupation tax on an office in El Paso, yet in an inventory of his effects, there were more pistols listed than law books.

On July 1, 1895, Hardin let his law practice lapse when he did not renew his license. It's possible he disposed of much of the paraphernalia attendant to his practice of law. If so, why did he keep this injunction? Did he attach importance to the document?

The answer is in a short note on the cover of the injunction written by Helen Beulah Mrose, who used the injunction to compose a hasty note to Albert. Hardin placed enough store in this note to hang onto it through the ups and downs of his relationship with Helen and his own moodiness and alcoholic fog.

The note says:

> My dear Albert,
> The only trinkets that I left in your power are yours, because I have made presents of them to you and under no motive deliver them to anybody. You can dispose of them as this is my wish, the wish of the woman that loves the most in the world and ever will be yours.
> B.M.

After further thought and probable discussion with Hardin, Helen corrected a Freudian slip by adding the word "you." The new version read:

> My dear Albert
> The only trinkets that I left in your power are yours, because I have made presents of them to you and under no motive deliver them to anybody. You can dispose of them as this is the wish of the woman that loves you the most in the world and ever will be yours.
> B.M.

Historians have used this scribbled note as the basis for a misconception about Helen. "Albert," so the reasoning has gone, must have been her son, the "boy" in the photograph "Mrs. McRose and Kid." It was a clue to research further details of Helen's life. For a hundred years, historians have studied census reports, documents, and other papers on the assumption Albert was Martin Mrose's son who grew up, had descendants, and possibly left a legacy that could lead to an understanding of his mother.

For a hundred years, researchers have looked for Albert, and they have learned nothing. As we have seen, Helen's child wasn't named Albert, nor was "his" last name Mrose. Helen and her "son" vanished from history.

The fact is Helen had a daughter named Laura Jennings. The note, therefore, is not simple after all, but this makes its true recipient a mystery. There is, however, additional proof the note was not written to Helen's child. Linguists call the first, "register," the way a speaker adjusts volume, style, word choice, and grammar to fit a listener's experiential level. Try reading the note aloud as a doting mother would say it to a four-year-old child. It doesn't work. It's too formal and mature for a child who couldn't read, besides the fact it's signed with initials and not "Mother" or "Mommy."

So, if the note was not written to a child, for whom was it written? Who was Albert? The note takes on mystery. Try reading the note as a woman would say it to a grown man, and it becomes more apparent who the intended recipient was.

Helen and Hardin lived in a fantasy based on whiskey and the hope Hardin's autobiography would rescue his declining fortunes. His career as a lawyer was, for all intents and purposes, finished. His career as a gambler was uneven. His plan to buy a saloon was uninspired. His only future was the autobiography. From the beginning, he and a few others recognized the marketability of his story.

The Old West was fading away around them. Jesse James had been shot in the back, and no one would ever know the truth about him. Wild Bill Hickok never took the opportunity to tell his story; the dime novelists had turned him into a fictional character while still alive. Bat Masterson became a sports writer, Doc Holliday died young, and who else of criminal stature, of gun-handling expertise, of sheer devil-may-care adventure was left? John Wesley Hardin was the last gunfighter who might leave behind a version of the truth. Of course, an adoring public would buy it, especially if Hardin traveled the lecture circuit and promoted it. The book would be a ticket to concert halls and theaters from London to San Francisco. It might sell better than any lecture by Mark Twain, America's most famous performance artist. Hardin could stand on stage and perform gun-handling tricks to amaze the audiences. His future was bright.

Helen thought so much of this dream she bought into it. The *El Paso Leases Deed Book* on June 18, 1895, records, "I, John Wesley Hardin, on this day

take Mrs. Bula Mrose as a full partner in my manuscript & all business matters…."
Helen advanced Hardin at least $1,500 in this partnership. She claimed a half interest in the manuscript as her right, but undoubtedly she also played a major role in writing it. What did she hope to gain? Fame? Possibly. A steady income with which to raise her daughter? Undoubtedly. A tie to Hardin? Certainly. Helen Beulah bought into Hardin's future. They planned a life together, though their relationship seemed doomed.

There are hints Hardin did not intend to stay in El Paso much longer. The saloon purchase was a frivolous gesture soon corrected when he sold his interest in the Wigwam. He was rumored to be involved in a few items of last-minute business—a settling of a few scores, perhaps even a robbery, but everyone knew he was going to leave the minute his book was finished.

Where would he have gone? Back to Texas and memories of his old haunts? Back to family and the grave of his wife, Jane? Back to the mess he'd created with Callie Lewis? Back to Florida? The answer is undoubtedly negative. In all likelihood, Helen and Hardin planned a life together in Arizona. Shortly after his motion for a retrial on gun-carrying charges was denied on June 2, 1895, Hardin disappeared from El Paso newspapers. In truth, it was hard to track him in the best of times, for newspapers preferred to call him "a stranger in town;" even so, the "stranger" disappeared from mention.

It was at this time Hardin and Helen Beulah traveled to Arizona to meet Helen's parents. There, they lived a deceitful scam as husband and wife. It was the first time Ann Eliza Williams had seen her daughter since 1893. Of course, as concerned parents, Bill and Ann Eliza Williams asked hard questions about Helen's husband, Steve Jennings; they must have inquired what Helen had been up to since she'd left Fredonia. Helen did not mention Martin Mrose. Instead, she painted a rosy picture of herself and the West's greatest celebrity, and the Williams family bought it wagon, tongue, and team. It's evident from this that Hardin and Helen considered her marriage to Martin Mrose history.[7]

Because of this, there is a slim possibility "Albert" was Hardin himself. It may have been an alias for a new life somewhere else. He and Helen may have planned on living anonymously on the royalties from his book for the rest of their lives. Taken this way, the note to Albert makes some sense. It's a note from a young woman to her lover: "[T]he wish of the woman that loves you the most in the world and ever will be yours." How romantic.

The relationship Helen had with Hardin, however, was anything but idyllic. Sex, arguments, drunkenness, violence, and fear are what they shared. Helen may have suffered from the mentality of a battered woman, which may explain why her affair with Martin Mrose was doomed—he was too nice to her. Hardin, on the other hand, was bad to her, though it's hard to say if he was worse than Steve Jennings. Hardin threatened to kill her; they had violent arguments, they separated, then got back together. There was an element of maternal concern in their relationship, too. That Helen cared for Hardin is obvious, and Hardin needed a steadying influence in his life.

Yet, if Hardin were Albert, the note introduces another mystery. "The only trinkets that I left in your power are yours, because I have made presents of them to you and under no motive deliver them to anybody." Was this a goodbye, hastily scratched on the first available paper Helen found in the room they shared? If so, what trinkets were they—the Confederate $50 bill? It doesn't make sense. Hardin was not Albert, but if not him, who else?

Consider this: "Albert" may have been Martin Mrose. It was likely his first name: Albert Martin Mrose. Few people must have heard it. Most never used any other name for him than Martin. Dee Harkey never mentioned it. Deputy U.S. Marshal Phillips, who claimed to have known him all his life, never mentioned it[8] nor did Mrose' partner, Victor Queen. In fact, there is not a single documented instance of anyone calling him anything but Martin. Albert was not a name he introduced himself to others with nor shared with anyone other than his wife, and then perhaps only during pillow talk. She must have used it as a pet name. It was the truth that lay between two lovers who had seriously plighted their troth to each other, in sickness and in health, until death do they part.

Helen used the name in the note to demonstrate her message came from the heart, but the message can be read two ways. Read it aloud as a loving wife might offer a message to her husband. There's nothing wrong with its wording or tone, but a question arises why a woman separated by a river and two sets of laws needed to write a note when she could more easily cross a bridge and rejoin her husband. For this reason, the truth is more sinister. Read it as a woman teasing him with the fact he needs to come see her if he is to regain what is his: his wife, his honor, and his cash. Helen's role comes more clearly into focus.

Helen Beulah and Hardin must have considered ways to lure Mrose across the river for a solution to their troublesome relationship. Only by getting rid of Mrose could they gain legitimacy as a couple and spend his money without fear of retribution. The trouble was, however, Mrose was unpredictable. Hardin's skills as a gunfighter were unknown. He hadn't killed anyone since 1877. Though he practiced daily and could awe crowds with his speed, he had not faced a confrontation in eighteen years. His incarceration had isolated him from the real world and protected him from certain death in a saloon somewhere.

Mrose, on the other hand, had thrived in a turbulent world. He had gone through violent times in Lincoln County, Phenix, and Seven Rivers. He had made Bob Ford turn tail in Colorado. He had bragged, or so Dee Harkey claimed later, he had killed at least two men, yet his reputation was not based on known actions but on a suspicion of his competence. Undoubtedly, his sheer Wendish obstinacy added to this perception. Rather than being cowed by Hardin's reputation, Mrose openly grumbled. It is significant that after Mrose's release from jail, Hardin did not cross into Mexico to settle scores even though he had stolen Mrose's money and wife.

Somehow, Mrose had to be tricked into forcing his hand. The waiting game had to end. What better way than to draw him across the Rio Grande? The lawmen could take the risks, get the credit for apprehending him, and collect a reward. The trouble was, however, Mrose was too smart. There were twenty lawmen eager to arrest him. He faced the guns of Beauregard Lee, Jeff Milton, George Scarborough, Dee Harkey, "Uncle" John Selman, Charles Perry, Johnny Behan, George W. Baylor, George Curry, and a host of others. As long as he stayed in Mexico, he was safe.

But the woman he'd rescued, a woman he'd cared for and married, with an adorable little daughter he had taken to heart, was the same woman who held a lot of his money and was taunting him, making him a cuckold not only in front of his friends but in the newspapers. Even so, he dithered. George Scarborough tried to convince him a meeting with his wife could be arranged. George Look, a saloonkeeper claimed "Uncle" John Selman arranged a room for the meeting. Despite the talk, Mrose waited.

How could he be brought across the river to end the impasse? There was no better way than a simple tease from his wife, "the wish of the woman that loves you the most in the world." All he had to do was cross the bridge and take what was his.

It was not the first time Helen thought about turning on her husband. An article describing Mrose's arrest in Mexico by Beauregard Lee offered a clue about Helen's loyalty. Lee "saw New Mexico officers going up and suspected something."[9]

Who, other than Beauregard Lee, knew Beulah was in Juarez and she was the key to arresting Mrose? Who were these mysterious New Mexican officers? Sheriff J.D. Walker? Dee Harkey? Charles Perry? Les Dow? There were not a lot to choose from. Although they were competitors for the reward in this instance, the lawmen were potential allies later, and Beauregard Lee did not name them.

With a simple note to Albert, however, Helen Beulah lent her support to a complicated plot to separate Mrose from his cash ... and from her. She and Hardin planned the enticement; the lawmen plotted the solution. She must have practiced the wording of the note on a handy piece of paper, the back of the Terrassas Injunction, and afterward she produced a finer copy for delivery to her husband. For a hundred years, historians have speculated on Hardin's role in a conspiracy with the lawmen to catch Martin Mrose on the American side of the border. The Terrassas Injunction is probably the "smoking gun."

Helen Beulah and Hardin's involvement in a conspiracy to end the suspense was designed as a simple enticement to cross the Rio Grande River. It would be interesting to know how Helen closed the final, rewritten missive. Surely she signed her name, not just her initials as in the draft, but the closing itself would reveal much about her.

Did she write "Sincerely?"

Probably not.

Did she write, "Fondly," "With Love," or "Ever Yours?"

Again, probably not.

She and Hardin must have cackled conspiratorially in their room at the

Herndon Lodging House as they drunkenly considered the wording. They must have thought it over very carefully. It couldn't be too warm or friendly, but there must not be a hint of danger either. Perhaps Helen cynically ended the note with "Your loving wife."

17
THE SANTA FE DUMP
JUNE 1895

"By God, I believe I will go over tonight."[1]

I t was inevitable Martin Mrose cross the Rio Grande River to see his wife or try to kill John Wesley Hardin, but the manner of it was in doubt. Going to El Paso was a dangerous proposition, but even so, Mrose, helpfully escorted through the darkness by a sympathetic Deputy U.S. Marshal George Scarborough, crossed the Mexican Central Railway bridge from Juarez, Mexico, to the weedy outskirts of El Paso, a half hour before midnight on June 29, 1895. While threading their way through mounds of trash and construction materials in the midden known as the Santa Fe Dump,[2] Scarborough stopped suddenly and whirled around. Realizing he was betrayed, Mrose pulled his pistol and fired, not understanding until too late he was flanked in the darkness by Jeff Milton and Deputy U.S. Marshal Frank McMahan. In a burst of gunfire from his left, Mrose was shot in the heart, fell, jumped up, then was cut down again. By the time a doctor was summoned, Martin Mrose was dead.[3]

Justice of the Peace W.D. Howe wrote the death certificate, locating the death "by side of RR track near Mex Central Bridge," cause of death "gunshot wounds," and "duration of last sickness: one minute."[4]

Dr. Alward White, in an affidavit prepared for the court, noted Mrose died as a result of "seven penetrating wounds all but two of which were made by bullets of large calibre. [sic] [T]wo of these large bullets [...] passed directly through the heart. [...I]n addition there were six or seven shot wounds in the left arm."[5]

"One of the pistol shots was fired at such close range that his face was powder burned and around the hole where the ball entered his right chest, it was also slightly powder burned. [... T]he body of the dead desperado was conveyed to the Star Stables and undertaking rooms where [it was] laid on the cooling board and viewed [...] by a number of people. The clothes were also there just as they had been removed from the body and were covered with a solid coating of his blood."[6]

Born in Texas the spring of 1856, Martin Mrose was 39 years old at the time of his death.[7]

These are the facts, but almost everything else about the shooting was, and is, controversial. If it were not so meaningful in light of later events, the death of Mrose would not have been remembered much beyond his burial in a desolate plot at the bone orchard of Concordia Cemetery.

The shooting of Martin Mrose, however, determined the fates not only of some of the most feared gunmen of the time but the reputations of respected lawmen. With this in mind, it is appropriate to examine the shooting in detail.

The participants:

Martin Mrose, the aggrieved husband
Deputy U.S. Marshal George Scarborough
Jeff Milton, former Chief of Police of El Paso and now a Deputy U.S.
      Marshal
Deputy U.S. Marshal Frank McMahan

The Witnesses:

Victor Queen, a friend
Charles Newman, customs inspector
Two Mexican smugglers
Dr. Alward White
Deputy Sheriff Jones
W.D. Howe, Justice of the Peace
The coroner
A man with a lantern
Dwyer and Bendy of the River Guard
The undertaker

Other concerned parties:

Helen Beulah Mrose, the wife

John Wesley Hardin, the correspondent

John Selman, Sr., who, arguably, closed the "back door" over the bridge.

First, George Scarborough, described as "a light complected [sic] man about [...] five feet eight or nine inches tall, rather heavyset, with [...] hair [...] sandy, almost red [...] there was something about him that [...] caused you to look at him a second time if you should pass by. He was a very [...] dangerous looking fella [sic] and yet pleasant enough to talk to...."[8]

The shooting in Scarborough's words:

M'Rose wrote me two letters, one while in jail in Juarez, and the other after he was released from jail. [... H]e expressed a desire to come to this side of the river that night and see a party. [...] He asked me if I would meet him in the middle of the Mexican Central bridge, just before the moon went down and before the electric light on the bridge was lighted. I told him I would meet him there at that time.

I then came over to this side and saw Milton and McMahan and told them to get ready. That night, we met here in town for about an hour and a half before the moon went down and we went down to the Santa Fe dump just this side of the bridge. I left Milton and McMahan stationed on this side of the dump, with the understanding that when I returned, I would come over the dump at a certain point and stop with M'Rose. I told them to be very careful and not to hurt him if they could avoid it. I then went out on the bridge to where I was to meet M'Rose. When I got there he was waiting for me with his pistol in his hand at full cock. As I came up, he let down the hammer and then revolved the cylinder several times by cocking it and letting it down. We sat down and talked for about ten minutes and then he remarked, 'I'm afraid to go over the river.' I answered him by telling him to go back to Mexico and I would return home. He studied a few minutes and said, 'By God, I'll go,' and asked me to lead the way. We came over and got off the bridge at the lower side and took the trail leading up to the dump. He had his six-shooter in his hand all the time but then shoved it down the front of his pants. He wore no coat, only a vest. He then said, 'Lead out and I will follow.' I started and when we got to the dump and at the place specified with Milton and McMahan I stopped with him about three steps behind me. Just as I stopped Milton and McMahan yelled, 'Throw up your hands!' At that instant, I wheeled and jerked my six-shooter and as I dropped my gun on him he pulled his gun. I said, 'Don't make any play—we don't want to hurt you.' He never spoke, but cocked the pistol and dropped it on me. As he did this I fired. The shooting then commenced. I could not say positively that he fired, but he had his gun down on me. I fired four shots. At my third shot he said, 'Boys, you've killed me!' I said, 'Stop trying to get up and we will quit shooting.' He had tried to get up several times with his gun still in his hand. An instant later he fell over on his back. I then asked McMahan to go to town and get the doctor and the sheriff and bring them down. About that time, Dwyer and Bendy of the river guard came over to us. Shortly after, Dr. White and Deputy Sheriff Jones came down. Then the hack was sent for the justice and the undertaker and the body of M'Rose was then carried over to the lower bridge.

Scarborough's account has plenty of holes. Most damaging is, "I left Milton and McMahan stationed on this side of the dump, with the understanding that when I returned, I would come over the dump at a certain point and stop with M'Rose." What he is admitting here is the officers had arranged clear fields of fire toward the river. Mrose was not going to be surrounded and given an opportunity to surrender; he was going to be cut down with shotgun and pistols, and no one would be hurt with crossfire.

Jeff Milton testified, "I wired Sheriff Walker to find out if M'Rose was still wanted. Finding that he was, Mr. Scarborough and myself undertook to capture him. Scarborough made arrangements with M'Rose to come over to this side and meet somebody whom M'Rose wanted to see. Knowing M'Rose to be a very desperate man from general reputation, we got McMahan to assist us so we would have no trouble in arresting him, thinking he would give up quicker to a large number. [...] We went to the place where he was to cross the river and Scarborough placed McMahan and myself alongside of the trail where he was to come up the Santa Fe dump so we could get the drop on M'Rose. Scarborough came along the trail with M'Rose following him and stopped on the dump. At that instant, McMahan and myself arose and yelled to M'Rose, 'Throw up your hands and consider yourself under arrest.' All of us told him to throw up his hands, but instead of throwing up his hands, he pulled his pistol and either him or Scarborough fired. I thought he would kill Scarborough or some of us, and that was the reason I fired. I shot him once."

Since no warrant was filed in New Mexico, Milton "produced a warrant issued out of Justice Howe's court in El Paso for the arrest of Martin Mrose. The warrant was issued on June 28, 1895, charging M'Rose [sic] with being a fugitive from justice from the territory of New Mexico."[9] This, of course, was irregular, but the paper did give the enterprise some authority.

Frank McMahan gave much the same story, with an interesting exception.[10] He testified he "was called on by J.D. Milton, a special ranger, to assist in arresting M'Rose." Why would he be asked by Milton and not his brother-in-law, George Scarborough?

Milton and Scarborough were careful not to let on whom Mrose wanted to see in El Paso. At the same time, Milton and McMahan were careful to put the planning on Scarborough's account. Why?

A witness to the shooting was Charles Newman, a customs official standing at the Stanton Street side of the customs station, a half block away. He said, "I had walked out in the dump to urinate. [I] was standing there looking toward the RR bridge when [the] shooting started [...] the 1st shot come from the river side, toward Mexico, and the others then opened up [...] showed M'Rose had fired first."[11]

W. H. Burgess represented the three men in court. He said Newman "was looking up toward the guard's room on Santa Fe Street, up river two blocks. Everything dark, then a shot, followed instantly by another. The first shot came from next to the Mexican side of the river, from south. 2nd shot from [the] north, then another from [the] south side, and also from north. Charles was positive about it, and he was only 1/2 block away."[12]

Within minutes, the river guards, Deputy Jones, a doctor, a hack driver and others arrived. In this age of flashlights, whose beams face only one way, it's hard to remember in 1895 only lanterns were used. Such lights were as blinding as they were illuminating. This fact must be kept in mind when considering the account of two Mexican smugglers who may have witnessed the shooting.[13] In addition, the issue of a lantern was expanded upon years later by W. D. Howe, who said, "Some fellow came up behind us with a lantern, and we were between the lantern and the river, and Jeff [Milton] kicked it out, and said, 'What are you trying to do, skylight us[?]'"[14]

In a story on the death of Mrose, the *El Paso Herald* quoted Victor Queen, Mrose's partner in Juarez:

> After I missed Mrose, I went to hunt him up. I went to the Santa Fe Bridge and then towards the railroad bridge just as the shooting began. A little while after the shooting, two men came running over the railroad bridge.
>
> I stopped them and asked who was shot and they were afraid to talk to me. I then went to the lower bridge and sent a policeman over and he returned and told me it was a Mexican that was killed. I then started out to find M'Rose a second time and when I got back up town I learned it was my friend that was killed, so I went back and crossed the river to see if I could get to him. On that trip, I met the same two men who had crossed the bridge just after the shooting. They were making their way back to Mexico with small sacks. I talked with them a few minutes and they said that when they crossed the river they would tell me what had happened. I came back with them and they took me in their house and gave me their version, which is as follows:
>
> We were taking over a few things to make a little money. When

we were going up the track on the side of the dump we [saw] some men coming and laid down in some weeds so they might pass, but they stopped and talked for awhile and then one of them—a tall slim man—went towards the bridge. In about half an hour he returned, followed by a big heavy-set man who was walking five or six steps behind. When the first man passed the two that were in hiding he coughed twice and one of them that was crouching down shot twice at the back man. He staggered and fell; at that moment, the man in front that went to the bridge turned and ran back and as the back man tried to rise the tall man fell back, but sprang to his feet like a cat and pulled his gun. Then the fat man with the long gun let fly and the other two at the same time began firing. Then the big man kept trying to get up; then one of the men went towards the streetcar bridge and another lighted some matches and found the dead man's pistol and took it and lay it close to his hand on the ground. Then the man that was shot tried to rise again and the fat man put his foot on him and held him down until he died. The two men that were left were talking very fast, but there was no word said by anyone until after the shooting. By this time, there was a man coming with a light and we dragged our sacks away about 100 yards and hit [sic] them and then crossed the bridge back to Mexico, and in about two hours went back to our sacks and brought them back to Mexico.[15]

Angry at the turn of events, Victor Queen could not let the murder go. At the first opportunity, he accosted Beauregard Lee. "Queen immediately wanted to know if Mr. Lee was not the man who first arrested M'rose at Magdalena, and he replied that he was; whereupon Queen started in his chin and declared with a varied flow of profanity that he did not want to have anything to do with Mr. Lee or any such people as he was. The detective [...] did not propose to take any abuse from him, and he wouldn't. [...] Mr. Lee then went over to the office of Chief Haro, who [...] told him in an unvarnished flow of emphatic Spanish that if he tried any such racket as that again, he, the chief, would boot him clear across the river into El Paso.[16]

Interestingly, "A letter was found on the body of Mrose. It was directed to Miss Beula [sic] Mrose…. The envelope was covered with blood and had been struck by two of the pistol bullets. The letter was opened and read by District Attorney McGowan and then sent to Mrs. Mrose, for whom it was intended. Mrose also had seventeen .45 calibre cartridges in his pocket, and a small pocket comb." Helen Beulah explained, "The letter I received after he was killed was a request for me to meet him at a certain place in El Paso, but I did not get it until after he was dead. There was nothing more in the letter, except of a private nature."[17]

Robert K. DeArment, in his biography of Scarborough, discounts the story of the smugglers. "It is highly unlikely that two smugglers with sacks of contraband could be hidden this close to the scene of the shooting without ever being detected by either the officers involved in the shooting or the river patrolmen."[18]

Despite this story's hearsay nature, and in spite of Queen's obvious desire to challenge the men who had killed his friend, one fact stands out. Queen's reportage of the Mexicans' version of events was published the same day as the lawmen's and it agrees in substantial detail with them. How this could be possible if he were inventing a story is hard to imagine. It's one thing to dispute a story, but it's another to anticipate an adversary's tale before it's published. For this reason, some credence must be granted to the story of the two Mexicans.

Several other details must be explored. First, the Mexicans claimed that after passing Milton and McMahan's hiding place, Scarborough coughed twice, a signal. This was followed by two shots, and, while Mrose was down "the fat man with the long gun let fly." There was no opportunity to surrender. Second, one of the officers tampered with the evidence when he "found the dead man's pistol and took it and lay it close to his hand on the ground." Third, the sad detail, "Then the man that was shot tried to rise again and the fat man put his foot on him and held him down until he died."

Deputy Jones said of the pistol, "His pistol was lying by his right hand cocked. There was one empty chamber and one shell that had recently been shot and four cartridges were in the pistol. The pistol was lying about an inch from his right hand."[19]

Justice W. D. Howe made a significant comment about the shooting. "Jeff

Milton told me he though[t] Hardin was pretty quick with a gun but thought M'rose [sic] was quicker, that he never saw a fellow so quick."[20] For this reason, it might be good to ask, how well did Mrose do with his one shot? "Mr. Scarborough was wearing a Mexican hat [sombrero] at the time of the shooting and the brim of his hat was pierced by a pistol bullet about an inch above his left ear."[21]

And the pistol? Justice Howe kept a small collection of evidence from some of his cases. "Among these is a letter he received from Victor Queen after the notorious Martin Mrose had met his death. It is a request that the Justice turn over to Vic the revolver that Martin had on his person when he kicked the bucket, the writer claiming that it belonged to him. He gave an accurate description of the gun all right, but as Mrs. M'Rose also claimed it, the Justice turned over the death breeder to the sheriff. It is a Colt's .45 calibre."[22]

Scarborough, Milton, and McMahan were charged with murder—standard procedure in those days. The shooting, however, was a turning point in the lives of these men. At the time—and even now—something was wrong, and the fishy smell of it clouded the reputations of all involved. As time passed and careful men considered the shooting carefully, they formed a consensus, the verdict of history:

"George Scarborough began a systematic course of deception to inveigle Martin Mrose into going across the river."[23]

"[H]e decoyed the fellow across the river."[24]

"[T]he officials at El Paso [...] did wrong in inveigling Mrose to the point they did [....]"[25]

"[T]he officers [...] did wrong in inveigling Mrose [....]" [26]

Mrose "was induced to come to the American side."[27]

"[T]hey got him to go on the bridge there and killed him."[28]

"Mrose was lured to this side...."[29]

"M'Rose was induced to come over into El Paso one dark and stormy night [...] and then received a sudden and anonymous ovation in the shape of sixteen buckshot."[30]

"Yes, I think Scarborough towed him over here."[31]

"[Mrose] was murdered at the bridge."[32]

"It was rather cold blooded...."[33]

But the verdict of history also included Hardin and Helen Mrose. The *Gonzales Inquirer* called Hardin "the leading figure in a case [...] to induce a fugitive from American justice to come back to this side of the Rio Bravo...."[34] And Harry Epperson recalled, "Martin had a sweetheart in El Paso, who made a date with him to meet her on the bridge between El Paso and Juarez. She inveigled him to step a few feet across the line into the U.S.A. and he was shot and killed for the reward."[35]

Even W.H. Burgess, who defended Scarborough, Milton, and McMahan at their murder trial, admitted Scarborough had "[t]old [Mrose] where he could get a shot at Hardin. [... Mrose] came over here to kill him about the woman."[36]

Another account, recorded a few years after the event, but long before Hardin stories had become marketable, was written by George Look, a saloon owner, just before his death. Look's memoir, which relegates the Hardin story to pages nine and ten, says:

> John Sellman [sic] came to me and said that he had a cowman friend over the river, whose name was something like McRose, whose wife, he said, he would like to meet, and if I could give them one of the old rooms back of the Gem [Saloon], where he could get them together. McRose was under cover, and daren't show up on this side of the river. I don't remember whether Spellman [sic] got them together that time or not, but within a day or two Scarborough got McRose to come across the Mexican Central bridge with him under the pretense of meeting his wife on this side. On coming across the bridge with him, they met John Wesley Hardin, Milton and John Sellman. McRose was killed by those men at the foot of the bridge. Then Hardin got to him first and took $3,700 out of his pocket. The next day or two John Wesley Hardin and McRose's wife [were] riding around in a hack. [37]

George Look did not sensationalize Hardin or the Mrose shooting. Instead, his recall of events was at the end of his short manuscript. Because of this, the author believes Look is one of the best sources available on these events.

There are questions about the shooting that linger today. Why were all the killers careful not to identify Hardin or Helen in the newspapers? Scarborough calls him/her "a party on this side of the river." Were the officers afraid Helen and Hardin might be questioned as part of a larger conspiracy?

If the lawmen's avowed purpose was to arrest Mrose, why did they arrange it in an isolated dump with all of them facing no-man's-land and the Rio Grande River? Why did they attempt an arrest in pitch-black conditions? Why not do it in a well-lighted street, where all the lawmen could step into the open and Mrose might surrender? The answer to these questions, of course, was that surrendering was not an option the lawmen wished to extend him. That being the case, the shooting of Martin Mrose was an assassination.

Why would three lawmen become involved in a conspiracy to murder someone, who, at the time of the shooting, was not a fugitive and was living as a law-abiding guest in another country? The answer may simply be they needed money. Scarborough had a family to support. Frank McMahan was newly engaged, and a little over two months later, on September 1st, would marry Alice Hunter of Mason, Texas.[38] And for six weeks prior to Mrose's murder, Milton's embarrassing financial straits—garnishment of his effects for nonpayment of bills and flight across the Rio Grande to elude creditors—was the subject of news reports.[39]

The effects of Mrose's murder reverberated for weeks. Tom Fennessey, one of his closest supporters in Juarez, "says he has quit the Pecos valley for good."[40] Though one lawman, Col. G.W. Baylor remarked he would have liked to have killed Mrose[41] almost everyone else expressed remorse things had turned out so unfairly.

Helen "felt badly about the sudden death, but did not blame the officers."[42] She was about the only one who did not. "Ever since the killing of Martin Mrose, there has existed a bitter feeling between the friends and chums of Mrose and the officers who killed Mrose. [...] This state of affairs will ultimately result in someone being killed as all of the parties are high strung and fearless and should they meet a shooting scrape is sure to occur."[43]

Victor Queen wrote the *El Paso Daily Herald*, August 13, 1895, "[M]y friends have not in the least encouraged me to stay in Juarez or seek revenge, nor do I permit them to interfere in my private affairs." Earlier, Queen tried to patch things up with Helen. On July 30th, he wrote:

> I want to see you on some business and I don't want anyone else to no [sic] anything about it. I have been trying to get to see you for some time but have failed now Bula if you will come over let me no [sic] at once it is for your own benefit it will save you a grate [sic] deal of trouble over there and there ant [sic] against you over here for if you can come over and see me Please Do so at once So no more for this time as ever your friend
>
> Victor Queen[44]

With Martin Mrose dead, all that remained was the funeral. Showing no remorse at the recent turn of events, "Hardin and the blond didn't help matters any by their conduct. After Mrose was killed, they drove by the undertaking parlor across the street from the city hall and both were pretty well lit up. The body of the slain Mrose was even then lying in the funeral parlor."[45]

One of Mrose's friends, "J.J Rascoe, [...] went to El Paso Sunday night of last week to identify the body of Mrose [....] Not a person attended Martin's funeral and the undertaker was compelled to solicit four men to go out to the grave and cover the body. At the grave they met Wesley Hardin and Mrs. Mrose."[46]

Helen allowed herself to carouse with Hardin after the death of her husband, but things may not have been so rosy. There was a rumor in El Paso she tried to kill herself the next day.[47]

Finally, we must wonder what Mrose's ultimate purpose was: to visit his wife, regain his cash, or kill Hardin? The best clue as to his intentions is demonstrated by how he armed himself. In the photograph taken of Mrose and Fennessey, Mrose may be packing a pair of pistols, but the night he was murdered, he carried only one, a Colt single-action .45 with a short barrel. The front sight had been removed, making the gun a second faster than guns like the Smith and Wessons Hardin was carrying. More importantly, however, was Mrose's handling, which Scarborough remembered, "He let down the hammer and then revolved the cylinder several times by cocking it and letting it down."

It was the custom to leave an unloaded chamber under the hammer to prevent accidents such as John Wesley Hardin's kinsmen, Mannie Clements and Martin Q. Hardin, had recently suffered. Hardin himself was known to keep one cylinder empty, but NOT Martin Mrose, despite testimony to the contrary. By spinning the cylinder, he proved to Scarborough's trained eye he had loaded all six chambers. Was he loaded for his wife or his money? No, he had loaded in deadly earnest for the greatest living gunfighter, and he needed every advantage he could get. The revolver, made without an ejector rod, was difficult to reload. It was made for a fast, close-range encounter. Shorter barrel to clear his waistband, lighter to come to bear more quickly, six bullets rather than five—three small advantages in a fight to the death. Of all the guns of the Old West, the revolver Martin Mrose carried the night of June 29, 1895, is perhaps the only one intended to kill one very special man.

18
HELEN BEULAH
JULY–AUGUST 1895

"[T]his goddess of war ...."[1]

Tucked away under a bed somewhere or waiting in a safe deposit box may be a priceless manuscript written on a yellow legal pad now gone gray after all these years. It is about a hundred pages long, margins filled with corrections. Without a doubt, it is in a woman's handwriting, with some corrections a man's. The manuscript may be the most valuable literary work from the Old West—if it still exists, of course.[2] It is the autobiography of John Wesley Hardin. Lacking the manuscript, two mysteries have emerged: how much did an editor change it before publication, and how much came from Helen Beulah Mrose?

The concept of recording Hardin's story began very early. Not long after his arrest in 1877 for the murder of Charlie Webb, his attorney, J.A. Lipscomb wrote, "Don't let any one [sic] write your life. I want that job myself."[3]

Years later, after Hardin had moved to El Paso, a friend, Jeff Hargis, wrote, "[W]hen you get your life [story] out I want you to give me all the territory down here that I can possibly work[.] I believe I could sell 2,000 [copies] in Gonz[ales] Co[unty.]"[4]

Among those who may have seen the original manuscript was J. Marvin Hunter, later in life the publisher of *Frontier Times*. Frank McMahan's brother-in-law, Hunter said he "met John Wesley Hardin at Mason, Texas in the early part of the year, 1895, when he came into the Mason Herald office to get an estimate on the cost of printing a small book, the story of his turbulent life."[5] Later, in an introduction to Hardin's autobiography, he said Hardin "was at Mason in 1895, and to me he appeared to be a very mild mannered gentleman, not of the desperado type whatever."[6] Born March 18, 1880, Hunter would have been only 14 years old at the time of the alleged encounter.

The incident (J. Marvin Hunter meets John Wesley Hardin) probably never happened like Hunter claimed. Though Hardin was in the area, it would have been at least a three-day round trip from Junction City to Mason. A stagecoach traveled the route every day. It took twelve hours one way and arrived in Mason in the evening.[7] There were two bitterly competing newspapers in that town, the *Mason County Herald* and *The Mason County News*. Copies of the *Herald* have not survived. Having come by stage to present his proposal, only to get turned down, Hardin would naturally have sought out the competitor, yet the *News* never made a mention of his visit. The greatest celebrity in Texas, and he doesn't merit a line of coverage? Inconceivable!

A more likely account of Hunter meeting Hardin comes from El Paso. Hunter had moved there and worked for W.W. Bridgers at the *Graphic* newspaper. Though he claimed this was in March 1899, famed writer Ed Bartholomew recalled Hunter "related to me how he had seen Hardin, while in El Paso, as he came into the printing shop in which Hunter was then working, in an effort to get his life's story published. Mr. Hunter stated that Hardin carried the manuscript about in a black handbag."[8]

Hunter's sister married Frank McMahan in El Paso in September 1895, and Hunter claimed he attended the wedding. What it all suggests is Hardin's progress on the manuscript was haphazard at best. He talked about writing a book in Gonzales; in Junction City, he was distracted by his marriage to Callie Lewis. In Austin and San Antonio, he made inquiries. One man wrote, "This will introduce to you Mr. John Wesley Hardin of Frontier Days fame. He is getting estimates on having some book published. You may rely on him as a thoroughly reformed and reliable gentleman."[9]

In Pecos and in El Paso, he played attorney and drank, but about May or June 1895, he became serious. "Hardin has [...] quit drinking and gambling, and will apply himself to the practice of law and to writing a history of his life."[10]

Hardin's resolve had to do with two factors. He had a woman who was literate and determined, and through her, he had the funds to pursue his writing full time. Even so, why did Helen throw herself so completely into the arms of John Wesley Hardin? The explanation comes from John Selman, Jr., who said, "It became known Mrose had left five thousand dollars in insurance to his widow, and Hardin, acting as her attorney, left town, presumably to attend to the matter. He had to go up to Eddy, New Mexico to collect the insurance." Helen could not have been popular in Eddy with Mrose murdered, and she would have had a hard time collecting insurance on her own. A gunslinging lawyer acting on a power of attorney, however, had a chance of gaining the money. Though Hardin had also agreed to represent a plaintiff in a minor adultery case in Pecos,[11] even so, there was almost no good reason to leave El Paso.

The only discipline Hardin had was when they were together. Without Helen Beulah to moderate his urges, Hardin would make a fool of himself. The same would be true for Helen, for Hardin's absence opened the door to trouble. Hardin "had hardly got out of town'" said John Selman Jr., "when the queen went on a big spree and wound up down on San Antonio Street in Billie Ritchie's restaurant. There she made a big gun play. I was passing at the time and saw her through the large glass window. Billie was standing facing the street with his hands up. The queen was holding a pair of guns on him. The door was open so I walked in, very quietly, and stepping up behind her, I encircled her with my arms and squeezed her so hard she dropped the guns on the floor. They were a beautiful pair of matched forty-ones, pearl handled Colts. I took her to jail and had the jailer hold her in the office for a couple of hours and then release her on a cash bond. The next evening, she pleaded guilty to carrying a gun and paid a fifty dollar fine."[12]

Selman's unusual method of disarming this attractive, bosomy young woman had an impact on both of them. Helen, Selman recalled, "did not hold any ill feeling toward me and treated it as a huge joke. A few days later, it was Saturday afternoon, in fact, I was standing in front of the Parlor Saloon. She drove by in an open hack. When she saw me, she called out, 'Come on and take a ride with me.' I shook my head. She then stood up in the hack and waving a large roll of bills at me, she called, 'I'll give you five hundred dollars if you'll take a ride with me!' My friends began to laugh and enjoy the fun, but I cut it short by dusting around the corner, and if my face was as red as it felt, it must have been scarlet."[13]

The *El Paso Herald* reported, "Mrs. M'Rose [...] drank too much Texas rabbit's foot last night and became decidedly bellicose. At the hour of murky midnight this goddess of war camped on officer Sellman's [sic] trail in front of Charlie's restaurant on San Antonio street[14] where she made a few cursory remarks in the way of general compliment and then invited the officer to pull his gun or be made a target of. Sellman noticed the glimmer of a gun in the madame's parasol and straightaway made a [dive] for the same. She was not quick enough and he got it away from her. Then she riz [sic] right up in her wrath and turned her vocal batteries loose on the officer's head until the air was of something more than a Cerulean hue and the paint scaled off the neighboring woodwork."[15]

Helen Beulah was fined twice as much as Hardin for the same offense,[16] but when Hardin was arrested by Sheriff Simmons on May 6th on an outstanding warrant, he had only one gun; Helen twirled two, and they were both fined $25 per pistol.[17]

At this point, one must wonder what was going through her mind. Did she feel under the protection of a powerful and dangerous—though absent— lover? Or was she just letting loose without the old man around? Sadly, it was probably the latter. Helen's problem with alcohol was coming to the surface. The blood of outlaws and lawmen coursed through her veins, and she was a child of the frontier where hurrahing a town was an honored tradition. Surrounded for the last three months by dangerous men with guns, she probably felt she had a right to lay waste the town of El Paso. It's fortunate no one was killed.

Young John Selman acted properly in disarming her, but did he throw his arms about her waist and shake the guns from her hands? No, it would have been dangerous. Her lower ribcage to knock the wind out of her? Again, her arms would have been free; it was too dangerous. Selman must have wrapped his arms over her shoulders and forced her arms down, his hands locked over her bosom. Forty years after the encounter, he was still breathless describing it. It was not just an arrest, and Hardin knew it shortly after his return. Helen must have described it to him in detail, perhaps even acting out how she had grappled with young Selman. Hardin didn't take that well, and trouble began.

Unfortunately, Hardin hadn't behaved any better when beyond Helen's influence. He had gone to Eddy to collect Mrose's life insurance, but that didn't preclude a side trip for recreation. Undoubtedly drinking, he forgot an essential item: months before, his cousin, John Denson, had assaulted Deputy Sheriff Lon Bass in Phenix. By the time Hardin returned in August, Denson was gone; Martin Mrose, who had put up bond for Denson, had been murdered; and Helen Beulah was Hardin's lover … but Bass was still there, waiting.

Bass had been town marshal of Phenix, but when J.D. Walker took over as sheriff, he was appointed a deputy. His beat, Phenix, was out of control. Bass had, therefore, arguably the most dangerous job in the Old West, trying to enforce law where it was not wanted. For that reason, we must believe he was competent with a gun. He was about to have his greatest test.

Deciding to gamble in Phenix, Hardin "tried to work his El Paso game of picking up money from a gambling table, [but] was made to put it back at the point of a revolver in the hands of Lon Bass. John Wesley only tarried in Eddy between trains that day."[18]

One oldtimer said, "Bass outdrew John Wesley Hardin, and he walked him at the point of a pistol back to the train station and made him sit until the train pulled out."[19]

Hardin must have been mortified, and he can't have been in a good mood upon his return to El Paso. Did he get the insurance money? He may have left some of it on the gaming table in Phenix, but Hardin and Helen continued to spend unwisely in El Paso, so it's likely he brought at least some of the money back with him.

By this time, Helen and Hardin were living together in the Herndon House. Weather reports tell us it was a normal summer in El Paso, that is to say, it was hot as hell. Dust storms provided the only relief. There was, of course, no air conditioning. Hotels and boarding houses' draws were the quality of their menus and the coolness of their rooms. Among the smaller boarding houses was the Herndon, run by a wiry firecracker named Annie Williams.

The Herndon House was located upstairs from 207/209 Overland Street between Utah and Stanton Streets. The site of the hotel is next to the California Furniture Company at 201 Overland Street, today misidentified as the Herndon because of its hotel-like structure and second-story block of windows. The actual Herndon, next door to the east, according to Lawrence Reidman, the owner of the California Furniture Company, was torn down in the 1960s and replaced by today's structure, a locked and shuttered sporting goods store.

The Herndon House had been taken over in late 1894 or early 1895 by 32-year-old Annie Williams. Her husband was living several blocks away, so the relationship must have been acrimonious. On May 28, 1895 the *El Paso Daily*

Times reported Annie and Thomas Williams in court over a divorce. About this time, Annie's sisters and their children arrived in town to give her moral support. On June 6, the divorce was finalized, with Annie getting custody of her children.[20] In future El Paso city directories, she had herself listed as "widow of Thomas."

Annie had three children living with her at the Herndon: Alfred S., born in 1879; Thomas Jr., born in 1881; and Sarah, born in 1883. So, at the time Helen Mrose and John Wesley Hardin lived there, Annie Williams, her sisters, her three children, and perhaps her sisters' children were also living there, this in addition to the paying guests. Meals, served boarding-house style at a main table, must have been crowded, not to mention the other facilities of the little hotel. Noise was constant as people moved up and down the hallways and stairs. Children may have been playing underfoot, and privacy was at a minimum. Every window was open for ventilation. There may have been electric ceiling fans in the rooms, but the walls were thin and poorly insulated. Everyone in the building knew everything about the others, and tensions must have been awful during the rising temperatures of summer.

It was at this time and in this crowded place that John Wesley Hardin worked to finish his autobiography. Helen brought a sense of purpose to his project. Desperate for money, Hardin signed her as a full partner in the enterprise, and she moved him along in the project. They spent hours drinking and writing.

Martin Mrose's murder, however, was a turning point in Helen's relationship with Hardin. They began to bicker. Hardin drank more heavily and gambled away their money. Through all of this scandalous behavior, landlady Annie Williams held her tongue.

Though the paper reported, "When John Wesley discovered that Mrs. Williams was not afraid of him, not even a little bit, he felt a high admiration for her and would sit for hours talking to her of his past life and his hopes for the future...." Even so, Annie disliked him. She said, "I did not hesitate to talk saucy to him when he got drunk and damaged my furniture, and yet I know I feared him for I would feel my very bones chill when he looked at me with his little darting serpentine eyes. He would bring his whiskey up here by the gallon and I could hear him at all hours of the day and night stirring his toddy. But I never did see him staggering drunk and could only tell he was drunk by his extreme politeness and the peculiar snake-like glitter of his eyes."

It was a strange time to know Hardin. Busily writing, he seemed unnaturally insightful. The blackness of his character bothered him. "He declared to me," Annie said, "that he had no credence in human nature; that the human heart was rotten and that everything living was deceitful and he made me shudder when he said: 'I would not trust my own mother but would watch her just as I watch everybody else.'

"I tell you those two, Mr. Hardin and Mrs. M'rose [sic], made life a burden for me and I tried in every way to get them out of the house before they finally left. Hardin would walk the hall for hours at night with a pistol in his hand. I think he was crazy with fear, for no matter who knocked at his door he would spring behind a table where a pistol was lying before he ever said 'come in,' and he never allowed a living soul to enter his room while he was sitting down. Mrs. M'rose carried a gun also, in some kind of stationary pocket in the folds of her dress and I tell you she could pull it out in a hurry."

Another glimpse into life at the boarding house was provided by a newspaper boy.

> Carl [Longemare] got a delivery route for the *El Paso Times*. [...] When it came time to collect, he approached the landlady and said he would like to collect from Hardin. So the landlady took him up the stairs, back to the very end of the hall, and gave a code knock on the door.
>
> "Who's there?" Hardin asked from behind the closed door.
>
> "It's me and I've got the paper boy. He wants to collect," replied the landlady.
>
> "Just a minute," replied Hardin, who unlocked the door, then said, "Come in."
>
> They went in to discover Hardin holding two revolvers on them.[21]

Hardin had prearranged a particular knock. Even so, he didn't trust anyone. "Mrs. Williams told Carl that Hardin always greeted her that way. He feared an enemy might force her at gunpoint to use some such ruse to gain entrance to his room."[22]

Hardin gave the boy a generous tip, and, then, in an example of how charming he could be, invited the boy to watch him practice the maneuvers that had made him famous. For two hours, Carl watched in fascination as, "Hardin put his two loaded pistols on the dresser, within easy reach, and took two unloaded ones from a drawer. Then he positioned himself in front of the mirror and began his daily practice. [...] Concentrating intently, Wes Hardin watched his every move in the mirror, searching for flaws in his technique. If something was not quite right, he'd do it again and again until satisfied. [...] This dedication to perfection and the compulsion to attain it enabled Hardin to become a rarity in the Old West—a middle-aged gunman."[23]

Practicing in front of a mirror is a curious technique and certainly not necessary for fighting, because it's not one's appearance which wins a fight. Hardin seemed concerned with how his maneuvers looked, and it is for this reason we must believe it was part of a larger plan. The autobiography of a gunfighter might sell, but in those days, performance art sold better. There was a fortune to be made on the lecture circuit. Hardin had a built-in gimmick. While Helen sold books out front, he could perform on stage, whipping out guns and telling stories like a mini Wild West show. It was a potential goldmine, and Helen encouraged him.

But Hardin was becoming unmanageable. "Hardin had become louder in his abuse and had continually been under the influence of liquor and at such times he was very quarrelsome, even getting along badly with some of his friends...."[24]

As tension built in El Paso, it began to affect the lodging house. Annie Williams had difficulty carrying on her work; it was inevitable something would happen. On the evening of August 6, 1895, she said, "I went into the room where they were quarreling and she drew a gun on him, but I grabbed it and told her for God sake not to have a killing in my house. Hardin would have shot her then and there but his pistol was on the table across the room and I believe he feared to attempt to reach it."

It was an extraordinary confrontation, the greatest gunfighter of all time caught flatfooted by one woman and rescued by another. Annie Williams did not hesitate to take charge. "Mrs. M'rose then followed me out to my back steps and said: 'Mrs. Williams I hate to do it in your house, but I must kill that man tonight or he will kill me.' I told her if she did not mind he would kill her when ever [sic] she attempted to shoot him. She said she would wait until he went to sleep and then put her pistol to his head and blow his brains out. He told me that night in her presence that he intended to kill her. Then she handed me a letter and he snatched it out of my hands. She said right there in front of him: 'Mrs. Williams that letter is one he forced me to write, saying that I had committed suicide.[25] He wanted the letter found on me after he had killed me.'"

The *Daily Times* reported, "Hardin had her on her knees praying to him to spare her life, nearly the entire afternoon." It was August in El Paso, and it was too hot to carry on like this. Annie Williams snapped, "I was so completely put out that I just told them to please get out of my house to kill each other."

Downstairs, at 207 E. Overland, E.P. Lowe, publisher of the *Evening Tribune,* was balancing his books. Suddenly Helen Beulah ran through the office shouting Hardin was about to kill her. The editor, described by the rival *El Paso Daily Times* of August 7, 1895, as "not caring to have his office transformed into a stage for blood cardling [sic] theatrics [...] warned the lady to skip out into the alley [....] In the meantime the landlady and lodgers [...] had quit the building without waiting on the order of their going, and were hunting hiding places. They created quite a commotion on Overland Street."

A rival newspaper also had fun with the scene at the *Tribune.* The *Herald* said, "Hardin got very mad with Mrs. M'Rose for something she did Monday night [i.e. going out drinking without him], and he held an interview with her that resulted in the woman's rushing downstairs in the Herndon [...] where she rooms and through the *Tribune* office, where after 'scaring the life out of' Proprietor Lowe of the *Tribune,* hid in the back yard. Captain Carr was summoned, and a *Herald* representative overheard Mrs. M'Rose tell him an unvarnished tale of her troubles that indicated a serious state of affairs between her and Hardin."[26]

Back at the Herndon, everyone was running for the hills, but Hardin wandered out of the hotel unnoticed during the pandemonium he had caused and began to drink in the Acme Saloon. While he was there, Annie Williams accompanied her distraught lodger to swear out a warrant for his arrest before

Justice of the Peace George Harvey. The move was calculated to guarantee Helen's safety, as well as provide Annie Williams with a legal reason to evict Hardin.[27]

Chief of Police Fink, John Selman, Jr., Captain Carr, and Joe Chaudoin went to arrest Hardin.

> The Chief told us to be careful as Hardin was armed and intended to shoot it out. The Chief had been tipped off. We entered the Acme and found Hardin in a wine room. He was sitting with his back to the wall and with both hands under the table. Joe and I got on each side of the table, while the Chief and Carr did the talking. This time, Hardin was not so tame. I could see his eyes glittering, like those of a snake, ready to strike.
>
> The Chief said, 'You're under arrest.'
>
> Hardin looked us over, very cooly for a minute, and answered, 'All right.'
>
> He stood up and layed [sic] two forty-five six-shooters on the table and said, 'If it were not for Joe here watching me so damn close, I'd have killed the whole damn bunch of you.'
>
> He meant it, too. We took him to the city hall and booked him, but he was again released.[28]

A second version of the arrest said when Hardin was confronted, the officers "were expecting gun play. Captain Carr stood to one side of the Chief and [John Selman Jr.] stood on his other side, to be ready for action. To our surprise, Hardin offered no resistance. Instead, he begged the Chief not to take him to jail as he was suffering from a bad case of piles and he went so far as to expose himself to convince the Chief." [29]

While this account is utterly bizarre, Hardin did make amateurish mistakes that night. In his inebriation, he publicly claimed he had put lawmen up to killing Mrose, an accusation that backfired when Scarborough heard it on August 10.

A third version of the arrest said, "At the point of a pistol, he was arrested by a batch of [...] officers, who [sic] he made read the warrant twice over before he would surrender."[30] The arrest "created quite a sensation on the streets. Many persons looked on from a distance, expecting to witness a killing."[31]

Unfortunately for such a dangerous man, Hardin had a craven personality in face-to-face encounters. His style, long ago proven on the plains of Texas and Kansas, was the sudden jerking of a pistol, not a protracted face-down and an exchange of words. Hardin's boast that he had put Milton and Scarborough up to killing Mrose led to a sharp exchange with Jeff Milton.

> Milton walked up to Hardin [and said] 'You have told a lie on me and you have got to retract it.'
>
> Hardin said, 'Milton, no man can talk to me like that.'
>
> Milton said, 'You heard what I said.'
>
> Hardin said, 'You are taking advantage of me by the fact that I am not armed.'
>
> Milton said, 'That is not true. There has never been a day since you left the state penitentiary that you were not armed.'
>
> He said, 'I am not armed.'
>
> Milton said, 'Go get your gun, and I will be waiting here when you come back.'
>
> Hardin said, 'Milton, why do you want to talk to me like that, because I am your friend.'[32]

Perhaps to mend fences, Hardin bought Milton a bottle of whiskey at the Wigwam Saloon for 80 cents.[33]

After his argument with Helen, Hardin was not willing to spend the night in jail, so he put up $100 bond not to harm her. Though an unnamed officer was quoted as saying Recorder C.B. Patterson would surely get the bond—i.e., Hardin would inevitably break the peace—the trouble with Helen had burst Hardin's bubble. Next morning, the *El Paso Times*, and the following evening the *Herald*, went so far as to publish a wire service article praising Hardin's greatest rival, Wild Bill Hickok.[34] On the streets, gamblers were betting on Hardin's next move, but the bond worked, and on August 14,[35] seen off by Hardin, Helen caught a train west to Cartwright, Arizona.[36] She would detrain in Deming, wire Hardin "I feel you are in trouble and I'm coming back,"[37] which she did, only to be reassured by him and put on another train on August 16th.[38] Her torrid relationship with the notorious gunfighter was over.

19
THE UNLAMENTED
AUGUST 1895

"I've been widowed twice in six weeks."[1]

Among the legends that have arisen from the ruins of Helen Beulah's life comes a curious tale.[2] Due to the passage of many years, there is no way to know if it is completely true, but it is indicative of her character, and so it is reported here.

According to a family story, she and her parents were sitting on a porch in Cartwright to catch the Arizona breeze after the heat of an August day. Laura Jennings and other children were playing and the adults were talking, when along came a Western Union messenger on a bicycle. In a thoughtless gesture, Helen handed the boy a twenty-dollar gold piece and told him to keep the change. For the messenger, the coin was a sizable sum, but before he could pocket the bonanza, Helen's father, Bill Williams, stormed off the porch and snatched it from him. Turning to admonish his daughter for her spendthrift ways, he was surprised to find she had fainted, the opened telegram at her side.

Things would never be the same again, for the telegram brought shocking news: John Wesley Hardin had been shot to death by Uncle John Selman.

Next day, Helen started back for El Paso. Hardin was dead and buried, but she had to recover her money and the manuscript of the autobiography somehow. *The Arizona Republican* of August 23rd reported, "Helen Hardy for El Paso [...] passenger [...] on the outgoing M&P train[3] last night." It went on to say, "Mrs. J.W. Hardin, of El Paso, who has been in Phoenix several days visiting her parents, left last night for her home. She had not heard from her husband since her arrival and yesterday she telegraphed to him. She received a reply that her husband had died on Monday and was buried." A similar report in *The Arizona Gazette* reported, "For other points were [...] El Paso, Helen Harding...."

The whole world was in turmoil that summer. Dave Kemp walked out on his marriage to Lizzie Kemp on August 18, 1895, and though she implored him to come back, he refused to have anything to do with her. No reason has ever surfaced for this. Dave and Lizzie Kemp had been married for five years.[4]

In September, Tom Fennessey left his pregnant wife. No reason for this has surfaced either, but it is a peculiar fact that three prominent men of Eddy County, close friends all, married to three of the most beautiful women in Eddy—Martin Mrose and Helen Beulah, Dave Kemp and Lizzie, Tom and Adah Fennessey—all three marriages were over within three months of each other. Very curious.

Hardin's violent demise had been coming for a long time. His relationship with Helen was a major contributor to his death—but other factors were at work too. One man said, "Those who knew Hardin best [...] are of the opinion that he was a little off in the mind."[5]

Since putting Helen on a train to Arizona, Hardin occupied his time drinking. On August 19th, he announced he had "finished" his autobiography and set off on a spree. "The Wigwam [Saloon] ledger shows Hardin was drinking from eight or ten drinks a day to as many as twenty or thirty; these numbers probably included drinks Hardin bought for others, but those people probably reciprocated in buying drinks for him. He also bought whiskey and rye to take back to his room."[6] What's missing from this equation is the fact this was just one saloon—and Hardin liked to visit all the saloons. On the night he was killed, he drank at the Wigwam, but died in the Acme.[7]

As Hardin was drinking, a boy, 11-year-old Herman Hubbard, delivered a sealed telegram to him. Hardin put it in his pocket. "He was drinking a big glass of whiskey at the bar as I came up to him. He gave me a dime, put his hand on my head, and said, 'Son, don't ever do this.'"[8] Was the telegram from Helen? Maybe. An undelivered telegram to "Nellie Williams" was listed in the newspaper just after Hardin's death. Message not received?

At any rate, on the afternoon of August 19th, "Uncle" John Selman testified, "he met Hardin [...] outside the Acme Saloon and Hardin commenced abusing [Selman's son] for arresting the Mrose woman a few weeks ago. Sellman [sic] protested against the abuse and Hardin threatened to make him run out of town."[9] Selman later expanded on the abuse, saying Hardin had threatened "to make me shit like a wolf all around the block."[10] He also said "he had heard of

Hardin's threats and was all prepared for him. He had been informed of Hardin's statement to his landlady that he would … kill three more men ere he could finish with satisfaction the writing of the history of his life."[11]

Hardin drank in the Acme from afternoon to late night. Selman continued, "[We] met in the saloon and the talk was renewed. [I] told Hardin if he wanted to fight to go outside and get in the road. Hardin retorted that he would come out soon and that when he did come he would come out smoking. [I] went outside and waited until 11 o'clock when a friend came along and asked [me] to go in and take a beer."[12]

> Owen White recalled, "That night at about ten o'clock I passed the Acme Saloon and there in front of it, sitting on a beer keg and smoking a cigarette, was old John [Selman].
>
> 'Hello, kid,' he said. 'It's time you're gettin' home, ain't it?'"
>
> 'I'm on my way now,' I answered, 'but what are you doing here?'
>
> 'Nothin',' replied the old man. 'Just waitin', that's all.'
>
> I went on and had got no more than a hundred yards down the road when I heard a pistol shot. I looked back. Uncle John was no longer sitting on his beer keg. I ran for the saloon. When I got there I found him and John Wesley both inside, John had a gun in his hand, and John Wesley, stretched out on the floor and already as dead as a mackerel, had a bullet in his brain.[13]

Contrary to the above quote, however, Selman fired four times, the first shot hitting Hardin in the back of the head. Part of this bullet—or perhaps a fragment of skull—exited just above Hardin's left eye. He was dead before he hit the floor. Who knows if he ever felt the bullet? He certainly knew it was coming someday. Like Houdini, he had courted disaster for years, but when it came, he wasn't prepared. As his body crashed to the floor, bar patrons scrambled to get out of the way, and Selman fired three more times, only two of the shots hitting the body.

When it was over, Hardin lay sprawled on the barroom floor, a perfect place for him. He never drew his pistol. Though credited by one historian with inventing the shoulder holster, in fact, two .41 Smith and Wesson revolvers were removed from leather-lined pockets. Officer Chipman marveled, "Hardin's fabled shirt of steel has not yet materialized." Such a shirt would not have saved Hardin though, for he was shot in the head.

Said one observer, "I was close at hand when the shooting occurred in the Acme saloon, and was there immediately afterward. I covered Hardin's face with my handkerchief to keep away the flies which were gathering."[14]

John Selman, Jr. recalled Hardin had been back from New Mexico "only a few days, when, walking through the Plaza, I walked right into him and the queen.

'Here is where the test will come,' I thought.

[Hardin] spoke very pleasantly and didn't mention anything about the arrest. I passed on, but believe me, I breathed a little easier after I was safely away.

A few nights later, while I was with Frank Carr, I met my father and he told us that Hardin, while drinking in the Wigwam, had done some talking about the arrest of the queen. He warned me to keep out of trouble and attend strictly to business.

[A]bout eleven o'clock, I met [Officer] Joe Chaudoin and he said, 'Did you hear about your father and Hardin having trouble this evening? [...] They had it out over you arresting [Hardin's] woman. Hardin threatened what he was going to do to you and your father told him that if he had any quarrel [sic] with you, he'd take care of it himself. They had quite an argument, and your father wanted to shoot it out then and there, but Hardin wasn't armed, so your father warned him to go home and get armed and they'd shoot it out on sight.'

I answered, 'I'm going to find him right now. You know, Joe, he can't see very well after dark, and he won't have a chance with Hardin.'

We went to the Ruby and several other places, and I was getting into a blue funk when we met someone who told us he had just seen him going toward the Acme. We almost ran. When we got within a few feet of the Acme, I heard the first shot.

I ran through the swinging door with my gun in hand, but I wasn't needed. Hardin was lying on the floor face up and my father was standing a few feet away shooting at his body.

I sheathed my gun and took my father by the arm and said, 'Don't shoot anymore. He's dead.'

I took my father's gun and started out with him. Before I left, I looked at Hardin. His coat was open and I plainly saw the handles of two guns. I didn't look closely, but they looked like the selfsame guns I had taken from the queen a few days before. [...]

I went out with my father, and when we got a little way from the Acme, we stopped. While he rolled a Bull Durham cigaret [sic], I reloaded his gun from my belt. He never carried extra shells.[15]

In the modern world, this would clearly have been a murder, and a premeditated one at that. At the inquest and preliminary hearing in 1895, however, Uncle John Selman's account was accepted at face value. The only real issue was whether Hardin was shot from the front or the back. Selman said "front." No one thought to grill Selman's friend, E.L. Shackelford. Undoubtedly a "spotter," Shackelford could have provided information as to the set-up of the shooting. His account at the inquest differed from Selman's when he claimed he found Selman drinking in the saloon and walked him outside to advise him not to drink as he knew "the character of the man with whom he would have trouble. We walked out on the sidewalk and came back into the saloon, I being some distance ahead of Mr. Selman...."[16]

Despite Selman's assertions, however, Judge Howe closed the hearing with, "That [...] the death of said deceased was caused as follows...: That on the 19th day of August 1895, one John Selman of his malice aforethought ... did shoot the said deceased ...."[17]

Commenting on this controversy was Rev. E.H. Higgins, who was called to attend the body. "When asked how the body looked, he answered, "'Better than I ever saw him.' He added that if Hardin was shot through the eye from the front, 'It would be remarkably good marksmanship,' and if he was shot behind the right ear and not from the front, 'It was probably remarkably good judgment.'"[18]

Eyewitnesses supported Selman's version, as, for example, "At eleven o'clock last night as John Wesley was rattling his last throw of dice for a drink, which he never got, Sellman [sic] entered the saloon, and as John Wesley turned to look at him, he sent a 45-horsepower bullet crashing through John's brain."[19]

Mr. Burge, a photographer, declared "Hardin was shot directly in the face, and not in the back of the head. He says that had the bullet entered the back of the head, it would have torn the eye ball and environment in its exit, whereas the bullet hole in the left eye is so clean and well defined [...] there was where the bullet entered."[20]

The opposite view is represented by Frank F. Patterson, the bartender, who was standing close by. "Hardin was standing with his back to Selman. I did not see him face around before he fell or make any motion."[21] Henry S. Brown, who was was playing dice with Hardin, stood immediately to his right during the shooting. Hardin rolled a perfect score—perhaps the "Dead Man's Hand"[22] in that game—when he told Brown, "You have four sixes to beat." These were the last words Hardin ever said. Brown, in his testimony, reported "[A]s near as I can say his back was toward the direction the shot came from. I did not see him make any effort to get his sixshooter."[23]

Finally, three physicians who had seen many gunshot wounds during their careers, wrote, "We the undersigned practicing physicians hereby certify that we have examined the gun shot wounds on the person of John Wesley Hardin and its [sic] our opinion that the wound causing death was caused by a bullet wound. That the bullet entered near the base of the skull posteriorly and came out at the upper corner of the left eye."[24]

The single most significant recollection about Hardin's murder was made by George Look. There are several reasons the Look reminiscences are relevant. First, Look recorded his manuscript not long after the shooting but before Hardin stories became marketable. Second, Look attached greater importance to other matters; the Hardin story is relegated to the end of his manuscript. Third, it's a fairly straightforward story; there's no exaggeration apparent.

John Sellman came to me and told me that Wesley Hardin had

quite a roll—in fact, had McRose's roll. [...] 'George, you people may stand it, but I won't he has got to come across or I'll kill him.' He says, 'I believe that he has cut with Scarborough, but he has not cut any with the rest of us. What do you say—shall I get the son of a bitch?' We were in a very bad position. All the officers were either in the deal or afraid of John Wesley Hardin. Sellman, within a day or two killed Hardin, shooting him in the back of the head, in the Acme Saloon, because he would not give him, Sellman, his cut of the McRose money."[25]

The arrest of Helen Beulah by John Selman, Jr.; the murder of Martin Mrose; and Hardin's not sharing money with his co-conspirators appear to be the factors leading to the murder.

An interesting reaction to Hardin's sudden leave-taking was that of George Scarborough. "Years ago the late Gene Cunningham told me that at the time of Hardin's murder George Scarborough was aboard a train en route to El Paso. When the news of John Wesley's murder was received by the passengers, Scarborough flew into a rage. He had marked the gunman for his own tally sheet...."[26]

Another version has Scarborough asked by the conductor, "Have you heard the news?" he asked as he checked their passes.

"What news?"

"Why, Wes Hardin was killed."

"Who did it?" Scarborough asked.

"John Selman."

Scarborough nodded, unsurprised. "I'll bet he shot him in the back," he said.[27]

In the *El Paso Daily Times* August 20, 1895, Officer Chipman commented, "When I read in the *Times* this morning that Hardin was dead I drew a long deep breath of relief. Every day I feared I would be called into some saloon to arrest Hardin and run the risk of being killed. I never felt better when I saw him dead and I do not think Hardin ever looked better."

A man was asked by an acquaintance who had killed Hardin. "A fellow by the name of Selman."

"Do you know him?"

I said, "Goodness, yes."

He said, "What sort of man is he?"

I said, "A better man than Hardin, but much the same sort."[28]

Speaking of Hardin's reputation, another said, "An El Paso man was in Dallas "[... and said] the way John Wesley Hardin was carrying on, it would be a miracle if somebody did not put out his light within a month. This man said John Wesley had the town terrorized, did as he pleased, and was ready to shoot at the drop of a hat or anything else.

"The people all wanted him killed, but every fellow was waiting for somebody else to do the killing. Nearly every barkeeper in town kept a sawed-off shotgun for John's benefit, but whenever John came in and swiped the glasses off the bar with his gun, the bartender would ask Colonel Hardin what was his pleasure."[29]

W.W. Mills reported, "[P]eople, though not sorry at Harden's taking off, were shocked at the manner of it, but feared to condemn the act, because no one knew who would be the next victim. I was passing along the street, and a merchant friend called to me and said [...] 'What do you think about this killing of Harden?' I placed my hand at the side of my mouth and whispered, 'I'll tell you if you say nothing about it. I have just been down to the undertakers and I saw Harden [sic], and I think—I think he's dead!' I believe my friend kept the secret."[30]

Others felt compelled to comment. Jailer J.C. Jones, rumored to be on Hardin's "to kill" list for alleged involvement with the lynch mob that had hanged Hardin's brother in Comanche, Texas, laughed he was nowhere near there. Annie Williams, Hardin's landlady at the Herndon House, also had a lot to say.[31]

The body of the late gunfighter was conveyed to the Star Stables and Undertakers where undertaker J.C. Ross prepared it. Afterwards, "The body was photographed [...] in the morning, and in the afternoon photos found a big sale on the street. [...] The saloon where the killing occurred was an object of curiousity all day, as hundreds of people wanted to see where Hardin was shot and look at the bullet marks on the floor."[32]

A number of newspapers had a little fun at Hardin's expense. Said one, "Another of the men of Texas' earlier days, who agonized to get to bed with his boots on, has been gratified in his wishes. Constable Sellman [sic], of El Paso, was the instrument of Divine Providence by which Wesley Hardin obtained the rest that for years he so ardently courted. Peace to his ashes."[33]

The *Eddy Current* said, "John Wesley Hardin met the fate so richely [sic] deserved by any and every man who carries a gun. A gunman is dangerous and should be held up to ridicule by all law-abiding people."[34]

Another commented, "Since he was pardoned out he has been trying to get back into his old habits and get his old reputation again. But the country has changed and the fates were against him. So John Wesley passed in his checks and quit the game."[35]

One newspaper claimed, "more than a hundred men shook hands with and congratulated Constable Selman."[36]

Another editor wrote, "'At rest' was engraved on the plate on the coffin of John Wesley Hardin, the desperado killed in this city Monday evening. This is probably the first rest deceased has had since early boyhood."[37] Still another editor commented Hardin "had scarcely struck an attitude before he was ushered off [the stage] and his audience does not regret his hasty exit."[38]

On August 23, 1895, the *El Paso Daily Herald* joked, "Recent developments in mortuary circles have made it a proverb in El Paso that four aces will beat four sixes every time."

The *Mason County News* of August 23rd said:

John Wesley Hardin, the notorious desperado who served 17 of a 25-year sentence in the pen, and was pardoned some months ago, was killed at El Paso last Monday night by Constable John Sellman [sic]. The two men had had some words and were watching each other in a saloon, when Hardin reached for his pistol, but Sellman was too quick for him, shooting him in the head and shooting him twice more as he fell to the floor. Hardin has been terrorizing the people generally since his release from prison. His young wife whom he married about 6 months ago, lives at London, 20 miles west of here.[39]

At four P.M. on August 20th, Hardin's remains were loaded onto a hearse and conveyed to Concordia Cemetery for burial. In the cortege accompanying the casket were two buggies carrying relatives J.L. and Roberta Whitmore and Frank and Jennie Powers. Hardin was laid to rest in the second space from Martin Mrose's.

"Uncle John Selman, whose six shooter balanced Hardin's accounts, stood calmly on the street corner and watched the procession file by."[40]

20
THE ESTATE
AUGUST 1895–FEBRUARY 1896

"I'm a winter girl,
Ain't I a beaut?
I've got my new fall hat
And tailor suit.
Just a short time ago,
I had a summer beau,
For I was a summer girl then,
Don't you know... ?"[1]

Helen Beulah Mrose was remembered as a prostitute by nearly everyone who recalled her, and her decline into that line of work must have been awful to witness. Relatives can't bear to speak of it to this day, but the truth seems to be this beautiful farm girl, born into two of the great pioneer families of Texas, tied by blood and marriage to half the outlaws and lawmen of the Old West, became unhinged after the death of her lover. Unfortunately, her sordid path downhill included her four-year-old daughter, Laura Jennings, for she had brought the little girl back to El Paso when she'd come to settle Hardin's affairs. Years later, Laura claimed her mother had become "sick," and she left it at that, not caring to elaborate.[2]

The truth was always hard to take but harder to condemn. A woman encumbered with a child had no choices a hundred years ago. If she were uncommonly talented, she could work as a dressmaker; if unusually lucky, she could find a position as a postmistress; if unusually hardworking, she could work as a cook, laundress, or run a boarding house. Most women on their own, however, had no such alternatives.

In contrast to the lack of choices facing Helen Beulah is the case of Rae Wilmarth Lee, wife of Beauregard Lee, the man who had arrested Martin Mrose in Mexico. Rae traveled to Chicago in 1900 to have a baby in more civilized surroundings than Raton.[3] Rae Lee had a boy, whom she named Beauregard after his father, but she did not return to New Mexico. Sometime after Beauregard Lee's death, his brothers tried to retrieve the boy, but Rae refused to let them have him. Her father, according to family tradition, disagreed with her living as a single parent, and he may have thrown her out.

Luckily, there was a grand social experiment called Hull House in Chicago. Rae Lee spent time here and became a personal friend of Jane Addams, one of the founders. Later Rae reconciled with her father, and about 1909 the family moved to Los Angeles, where her son grew up to become a professional musician and a friend of Tom Mix and other celebrities.[4] Hull House had saved Rae Lee and her son from a fate that was to consume Helen Beulah and her daughter.[5]

Under the poem, "I'm a winter girl, Ain't I a beaut?" the editor of *The El Paso Daily Herald* wrote on October 1, 1895:

> A woman went into the [Acme Saloon] not long since, accompanied by her little daughter. The child was set upon the table and the mother proceeded to drink liquor and smoke cigars until she was in an irresponsible state, when the child was led out and the mother and a man—there ought to be some other word like brute for such a scoundrel—were left alone. [... I]t is not unusual to see men and boys standing in the alleyway trying to see what is going on inside."

While the editor did not blame her, he disapproved of what was happening; he railed at the authorities for not stopping it, and he urged them to close the saloons' wine rooms. Especially troubling about the story is the fact Helen carried on this way in the very saloon where her lover had been killed.

Soon afterward, the editor reported, "There is a certain handsome young woman in town who is not scrupulously careful of her morals, and she has set the hearts of some of the railroad boys and others in a flutter, and, at the same time has created pangs of jealousy to permeate the hearts of a number of maidens [....] One of these jealous fair ones ran across the gay and festive young woman [...] and a scrap ensued, in which the latter received a good drubbing, and not being satisfied, the angry girl turned and thumped the chap of whom she was jealous.

Of course, the affair created quite a sensation among those who heard of it...."[6]

Fights between "women of the line" were often reported humorously. For example, Annie Rooney was arrested "for telling another woman what she thought of her in the bacchantic dialect."[7] Such promiscuous behavior, however, was to backfire on Helen Beulah. Rather than being a celebration of her coming good fortune with the Hardin estate, it robbed her of sympathy at the moment others were moving to control the Hardin legacy.

The first of these was John Wesley Hardin's legal wife. On September 4, 1895 an attorney from Mason, Texas, wrote Frank Hunter, County Judge in El Paso:

> At the request of Mrs. Callie Hardin, widow of the late John Weslie [sic] Hardin, I beg leave to inquire whether or not letters of administration have been taken out or applied for on Hardin's estate by any one, and if so, by whom? Who has taken charge of Hardin's effects?
>
> The parties were married in Kimble Co. about the 19 of January of this year. [sic] Hardin's sister Nannie and brother Gip are cognizant of this fact. The papers giving a sketch of Hardin's life omit this part of his career....
>
> Rudolph Runge[8]

The Runge letter has two interesting points: knowledge of the autobiography, and a familiarity with its length and conclusion. Actually, others were also aware of its contents. An article in the *Gonzales Inquirer*, written August 19th, but not published until August 22, reported a 360-page "closely written" manuscript. This means someone had read the manuscript in its entirety before Hardin's corpse had cooled!

Helen, of course, felt she had the strongest claim to the manuscript. Not only had she lent Hardin money, but she had helped write the book. It was common knowledge Helen "was supposed to be [Hardin's] stenographer."[9] It's impossible, at this late date, to do a stylistic comparison between the autobiography and Hardin's later letters.[10] Hardin's writing improved in prison, but the author's impression is Hardin's letters are preachy and shrill in tone. The autobiography is not. It's rollicking good fun, a young man on fast horses killing people left and right all the way from the cow towns of Kansas to the Florida Panhandle. Perhaps an editor reworked the manuscript before releasing it, but it's more likely the manuscript was the product of Helen Beulah Mrose, as dictated to her, and edited by, John Wesley Hardin.

Interestingly, Hardin considered the manuscript finished just before his death. Indeed, his spree on the night he was killed may have been a celebration for completing the long task. One can't help but wonder why Hardin didn't bring the manuscript up to date. He ended his story in 1889, when he decided to study law. It's an abrupt ending. Hardin was still in prison in 1889. His greatest triumph, manipulating his release from Huntsville, was five years in the future. His failures in Gonzales, his doomed marriage to Callie Lewis, his move to Pecos, and his adventures in El Paso were left unrecorded. Why did he stop writing so soon?

There is evidence Hardin was not finished with his life story. The *El Paso Daily Herald,* August 26, 1895, reported, "[Beulah] had all the data with her with which to complete the unwritten parts. [...] She says she was very much attached to Hardin, and did not fear him except when he was drinking and jealous, and that when he was sober he treated her better than she was ever treated before in her life." She declared Hardin didn't want to be buried in the ground, but "in the ocean, and she would have taken his body and deposited it there, if she had been [in El Paso.]" She also made clear "that she did not return to El Paso for any trouble, but that she is here on business. She desired to secure control of Hardin's manuscript to reimburse herself for money advanced."[11] So, it appears Hardin stopped work on his autobiography simply because his collaborator had gone.

The author feels Hardin and Helen considered the autobiography the basis for a tour on the lecture circuit. If true, Hardin wouldn't have wanted to discuss the sheriff's race in Gonzales, nor his failures in 1895, so maybe the manuscript was "finished" as far as he was concerned. Helen felt the publication of the manuscript might be worth $10,000. With Hardin's demise, the money should belong to her.

There were, however, relatives of John Wesley Hardin living in El Paso. One was Roberta Whitmore, wife of Joseph L. Whitmore, a prominent contractor. Roberta was the daughter of John Dixon Hardin, and the granddaughter of Robert

Echison Hardin, Wes Hardin's "Uncle Bob."[12] Her sisters, Mary Sachs and Jennie Powers, also lived in El Paso. Probably one reason Hardin decided to stay after the Frazer trial was closeness to his cousins. Whether he stayed at their homes the first weeks of his residency is moot, but none of the three women could have been pleased with his antics with Helen nor his troubles in the saloons.

Roberta's name never came up in the fight over Hardin's estate. Her husband, J.L. Whitmore, fronted the action. His stated purpose was to secure the estate for Hardin's children, Mollie Billings, John Wesley Hardin, Jr., and Jennie Hardin. Another aspirant for Hardin's estate was T.T. Teel. Martin Q. Hardin, a very distant relative, and Hardin's brothers, Gip and Jeff, also put in appearances.

Hardin had died intestate, without a will. With sixteen-year-old Callie Hardin, twenty-two-year-old Helen Beulah Mrose, J.L. Whitmore, T.T. Teel,[13] and Martin, Gip, and Jeff Hardin—that meant seven people were fighting over the estate. Teel withdrew his suit after a couple weeks. Gip, Jeff, and Martin Hardin never filed papers, so it's likely they were satisfied Whitmore had the best interests of the "family" at heart. Callie Lewis Hardin may also have agreed to let Whitmore represent her interests, or she may have been ignored. There is no record of an answer to Rudolph Runge's letter to Judge Frank Hunter. That left two major players in the fight for Hardin's estate, J.L. Whitmore and Helen Mrose.

Whitmore moved quickly. Retaining Payton F. Edwards as attorney, Whitmore applied to be appointed temporary administrator of Hardin's estate in a hastily written petition on August 21st, two days after Hardin's death. Judge Hunter approved his appointment and ordered him to "pay out of effects, if money, funeral expenses, room rent, and such bills as may be a lien on his property."[14] Later the same day, Whitmore submitted a typed inventory of Hardin's property. Included among the effects were two rings, five guns, five law books, $94.85 in cash, photos of Helen Beulah Mrose and her daughter and the dead Martin Mrose, a 165-page manuscript, and a fifty-dollar Confederate bill— probably the one seized from Helen in Mexico at the time of her arrest.[15]

Helen and Laura returned to El Paso late on August 24th. Helen hired a lawyer the next day. "Mrs. Mrose has secured Patterson & Wallace as her counsel and will contest for the Hardin autobiography and a number of articles of personal property left by Hardin, as the litigant alleges the deceased was largely indebted to her for moneys advanced, and the autobiography was signed over to her as security."[16]

The selection of Patterson & Wallace was a wise move. The firm specialized in probate. Millard Patterson was the probate court reporter for Judge Hunter.[17] Because of a conflict of interest, George Wallace represented Helen.

Unfortunately, J.L. Whitmore was a formidable opponent. He was not only prominent in business circles, he was an El Paso city alderman. Helen was forced to play her best card early in the game.

> Mrs. Mrose filed this paper today with the county clerk: 'El Paso, Texas, June 18, 2895 [sic] I, John Wesley Hardin, on this day, take Mrs. Bula Mrose as a full partner in my manuscript and all business also as a confidential correspondence clerk.
>
> John W. Hardin
> Witness, Bula Mrose'"[18]

It was a bold, or a desperate, move. Did Hardin sign this IOU? Probably, else why would Helen have advanced him any money? But why, then, didn't she have the original? The answer must lie in the fact that Helen's departure for Arizona was hasty, in a period of intense emotional turmoil, the paper overlooked in their shared hotel room. That meant J.L. Whitmore held the original IOU now. He could either honor it, or withhold it at his pleasure.

Helen filed suit "in the district court, for the Hardin biography manuscript, for the dead man's watch, a revolver, and two rings, the total value of which she alleges to be $10,000."[19] Helen had the advantage now, and Whitmore was in the position of denying what was known throughout El Paso: Hardin's debts to Helen Beulah Mrose.

On September 3rd, Helen filed a hasty, handwritten petition contesting the appointment of Whitmore as temporary administrator. Then in a typed, carefully thought-out document, Helen applied to be appointed the administratrix of Hardin's estate.[20] In her petition, she declared, "[T]he said manuscript writing was near its completion, containing about 196 pages of legal cap writing which was written by said Hardin and this applicant, at the dictation of said Hardin.

That the same was soon to be placed upon the market for sale by said Hardin, and this applicant, and the funds so received by the sale of said book were to be distributed as follows: to wit: one half of said funds to be paid to this applicant as her share of the partnership funds in said book. The remaining one half to be paid to said Hardin, after [...] paying to this applicant fifteen hundred and seventy-five dollars, an amount of money loaned to said Hardin, deceased, to complete said book, and on which this applicant had a lien to secure payment thereof. That the total sum of money loaned to said Hardin by this applicant was fifteen hundred and seventy-five dollars. That the total value of said manuscript is about two thousand dollars."[21] Later in the same document, she notes, "the funeral expenses were paid with money loaned to said Hardin by this applicant, and found on the person of said Hardin."[22]

She also said, "J.L. Whitmore is in no way interested in said estate as a creditor, neither is he related by affinity, or consanguinity, that the deceased, at the time of his death was not indebted to the said J.L. Whitmore nor to any other person except Helen B. Mrose, this applicant, in any manner which rendered his property liable, therefore that the said J.L. Whitmore wished to procure the Administration for the purpose of defeating the right and claims of the said Helen B. Mrose."[23] There was a lot of truth in that statement, but the court did not rule on her petitions during the September term of court.

On October 4th, Helen filed another motion seeking to be appointed administratrix of Hardin's estate. In this document she valued the manuscript at a hundred dollars, and Hardin's debt to her as $1,175. No reasons were given for the changes. Whitmore responded in November with a similar petition, valuing Hardin's estate as a thousand dollars. This time, Whitmore added the family connection. "Your petitioner's wife is a relative of said Hardin, and his children have each requested your petitioner to qualify as administrator of said estate."[24]

October brought cooler weather, which in El Paso means dusty, harsh winds. Bill and Ann Eliza Williams came to support their daughter.[25] Their investments in Arizona having failed by this time, they probably owed money for the Gila Bend irrigation scheme, but Helen's situation in El Paso concerned them. Not only that, but Steve Jennings was beating the bushes in central Texas looking for his runaway wife and daughter. He was an angry and dangerous man, said by some to be "the meanest man that ever lived," and Helen and Laura's precarious existence in El Paso—and reports of her erratic behavior, were cause for alarm.

The fall brought new faces to El Paso. First to arrive was John Denson, Hardin's violent cousin, followed by Gip and Jeff Hardin, John Wesley's brothers.[26] Jeff Hardin declared he was there "on a peaceable errand, to secure through legal means, the possession of the biographical Mss. left by his brother [....] Mr. Hardin is stopping with his cousin, Alderman Whitmore."[27] Gip Hardin, however, was looking for a fight, according to the San Antonio News, which predicted, "Even money that he don't [sic] get the manuscript, ten to one he gets a fight if he seeks it, and twenty to one he loses the fight if he makes it."[28]

Criticized for not giving bail after murdering Hardin,[29] Uncle John Selman Sr., finally posted bail on November 14th. Selman's murder trial being delayed occupied most of the news later that month. From November 1895 to February, 1896, the "Great Fistic Carnival," a heavyweight title fight between Gentleman Jim Corbett and Bob Fitzsimmons, was news. Tensions and excitement were running high all over town, and while Helen waited for the next term of court, she must have felt threatened from all sides; she maintained a low profile.

Someone noticed. On November 14th, the El Paso Daily Times reported, "Some unknown person calling himself a 'Strange Man' left at the Times office yesterday a communication relative to Mrs. Mrose and her contract with John Wesley Hardin. The correspondent thinks Mrs. Mrose is not receiving fair treatment."[30]

Why did the "Strange Man" feel this way? On the eighth of November, five men were summoned as witnesses in the matter of the estate of John Wesley Hardin. Four of these names—Charles Russell, James Morse, M. Ward, and F.J. McMurray—appear out of nowhere, but one name leaps off the page: George Scarborough. Why did he and the other men appear as witnesses in the Hardin estate? What could they have contributed? It is unknown, but the effect was a direct threat to Helen Beulah's claims for the estate. Perhaps it had something to do with discrediting her.

The biggest threat, however, came on December 4, 1895, when Mollie Billings filed to be appointed administratrix. Hardin's daughter, "deposes that she is the oldest child of the deceased, and is anxious that the account of his life as *written by himself* [author's emphasis], should be handed over to her for disposal and publication. Petitioner avers that the value of this manuscript decreases every day it remains out of the publisher's hands; and as the children of the deceased are in straightened circumstances, they need this assistance."[31] Perhaps the surprise was a bit much for Helen; again Bill Williams, her father, came to El Paso to support her.

Things moved quickly after that. Judge Hunter appointed Mollie Billings administratrix on January 21, 1896. As she gained control, other news filled the newspapers. Victor Queen, who had found work in Mexico with the Corralitos Cattle Company, gave up in January and returned to Eddy County, New Mexico. No warrants, complaints, or indictments could be found accusing him of any crime—probably the way it would have ended up for Martin Mrose, too. Then, on February 1, 1896, *The El Paso Daily Herald* reported John Wesley Hardin had received a letter at the post office. Apparently, someone hadn't gotten the news....

On January 31st, Judge Albert J. Fountain and his nine-year-old son disappeared in New Mexico; the murder-mystery would be sensational news for weeks, but the bodies were never found. With the Great Fistic Carnival, the Judge Fountain disappearance, and the Selman murder trial dominating the news, Helen Mrose was pushed into obscurity. J.L. Whitmore got more press than she did; his move from the Wellington Hotel to a home he had built for his family was reported in the *Herald* on February 5th. Famed New Mexican attorney Albert Bacon Fall arrived in El Paso to help defend John Selman; Beauregard Lee came on February sixth to act as a bodyguard for the president of the Santa Fe railroad.

On February eighth, a jury was impaneled for the Selman murder trial; 248 candidates had to be interviewed before twelve impartial jurors could be found. The trial began immediately.

Frank Patterson, barkeeper for the Acme Saloon, testified to seeing Hardin leaning with both hands on the counter and with his back to Sellman [sic] when the latter fired. Dr. Sherrard testified to the ball's entering at the back of Hardin's head. Shorty Anderson testified to seeing Hardin suddenly throw his hand upon his gun and start to turn around;

and Captain Carr testified to finding the dead man's right hand resting near the handle of his pistol which had been caught in his clothing [....]"[32]

The conflicting testimony confused the jury. Next day the *Herald* reported the jury was hung, eleven to one for acquittal.

On February tenth, Helen Mrose withdrew her petition for control of the Hardin estate.[33] She hadn't won anything, but had she lost? The biggest clue as to what happened was that she withdrew her petition, rather than waiting to go to trial. This means she must have achieved satisfaction. She was probably reimbursed $1,575; she may have received more to dismiss her suit. Either way, her claim was finished, and J.L. Whitmore was free to close out the affairs of the estate.

Two days later, the Selman trial was over, the jury hung, seven for acquittal, five for conviction. Another trial date was set for fall. Uncle John Selman walked out of the court, a big smile on his face.

W. D. Howe recalled that Selman said, "'I guess I am free, white and twenty-one.'

"I said, 'I see you are free and over 21 and presume you are white, but as to being not guilty of any offense, from the facts I have, you are guilty of a cold blooded murder, shooting a man who didn't have a chance.'

Selman apologized the next day, explaining that he was drunk. Howe added, "[Selman] was not acquitted. [...] He had a hung jury. He went around and cussed out one or two of the jurors that had voted to find him guilty...."[34]

It was time now for Helen Beulah Mrose and Laura Jennings to leave El Paso. They headed west to follow Helen's dreams. She had money for a start, but for a spendthrift like her, it would not last long. J.L. Whitmore filed his final accounting of the estate of John Wesley Hardin on March 19, 1896. He asked the court to be reimbursed $96.95 for costs incurred during the proceedings, and on March 23rd, he was paid.

For Helen Beulah, it was another blow. The murder of Mrose, the unexpected shooting of Hardin, and the loss of the manuscript must have been emotionally devastating. Three times the rusty iron bell of history had rung for her, but she had not heeded it. It would ring no more. The shooting of her uncle A.J. Williams by George Scarborough, with supporting fire from his brother stationed in the shadows to the left, and the shooting of Martin Mrose by the same man, with Jeff Milton and Frank McMahan in the darkness to the left; the technically illegal, violent arrest and extradition of John Wesley Hardin on a train in Florida, and the awful arrest and transport of her husband Martin Mrose on a train in Mexico; the Terrassas Injunction to prevent Eulalia Terrassas from taking her daughter out of the state and her own sloppy mess taking her daughter and leaving Steve Jennings back in Fredonia—three times events had repeated themselves, and history could do no more for anyone. As she headed west in search of a new beginning, Helen Beulah was lost and on her own now.

With the Williams family's fortunes in decline, her daughter living as a tramp, and her granddaughter in California, the strain must have been too much for Ann Eliza Williams, Helen's mother. She died near Georgetown, Texas, October 29, 1898[35] and is buried at Berry Creek.

Items from the Hardin estate found their way to Amanda Clements, Hardin's cousin. Among them was the missing IOU, "typed on a yellow ruled legal pad using a blue typewriter ribbon [...] signed by John Wesley Hardin. [...] If this IOU is legitimate, and there is no reason to doubt its validity, Beulah was indeed cheated out of $1575," concluded Dr. Marohn in his biography of Hardin.[36]

And what became of the Hardin manuscript? Hardin's three children, Mollie, John, and Jennie, gained control of the much sought-after text. It's possible they deleted objectionable material; they added an appendix and some of Hardin's correspondence, his pardon, letters about their uncle, Brown Bowen, and a newspaper account of Hardin's murder.

Under the title *The Life of John Wesley Hardin From the Original Manuscript As Written by Himself*, the book was published by Smith and Moore in Seguin, Texas in 1896. The defiant title was a direct affront to Helen Beulah Mrose, but it's doubtful she ever saw the book. Shortly after its publication, Hardin's children regretted releasing it to the public, and they withdrew the remaining copies and stored them in a dank warehouse. Many moldered and were lost. Occasionally, one would surface in certain bookstores in San Antonio. In 1950, historian Ed Bartholomew tracked down the remaining copies—450 of them—and bought the lot for $1,000. They were marketed by J. Marvin Hunter, publisher of *Frontier Times* magazine, for ten dollars each.[37] Today, each of the surviving first editions of the autobiography of John Wesley Hardin is valued in the hundreds of dollars.

The VVN chuckwagon. The cowboy 8th from left may be Martin Mrose. Author's collection.

John Wesley Hardin, about age 40, the time of his release from Huntsville Prison. Hardin had been a Sunday school teacher in prison, studied law, and was thought to be reformed. Special Collections, Texas State University.

Photograph identified as Callie Lewis, John Wesley Hardin's teenage wife. Special Collections, Texas State University.

Jim Miller was married to Hardin's cousin, Sallie Clements. Miller's troubles with Sheriff Bud Frazer in Pecos, Texas, led to Hardin's move to Pecos and, later, to El Paso. Robert G. McCubbin collection.

A group of men in Pecos, Texas, including Sheriff Bud Frazer, far left. Note Frazer's size. Men of the 1890's were commonly under six feet, but Frazer looks smaller still, possibly only five feet tall! Courtesy of Gene Riggs.

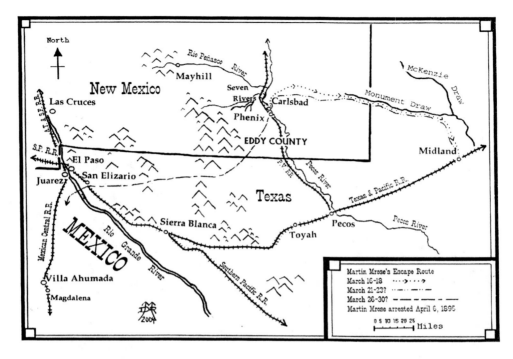

Martin Mrose's escape route, March 16-30, 1895.

John Wesley Hardin, El Paso, Texas, 1895. Hardin was in his prime. A lawyer, he was one of the greatest celebrities of the West, and his name was known across America. He was writing an autobiography and had a bright future. University of Texas at El Paso, Special Collections.

El Paso, Texas about the time of this story. Author's collection.

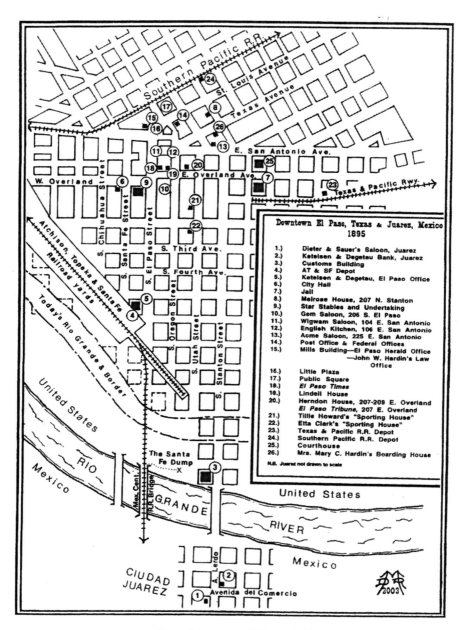

Map of downtown El Paso, 1895.
Note the site of the murder in the Santa Fe Dump is now in Mexico.

Helen Beulah Mrose and Laura Jennings, shortly after their arrival in Juarez, Mexico.
From an original in the author's collection.

Back of the photograph of Helen Beulah Mrose and Laura Jennings.
The D.A. mentioned is David Alonso Williams, Helen's brother. The photograph
belonged to Lois Freer, Helen's niece and D.A.'s daughter. Author's collection.

Martin Mrose and Tom Fennessey strike a defiant pose in Juarez, early June, 1895.
J. Evetts Haley Collection.

The gun Martin Mrose carried at the Santa Fe Dump, June 29, 1895. It's a short-barreled, single-action "Sheriff's" model. Note there is no front sight. Courtesy John Robinson.

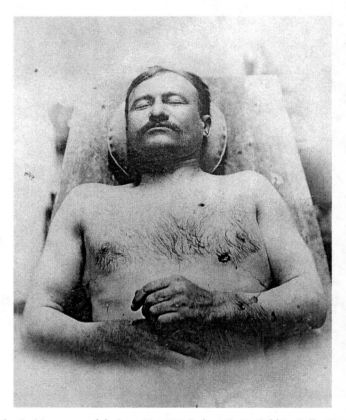

Martin Mrose on a slab, June 30, 1895. Robert G. McCubbin Collection.

U.S. Deputy Marshals Jeff Milton, on the left, and George Scarborough. Scarborough had killed Helen Mrose's uncle, A.J. Williams, in 1887. Both Milton and Scarborough were involved in the shooting at the Santa Fe Dump. J. Evetts Haley Collection.

John Selman, Jr. arrests Helen Beulah Mrose in front of the English Kitchen, August 1, 1895. This dramatic image by Robert Stanley illustrated an article "Death Wore Skirts" by David Dixon in an unknown 1950s magazine. Author's collection.

John Selman, Sr. about 1895. Like many gunmen of his day, Selman crossed back and forth from lawman to outlaw throughout his life. J. Evetts Haley Collection.

John Wesley Hardin on a slab.
Special Collections, Texas State
University.

Annie Londonderry,
bicyclist. During the
evening of June 29,
1895, Annie delivered
a lecture probably
attended by John
Wesley Hardin and
Helen Beulah Mrose.
Shortly afterward,
Martin Mrose was
murdered near the
Santa Fe railroad
bridge. Author's
collection.

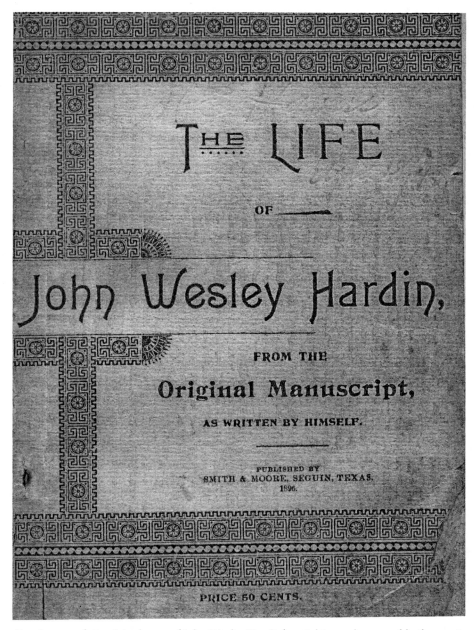

THE LIFE

OF

John Wesley Hardin,

FROM THE

Original Manuscript,

AS WRITTEN BY HIMSELF.

PUBLISHED BY
SMITH & MOORE, SEGUIN, TEXAS,
1896.

PRICE 50 CENTS.

Front cover of an original copy of John Wesley Hardin's autobiography, arguably the most profitable book ever written about the Old West. Author's collection.

21
THE HORSEMAN
1897

"[T]he bicycle is with us to stay and the overworked
horse can meander toward the sausage factory."[1]

Perhaps it was courage, the fire of anger, or spiteful tenacity, but one day Steve Jennings decided to get his daughter back. He had been patient long enough. Opinion in Texas had cooled, and there seemed more right now on Steve's side than his runaway wife's. People began to talk. Where Steve had encountered only stony silence, now he began to learn the truth about Helen.[2]

Steve quit his job and sold all his gear but the rig for one horse. Between him and his daughter, Laura, lay a thousand miles of desert. It was a violent land, and no one went unarmed. A lone rider carrying anything of substance had little chance of making it through the bandits, rustlers, and cutthroats between Fredonia, Texas, and Cartwright, Arizona, but a broke cowboy might make it.

Who knows what he took with him? A gun and every shell he owned, undoubtedly. A bedroll, hackamore, rope, hobbles, a few clothes, coffee pot, canteen, and what in Texas is called a "fry pan." It is known that when he rode out in 1897—nearly three years after the loss of his daughter—he was long on hope, short on means.[3] For the village of Fredonia, however, his departure was an event worth noting.

A curious spectacle occurred as he approached Fredonia on his way through. Some handed him money—whatever they could spare, for times were hard. One gave him a few cartridges; another exchanged slickers with him as his was newer and might give better service. A woman gave him a slab of bacon wrapped in a newspaper. Hardly anyone said anything. There were few well-wishers and no goodbyes at all, just a simple recognition something remarkable was happening. When Steve cleared the village and rode on alone, a half-dozen people silently watched him go.[4]

It is one of the conceits of our age to think the Old West was backward. To learn there were telephones as well as phonographs in use in the 1890s, to discover electric ceiling fans were becoming common in the saloons, to read that ice-making plants were revolutionizing meat packing and agriculture and that bicycles and bloomers were sweeping the nation by storm is to truly understand the West.

America had been swept up in a bicycling craze. In El Paso, bicyclists were riding at night without lights. Startled horses and disgruntled law officers were often reported in the papers. "Uncle" John Selman arrested all the bicyclists he could catch, which was surprisingly many, considering he walked with a cane. Bicycle clubs and races were front-page news, and it was inevitable someone test the endurance of a bicycle.

The first of these in El Paso was a young black man traveling coast to coast, but references to him are few, and his ultimate success is unknown.[5] Another cross-country adventurer was Annie Londonderry, a slight, wiry woman of Polish descent. Inspired by the adventures of woman journalist, Nellie Bly, Annie resolved to travel around the world on a bicycle.[6] She left Boston June 25, 1894. She appeared in France, Egypt, Saigon, Korea, and Japan. By the time she returned to American soil, she was a sensation. After crossing the harsh desert of the American Southwest, on June 28, 1895 Annie arrived in El Paso, Texas, the day before the murder of Martin Mrose. The McGinty Club hosted a widely attended lecture by her. Since Hardin and Helen Beulah were socially active in this period, it's probable they were in the audience as "the lady of the bike" described her adventures.[7]

The newspapers were full of Londonderry's escapades, since she appeared before crowds wearing what was, at the time, the most scandalous of women's fashion. Moved by Annie Londonderry's public example, women across the nation were beginning to wear bloomers, and perhaps even Helen Beulah bought a pair.

Despite intense interest in the bicycle, however, the traditional mode of travel across the Southwest was by more traditional means. A man had to be quite a horseman to attempt such a journey across the desert. One of the Army's best cavalrymen made a ride at about the same time as Steve Jennings. *The Arizona*

Daily Gazette reported, "An interesting test of the endurance of the native western horse for cavalry service was made this month by Lieutenant Cornelius G. Smith [...]. Starting from Fort Wingate [Arizona] April 10, he set out to ride 1,035 miles to San Antonio, Texas, in one month's time."[8]

On April 26, the horseman passed through Eddy, then northwest and east to Midland, Texas, arriving on the 29th after having ridden through the same country Martin Mrose had ridden through on his flight from Eddy. Smith continued on to San Antonio. When finished, his journey was reported to have been "a rough one [...] The horse looked well and had lost but 54 pounds."[9]

Still another great ride "settled" once and for all whether cavalry mounts, saddles, and training were better than standard cowboy equipment. This test, a race north-south across Texas from Dallas and Fort Worth to San Antonio, was between Major Terry Allen of the Army and Key Dunne, a rodeo rider. Major Allen completed the 300-mile distance seven hours ahead of the cowboy.[10]

Another endurance test occurred in 1898, a race west to east in better countryside. "[T]he 1,000-mile Chadron to Chicago Cowboy Horse Race was a contest of courage and endurance. It [...] proved the hardiness of both western men and horses."[11]

A desert trip, however, was the supreme challenge for man and horse. The famed outlaw, John Ringo, traveled from Mason County, Texas, to Arizona in the late 1870s, but whether he did it on one horse is doubtful. Cowboys working the cattle trails had strings of horses on which to make the journey, but Steve Jennings had none of these advantages.

The typical mount of the time was fourteen or fifteen hands high, weighing seven or eight hundred pounds. The horse Steve had was probably a common hammerhead, used to working with cattle on the range. Another disadvantage was Steve had only a serviceable saddle, not a comfortable cavalry one for the ride.

Steve probably rose before dawn each day to fortify himself with a meager breakfast. By sunup, he was ten miles on his way, and by the heat of the day he had probably covered thirty miles. It must have been frustrating to stop about noon each day, but his horse needed grazing time and water. This is where a less experienced rider could kill a horse, but Steve knew what he was doing. His mount required ten pounds of hay per day, as well as oats or other grains if he could get them; even more critical while crossing the desert, his horse required eight or ten gallons of water, dust baths, and sleep. Steve must have sat for hours watching his horse graze what little grass there might be. At night, he bedded his mount as carefully as he made his own bed. In storm and wind and thunder, he babied it. He had to: it was the only way a man could expect a horse to survive the desert ride.

Somewhere on this terrible journey, it must have occurred to him his wife Helen had made a similar trip, alone but for a three-year-old daughter on the saddle in front of her. Whether the difficulties he faced created an empathy for his wife's ordeal three years earlier is unknown, but probably an intimacy with the conditions his wife faced—and conquered—made him angrier than ever that she had exposed his daughter to these hardships.

Undoubtedly, Steve rode from line camp to ranch headquarters, isolated cabins to chuckwagons. It was the custom for cowboys to be fed by everyone they met. Some of the better outfits might offer a little work, and it's possible Steve used the opportunity to ride their stock and rest his. Pioneers were used to receiving strangers thus, for an in-coming rider brought news from afar. Steve must have memorized names and stories from one camp to report in the next. It was payment, the only kind he could afford. He would have recalled the weather, range conditions, state of the livestock, brands he'd encountered, not to mention whom he had seen. Like a troubadour of old, he was welcome in every camp.

Without doubt, he went through El Paso. He must have found it satisfying to hear details of Hardin's death,[12] and he probably heard of his wife's antics, too. A single hour spent in any of the saloons would have given him enough stories about his wife to poison a lifetime. Certainly, he was more determined than ever to find his daughter, and so he rode west into the New Mexican desert. By this time, Helen's brother and his family were at Cartwright, Arizona. Some of the Ellison in-laws—the Hurts, Brattons, McCarleys, and Glossbrenners—all from Fredonia and neighboring San Saba County, Texas, were there with them.

One day, a dusty Steve Jennings rode up to their farm, and as they gathered around his weary horse, they must have been surprised. A broke cowboy had followed his heart, ridden across a thousand miles of desert, and made it to their homes safely.

Unfortunately, the bitter ride across the desert was for naught. Helen Beulah Mrose had taken their daughter to California. In the end, the stalwart horse Steve Jennings had ridden across Texas, New Mexico, and Arizona brought only enough money for a train ticket home. As his in-laws and their friends crowded around sympathetically, they knew he had waited too long and his daughter was gone.

PART FIVE
Heartbreak

"She used to sit up there on the roof of an evening, ever [sic] time it was clear, just to watch the sun set over California."

—Anonymous #2, March 1998

22
THE CHARMED CIRCLE
1896–1903

"[M]ilk and butter to burn."[1]

The afternoon of April 16, 1866, a pair of damaged pine crates arrived at the San Francisco headquarters of Wells Fargo & Company. The boxes, one containing silverware, the other, a leaking box addressed to William H. Mills in Los Angeles, were refused by their consignee, due to their condition. Both crates were stained; they smelled gaseous and slightly acidic. Sent from somewhere in Europe to New York, the crates had been shipped by sea to Panama, thence by rattling train across the Isthmus, and roughly transferred down a slide into the hold of the steamship *Sacramento*, where they slid off onto the deck and were damaged. On arrival in San Francisco, the boxes were roughly unloaded onto a wharf and transferred by wagon over bumpy, cobbled streets to Wells Fargo.

Francis E. Webster, freight clerk for Wells Fargo, and William S. Haven,[2] a bookkeeper, decided to survey the extent of damage. They knew the *Sacramento* had brought a shipment of forty cases of nitroglycerine from Panama. These two crates were not part of that shipment, but the men were concerned. Was the damage to the crates external in origin, or was it a sign of internal damage? The men didn't know, but a claim would have to be filed. They summoned an assayer from an office at the back of the Wells Fargo compound. Workmen gathered around. A hammer and crowbar were produced. One man forced the point of a pry bar into the lid of a box and raised his hammer.

Meanwhile, a New York *Times* correspondent had business with Andrew Forbes at Wells Fargo. Samuel Knight, Jr., Superintendent of Wells Fargo & Company's Express, who was overseeing work on the packing crates, directed him to the Union Club next door. Minutes later, as the correspondent walked away, he encountered a friend, who remarked the weather felt "earth-quakey."[3] At that moment, an explosion erupted from the Wells Fargo building, and a plume of dust and debris rocketed four hundred feet into the air. Broken glass and debris rained down from the sky.

It is the nature of explosives to blow away from what confines them. In this case, the solid granite walls of the courtyard focused most of the blast of the nitroglycerin contained in one of the mislabelled boxes upward into the open air, but even so, damage was horrific. The explosion took out the back wall of the Union Club. The Wells Fargo building was shattered. Sidewalks in every direction were covered in broken glass.

"[B]lood was visible in many places where it had dropped from the wounds of people injured on the streets by flying debris [....] More terrible than all else, fragments of human remains were found scattered in many places."[4]

Sightseers crowded the streets; firefighters fought through the crowds. From near and far came the call as pieces of human flesh were discovered. Unique among the bodies, however, Samuel Knight's body was intact, though "his lower limbs looked as though driven into the body."[5] Everyone else was either vaporized or pulverized by the explosion.

Knight, who had opened Wells Fargo & Co. routes into the Idaho gold fields and was one of twenty-three incorporators of the Bank of California, left a pregnant widow, Elizabeth Stuart (née Haight) Knight,[6] and three children, Elizabeth, Fletcher Haight, and Samuel Dexter Knight III. Another son, Robert Stuart Knight, would be born six months after his father's death. The Knights were one of the most illustrious families of San Francisco society. Elizabeth Knight's father, Fletcher Matthews Haight, had been appointed the first federal judge for the Southern District of California by President Abraham Lincoln. Her father-in-law, Samuel Knight, Sr., was a judge. Her brother was California Governor Henry Huntley Haight.[7]

Despite the death of his father, Samuel Knight III, born in San Francisco on December 28, 1863, was raised in privilege. He was educated in the best schools, and he graduated from Yale in 1887 and Columbia Law School in 1889. After graduation, he became the Assistant U.S. Attorney for the Northern District of California from 1893–1895 and U.S. Attorney from 1896–1897. He was a member of the California Bar Association, and in 1899, he and Federal

Judge William Morrow of the Ninth Circuit Court of Appeals founded the San Francisco chapter of the Red Cross.

Samuel Knight's brother, Robert Stuart Knight, became a businessman, but his most notable accomplishment was marrying well, in this case to Henryetta C. Chabot, daughter of Remi and Emilie Chabot, wealthy society patrons of Oakland. Remi's father, Anthony Chabot, had made a fortune in hydraulic mining and other water projects.

Influenced by his brother's in-laws, the Chabots, Samuel Knight found a career niche. While other lawyers huddled in courtrooms, Knight sought out the fading gold fields of California. Here, he discovered his calling: environmentalism. Challenged by destructive silting on the Sacramento River, he published an article discussing the environmental destruction of hydraulic mining and the legal consequences of such damage.[8]

Later, as a partner in the firm—Page, McCutcheon and Knight, specializing in claims from silting and other environmental matters—Samuel Knight was hired by Charles D. Lane of Missouri to combat a corrupt federal judge and receiver in the goldfields of Nome, Alaska. The sensational case, "The Crime of 1900," gave Knight fame and fortune the rest of his days.[9] His greatest honor, however, came from a young down-and-out sourdough named Rex Beach, who left Alaska in poverty and embarked on a meteoric career as a writer. Beach's first novel, *The Spoilers*, used Knight's experiences in Nome as the basis for an exciting story. The book was made into five movies, one starring John Wayne, Randolph Scott, and Marlene Dietrich.[10]

Another prominent family of San Francisco was the Holbrook family. Charles Holbrook,[11] born in New Hampshire in 1830, came to San Francisco in 1850. Like most young men during the Gold Rush, he tried his hand at mining, but after a year, he began work at a hardware store in Sacramento. By 1859, he was a partner, and in 1863, he opened a branch store in Austin, Nevada. He achieved fame in an Austin mayoral race. The loser of a bet on the race was Reuel Gridley, who was forced by terms of the bet to carry a fifty-pound sack of flour from Clifton, Nevada, to Austin and present it to the new mayor. Holbrook, a successful store owner, decreed, however, he didn't need the flour, so Gridley conceived the notion of auctioning it, with proceeds to go to the Sanitary

Commission, an organization caring for wounded Union soldiers. Over and over the sack was auctioned. Gridley toured California and later the East Coast, eventually collecting over a quarter million dollars for the charity.

By 1864, Charles Holbrook had his own company, and he took on two partners, John Francis Merrill and James B. Stetson. As Holbrook, Merrill & Stetson, the company specialized in imported stoves, hardware, and plumbing supplies. In 1866, Holbrook married Susan Maria Hurd, the beautiful, frail daughter of a Sacramento merchant. Not long after that, they moved to San Francisco. The couple would have four children: Harry Morgan, Olive Mellen, Susan Maria, and Mary Hurd Holbrook.[12]

After the perfection of San Francisco's streetcars, wealthy families built mansions on Nob Hill. Charles Holbrook sited his mansion on Van Ness. "Every possible convenience was built into the house.... There was a master clock in the basement from which, by compressed air, the dials in twelve of the rooms showed the time of day...."[13] The house had high-ceilinged rooms, seven baths, and large basement vaults for jewelry and silver.

Holbrook wanted to live in the country for his health, and he built an estate in Atherton, a wealthy landowners' district some thirty miles south of San Francisco. Named "Elmwood," the home was landscaped with American elms, sequoia, and bunya-bunya trees, as well as copious plantings of wisteria.

Raised according to the theory children are best seen but not heard, Mary Holbrook and her brother and sisters were kept separate from family and social activities. Olive remembered, "I slept on the fourth floor with my nurse, had my play room in the adjoining room, and no meals with the family except on rare occasions. After [a trip to Europe] I moved downstairs and my status in the family life changed."[14]

Olive Holbrook was skilled in riding and driving a team. An athletic young woman, she scandalized proper society by riding bareheaded on the beaches south of Golden Gate. "No automobile, to my mind, has ever had the beauty or style of a fancy team, and I am glad I grew up in a horse age," she said proudly.[15]

Mary Holbrook grew up more studious than her sisters, but she was a noted socialite often mentioned in society pages. She was also an early practitioner of bicycling. "Women's bicycling received its real impetus when the smart set took it up. Once the seal of fashion was set upon the sport, the pace of its success was designated."[16] Before long, the Holbrooks hosted bicycling excursions from their home on Van Ness to Golden Gate Park.

It wasn't long before suitors showed up at the Holbrook door, among them a promising young attorney, Samuel Knight. Though the three sisters had an agreement among them to not have children in order not to pass on their allergies, Samuel Knight fell in love with Mary Holbrook and proposed. They were wed on October 8, 1895. Their early married life was filled with travel and adventure, but in 1898 they began development of an estate in Hillsborough.[17]

The Holbrooks, Knights, Palmers, and Chabots, all part of the glittering society of San Francisco and Oakland, subscribed to the belief they must live well, but they were conscious of those who didn't have such privileges. Like all of San Francisco society before the Earthquake of 1906, they supported worthy causes. Mary Knight was interested in orphanages. She was also a patron of the arts. Among the recipients of the Holbrooks, Palmers, Knights, and Chabots' generosity were Stanford University, the University of California-Berkeley, Yale University,[18] the Pacific School of Religion, Chabot College, the University of California, women's groups, and social organizations,[19] the town of Atherton, California, and the California State Redwoods Park.

The charmed circle of San Francisco society represented by these families was the glittering spear point of the Gold Rush and the agricultural wealth of California's central valleys. Such wealth, however, did not extend to all levels of society, and it is at this point we must put blame aside in our hearts for a while and think of this: as Helen Beulah Mrose arrived in San Francisco in 1896, she knew she was a bad mother, a poor example for her daughter to follow. At the same time, Laura Jennings was becoming precocious. She was asking questions.

The money from El Paso was probably gone soon after they rode into town. Helen had suitcases of clothes … and no prospects. Working ten hours a day, six days a week in a sweat shop, she could earn thirty dollars a month, but who would take care of Laura? Laura was an active little five-year-old; she had an ear for music. She had to start school soon.

There were places her mother could take her, not daycare as we know it, but squalid, noisome warehouses for the children of working mothers: the San Francisco Nursery for Homeless Children was an example. The children would be fed, but no one controlled them. They were a mob in confines. The better places put children to work to occupy their minds: The Girls Training Home or the Presbyterian Orphanage and Farm. Laura was too old for the Golden Gate Foundling Asylum or the Little Sister's Infant Shelter, so that left orphanages like the Children's Home Finding Society.

A decision had to be made, and Helen must have agonized over her choices. In the end, she opted to place Laura in a Catholic orphanage, of which there were a number in the area. Helen had converted to Catholicism before marrying Steve Jennings in 1889. She probably felt comfortable consulting a priest or orphanage official. She soon learned of the Sisters of Charity, who maintained several orphanages, or the Catholic Ladies Aid Society for Children, noteworthy for its successes: in 1904, the Society found homes for eighty children.[20]

Helen had to sign over her rights as the biological mother. The Catholics were adamant about this, for they didn't want to maintain and educate a child only to have the mother reclaim it years later. At the same time, since the Church controlled the orphanages, rather than the state, finding a child a home involved a process called "placing out," rather than adoption. "Placing out" was something like today's foster care. The Church had moral, religious, and ethical concerns, among which it wanted the children to be raised as Catholics, and it maintained control over the "adoptive" parents with a vague threat the child might be recalled by the Church and placed in different circumstances. The threat was rarely carried out.

Laura was too young to know what the adults were talking about. Her mother was "sick," she remembered in later years, and she probably got the idea the priests and nuns were helping her. It's easy to imagine Laura heard a choir practicing down one of the polished hallways or an organ playing in the distance. She may have gotten distracted. What a wonderful place this is, she might have thought as she was led away.

There's a good chance Laura became angry—an adult anger, not a child's. She blamed her mother for abandoning her, for she was too young to understand her mother's problems. For sure, Laura was hurt, and she carried that hurt the rest of her life. In speaking about it, years later, she recalled she pretended her mother was actress and singer Lillian Russell. Russell was beautiful, romantic, tragic, an acclaimed star of the stage—a perfect fantasy for a damaged five-year-old girl. Lillian Russell cigars were hawked all over San Francisco. Laura wore a cigar ring on her finger that had a picture of the actress on it.

Soon, the terror of what had happened struck her. What if no one came for her? There were teenagers in the orphanage. No one had claimed them ... or ever would. Babies seemed to be gone overnight, and she probably saw new parents cooing over toddlers and tots as they took them away. Who would want a five-year-old girl? Laura's fear came to a head when she injured a finger. It infected. No one must see, she decided, for then they would never take her away. She wrapped her swollen finger and hid it whenever one of the nuns was around. However, a nun did notice, and Laura was treated, but the terror remained, for she recalled the incident many years afterward. Anger, blame, and hurt ... all common among abandoned children, but the worst, of course, is the terror they will forever be unwanted. So it was with Laura Jennings.

The orphanage, however, appears to have been good for her. It seems she had a chance to develop her musical talent, but whether singing or playing an instrument is unknown. Whatever her talent was, she must have been shown off at charity fundraisers or before prospective society patrons. One of these was a newly married Mary Holbrook Knight. From among all the children in the Catholic orphanages, Mary Knight decided she wanted Laura. Laura's fear of being unwanted had proven false. Samuel and Mary Knight accepted terms of "placing out" of a child and took Laura Blanche Jennings as their own child. She would live with them in the lap of luxury. Her every whim would be indulged. She would have dresses, tutors, and servants. Like the Holbrook children before her, Laura would be raised a lady, out of sight for now, but with a great future in store. Despite the odds, Laura Jennings had joined the charmed circle of San Francisco society.

23
DESTINY HAS CLAWS
1904

Oh! I betcha she was surprised when she opened
that door!"[1]

In studying others' lives, it's all so clear: history does repeat itself. It isn't predictable; it may be an echo of experiences or a shadow across the face of time, but it is curious that a defining phenomenon is repeated over the years. For this reason, if we cannot realize it in our own lives, we can learn from the destiny of others.

Helen Beulah Mrose and her daughter Laura Jennings Knight had traveled separate paths. Helen's world was sordid and painful, but Laura's life had improved dramatically without her mother's mistakes. Helen had given up her child. Laura had embraced the charmed life. Helen was a prostitute, Laura a socialite, yet they were both to learn hard lessons. The stage was set for karma to interfere.

They lived not far apart, really. For a time, Laura and the Knights resided on a semi-permanent basis in the Palace Hotel in downtown San Francisco. Weekends and summers were spent in travel or at Elmwood, the Holbrooks' palatial mansion. With Samuel Knight's fortune assured after his triumphant return from Nome in 1900, the Knights leased lodgings in upscale neighborhoods. For a time they lived at 2106 Van Ness, and, for about a year, they lived at 2621 Pacific. They also purchased land in Hillsborough and joined the Burlingame Country Club as founding members, but it took several years for a home to be built and the grounds landscaped. They had only a few servants, but their needs were met the moment they arose. Money was never a problem. The Knights lived in luxury, and Laura benefited by association.

Blocks away was San Francisco's infamous Tenderloin, and it was here Helen Beulah settled. She may have been an embarrassment, for "she was in receipt of an income of $75 a month from her relatives, who gave her that amount to stay away from them."[2] If so, there may have been embarrassing confrontations in the vicinity of the hotel. Who knows how each felt? Laura may have been mortified at her mother's decline; Helen may have been thrilled to spy her daughter, but it's possible Helen demanded recognition, and Laura yearned for her mother's touch. Either way, the Knights can't have been pleased, and $75 a month was a pittance to pay for Helen to stay away. Even so, there is evidence mother and daughter exchanged letters.[3]

Though Helen Beulah's path was ever downward, she still had sparks of decency which were proven the night of April 19, 1903. Jack Macon, improbably described as a "strolling piano player," tried to peddle a newborn infant in the Tenderloin.

"Help came from one whose help might least be expected. [...] Hazel Williams is better known in the Tenderloin [...], but the smothered cry of an infant levels all social differences, and Hazel Williams became at once the protector and guardian of the abandoned babe. [...] No mother with natural love for her own child could have cared more tenderly for the helpless bit of humanity as she bore it in the dull, uncertain light of the morning to the hospital."[4]

She recalled, "I was standing at the corner of Mason and Eddy streets, talking to a cabman, [...] when Macon came up with a covered basket. He placed it in the cab and then took the driver across the street to get drinks. Macon was already intoxicated but wanted more liquor. [...] While they were gone I heard a baby's cry, and opening the basket which had been placed in the cab found an infant wrapped in cotton. When Macon and the cabman returned, I asked him what he had in the basket.

'A baby. [...Y]ou can have it for a dollar,' he replied, but when I offered him the money, he said he wanted $5 for it.

[...] The baby was crying, so I took it to the home of a friend on Fulton street. There I was advised to take it to the Emergency Hospital, and was on my way there when I met two policemen. The baby was crying, and they heard it. They asked me where I was taking it, and when I told them, said they would go with me. The baby was cared for at the hospital and I was taken to jail."[5]

A newspaper explained, "At the hospital the police made a simple blunder. They mistook Hazel Williams' sympathy for sham and set about to prove she was the mother of the child and had planned to abandon it."[6]

On April 22, 1903, Hazel Williams testified against John Macon. Unfortunately, the San Francisco earthquake and fire in 1906 destroyed court records, so there is no way of knowing what became of the baby, but for Helen Beulah Mrose, a.k.a. Hazel Williams, it was a high point. She dressed to the nines and exulted in the attention of the newspapers. It was, however, an ironic turn of events for one whose life was touched so intimately by child custody problems of her own.

Meanwhile, Laura continued to live as a "placed out" child with the Knights. Child custody and adoption cases filled the newspapers, for laws to regulate an orderly system of child protection were only beginning to be enacted. The largest provider of social services remained the Catholic Church. The Catholics maintained hundreds of children in the San Francisco area. Adoptions, as we know them, weren't the rule. Instead, the church "placed out" children— and foster parents had as many rights as such parents do today.

"Placing out" seems to have worked on the whole, but there were problems in the system. A book, *The Great Arizona Orphan Abduction*, illustrates what could happen. Well-meaning nuns from the New York Foundling Hospital took forty orphans[7], most red-faced Irish kids, to Clifton-Morenci, Arizona, to be placed with Catholic families. Unfortunately, the receiving families were Mexican, and the situation resulted in a racial flare-up that engulfed the communities. Nineteen children were seized by Anglos and given to Anglo parents in the area.

Technically, mothers couldn't permanently give up rights to their children, so the biological tie remained a serious problem. "Two principles of law concerned child custody in California at the turn of the century, best interest of the child and *habeas corpus*. [...] The 'best interests of the child' doctrine had been developing in the United States since the 1830s, as a rule of thumb for adjudicating child custody disputes which broke with patriarchal assumptions that children belonged to their father. [...] '*Habeas corpus*' refers to a variety of writs used to bring a person before a court, and their main function is to release someone from unlawful imprisonment." In the Arizona case, an opinion from the U.S. Supreme Court was, "*Habeas corpus* rights against unlawful imprisonment[8] did not apply to children. Children have no right to freedom, only to care and custody."[9]

At the turn of the century, news stories illustrate a variety of problems with child custody. In addition to child stealing[10] and divorce and custody battles[11] exactly like those today, there were unusual battles, too.[12]

The first of these involved *habeas corpus*. Despite the Supreme Court's ruling in the Arizona case, *habeas corpus* was still a common tactic to regain custody of a child. Indeed, in 1904, one man tried to gain custody of his daughter from his sister-in-law with a *habeas corpus* proceeding before the Supreme Court.[13] In a divorce in 1903, a father used *habeas corpus* to regain possession of his daughter from a woman with whom the natural mother had entrusted the child.[14] A grandmother invoked *habeas corpus* to gain custody of her granddaughter from the girl's stepmother.[15] Another example involved a couple who divorced, resumed marital relations, then the mother stole the child and demanded half her husband's business; the father filed *habeas corpus* to have the child produced in court.[16] In another case, parents spirited away an adopted daughter and demanded money to return her to her mother. In this case, *habeas corpus* worked, and the child was brought to court, custody being awarded to the mother.[17]

Perhaps the most difficult custody battles, similar to today's conflicts, involved natural parents who resorted to parental kidnapping. One of these, involved two kidnappings, the mother restealing the child from its father.[18] Another example was a father kidnapping his daughter, then hiring men to steal his other children from their maternal grandmother.[19] In another bizarre case, parents kidnapped their daughter from her grandparents; this started a violent fight in which four men, three women, and a policeman became involved.[20]

Most cases of parental kidnapping happened after courts had granted custody to one of the parents.[21] One case resulted in the kidnapper gaining custody over her daughter, the father eventually accepting the situation[22], and in an action similar to such cases today, a woman was jailed for contempt of court for not revealing the whereabouts of her daughter.[23]

An outstanding example of parental kidnapping was the case of Mrs.

Marion Thornton Egbert, a stunningly beautiful woman from Chicago, whose husband violently stole their two-year-old daughter from her in September 1900. Following him doggedly, Mrs. Egbert dressed in disguise and tracked her ex-husband from train station to hotel across Illinois, to England and France, then to Egypt, and finally to India, where he had found work as a physician for English officers. Her search took three years, but she regained custody of her daughter.[24]

More clear-cut custody cases involved guardians, foster parents, or adoptive parents caught up in litigation with natural parents. Most such cases resulted in a natural parent winning custody over his/her child[25], but in one unusual case, a natural mother lost to a guardian, the guardian producing evidence the mother was not a fit parent.[26]

It's apparent from these cases that adoption and "placing out" were judged on the merits of: 1.) best interest of the child and 2.)the biological claims of a natural parent. *Habeas corpus* and other tactics to gain custody rarely worked. Since "placing out" was undoubtedly done in the best interests of the child, only the biological tie of a natural parent could break it.

In Laura Jennings's case, being placed with the Knights was in the "best interests of the child." It was undoubtedly the finest thing that had happened in her life. Being "placed out" by a Catholic orphanage created a perfect little world for her: a wonderful home, parents who loved her, and things that money could provide, but for the Knights, it could have been a trap. How many times did they wonder at the traumas their foster daughter had undergone? What bitterness and hostility might she harbor in her heart? How could they keep her from following the footsteps of her no-good mother?

They probably tried to assuage these psychic scars with material things, and Laura—as is often the case in such situations—probably demanded their indulgence as her right. Certainly, the Knights instilled religion and discipline, but they may have also indulged her whims. When Laura was a small child, they bought her one of the first tricycles in California and took her to Golden Gate Park to ride it, much to the amusement and enjoyment of couples strolling there.[27] When she showed a desire for dresses, Mary Knight filled her closets with clothes. When she showed an interest in music, they bought her a piano; when she desired treats or candies, they lavished the best on her.

It's easy to imagine she became demanding. She probably threw tantrums. She may have indulged in all the ways and means of a spoiled girl, and the Knights were trapped in the knowledge they had a troubled child. Laura could be a perfect little lady in public, but she had a dark side, like teenagers do. She was, in short, a "handful," and it was toward the raising of this child the Knights devoted their energies.

Yes, it was a perfect world for a thirteen-year-old girl, but like all such worlds, it invited change. The indulgence of Laura Knight was about to end, and it is an example of a lesson we all learn: there is justice in this world, but it is always beyond our understanding.

Laura's world ended on an otherwise bright and sunny day in April 1904. It's likely she was practicing on the piano or attending to her concerns. Mary Knight was elsewhere in their apartment at 2621 Pacific. When she looked up, it's been said, she spotted a man looking up at the building from the street. He was a big, barrel-chested man, and on his face was a look of stern intensity. Dressed well but without style or grace, the man held his hat in his hands, his strong jaw set in a determined manner. She looked away. There were many men like him in this world, men whose look bespoke volumes about the trials they had faced in the settling of the frontier. He was dressed like a gold miner, laborer, butcher, stevedore, lumberjack, cowboy, fisherman, or railroader, certainly not the sort she associated with. The man appeared ready to move down the street, but about the time she began to feel relief, he approached the door.

The doorbell rang and Laura moved to answer it. Mary Knight jumped up to stop her, but she was too late. Laura had opened the door and was looking up in awe.

"Laura?" he is said to have asked, "Are you Laura Blanche?"

"Yes, I am," she answered.

"Then I'm your father. I've come to take you back to Texas."[28] A natural parent, the unbeatable biological tie, had struck, and with that, the floor fell out of Laura's little world. Things would never be the same again, not for her, not for the Knights, not for her mother, and certainly not for this big, dark man with startlingly pale blue eyes who called himself her father.[29]

24
HOME AGAIN
APRIL 1904–1907

"They had a hard time keeping that girl from the boys. They was [sic] afraid she'd end up like her mother."[1]

The evening Steve Jennings brought Laura back to Texas, he was met at the train station by his brothers Jim and Little Mike. The men had brought a buggy and two saddlehorses, and on the ride back to Fredonia next morning, Jim and Mike rode as armed outriders. Before they were in sight of Fredonia, other menfolk were saddling up or walking down to the road, and by the time the buggy reached the village, there may have been thirty people assembled. No one said a thing. It was a momentous occasion, not a happy one, because they had all lost a lot in the last ten years. Friendships had been realigned, some property had changed hands, people had moved away, relatives had been lost. For a tight-knit community, the search for Laura Jennings had been bitter, and there was no cheering its end. Who knew what the future held?

Laura probably rode through the gathering in bewilderment, but her father and uncles are said to have looked neither left nor right.[2] It was a private moment, a family affair, and they didn't so much as nod at any of the hatless throng. Instead, they rode in silence, and the clop and jingle of harness and hoof behind them grew to a roar as the men of Fredonia followed a quarter mile behind. The parade of horses and buggies wound its way along the road to a splashing across the ford at Lost Creek, where this had all begun, and the entourage held back at the gate to the Jennings homestead while the buggy drove on. Steve, it has been reported, grew sterner the closer they came to the house, the grandest in the vicinity.

There was a man sitting on the porch, watching them come. He was in shade, and it's been said he had difficulty getting out of his chair. Then, despite being nearly sixty-four years old, he ran like a teenager across the yard and down the path to meet them.

That was Laura's grandfather. Then a large, solid woman rounded the house. The news had been kept from her, perhaps due to the uncertainty that had beset the adventure from the beginning, and she was stunned to see them coming up the drive now, perhaps even more so at the sight of horsemen and buggies beyond the fence. Bridget Jennings sat down on the well-worn steps to await their arrival. Overcome with emotion, she bent forward at the waist, buried her face in her apron, and wept. For this stolid pioneer woman, it was the only emotional response she would give.

Laura Jennings had been gone ten years. As she stood taking in the tidy home, the fences marking Jennings land, the flowers and trees, it was hard to say if she remembered anything from her childhood in Fredonia. In later years, she showed confusion in her story,[3] and whether she had it straight as a teenager is doubtful. She was to discover her past was a forbidden subject here, and she learned not to ask questions about her mother.

From other families, we can glean what life was like on the Jennings homestead. The family itself has never spoken of it. Of course, we can guess Laura's first hours back in Fredonia were arranging the details. She was to share a bedroom with her aunt and was assigned her first chores, possibly the first she'd ever had to do. The farm in Fredonia was a cooperative affair. Though sons Mike, Jim, and Steve had property of their own, cattle to attend to, and places to be, they never outgrew their chores at the family homestead. There were animals to be fed, harness and fence to mend, gardens to hoe, and fields to tend. Bridget and Mary Ann took care of the home, and it was here Laura found her assignments.

There were always dishes to wash, meals to cook, clothes to mend, and a house to clean. There were few labor-saving devices on hand—except for Michael Jennings' hand-dug well, which he had enclosed as part of the house to give the family indoor water. Food had not only to be cooked and served in those days, it had to be prepared. Besides their own beef, pork, and lamb, wild game, fowl, and fish had to be dressed, butchered, and stored.

The family rose before dawn, the women to make biscuits from scratch, eggs, bacon, and coffee. There was milking to be done, chickens fed, and animals watered. Each had time to wash and dress, then they wandered off to milk, herd, hitch, and cook. It was a family routine, and much of it was done wordlessly.

For an undisciplined girl brought to live this rural life, it must have been baffling. There was no sense of accomplishment. A batch of biscuits would be wolfed down, then the men went off to their chores. Dishes were washed and put away, only to be brought out to serve the next meal. Clean floors were ruined by muddy boots. Milk was cooled, churned to butter, or fed to calves and pigs. In her spare time, Laura was taught to sew, knit, quilt, and crochet.

There was no joy in this drudgery, just a mind-numbing regularity, and she couldn't take it. She put her foot down. It must have been a surprise, and there is no way to know how they dealt with it. Perhaps they reasoned with her, but it's just as possible they quoted Scripture. It may have worked once or twice, but this was a headstrong teenager they were dealing with. The honeymoon of her homecoming probably did not last a week.

They had to crack down. In Texas, the best way to tame a mustang was to break it to saddle and bit, and Mary Ann Jennings was the rider to do it. Laura became her responsibility.

It was about this time the Jennings clan discovered Laura believed her hejira in Fredonia was temporary. She said something in an unguarded moment that set them thinking. She had much to learn about the family ... and about Texas. Perhaps it started when a stranger came to the gate. He was met by every gun the family had. "The Jennings were gunning fools with that Laura. Ever [sic] one of them would pull a gun if there was a stranger in town. They kept that up for several years. Miss Mary was the worst."[4]

As part of the regimen they put her through, they systematically destroyed every memory of her mother and California. She wasn't allowed to speak of the Knights, and she wasn't allowed to write letters. "Somehow, Papa Steve intercepted every letter they ever wrote," Laura told her niece. Able to assist in this, undoubtedly, was her grandfather, who, though illiterate, wrangled himself a job as Fredonia's assistant postmaster.[5]

Controlling her access to correspondence, however, doesn't seem to have been their only strategy. In later years, Laura showed an intense loyalty to the family, and most especially to Steve. It is a mystery how this was accomplished, but it was so successful that even after she had become independent, she did not initiate contact with the Knights.[6] In later years, though she still called them

"Mama" and "Papa," she affectionately called her father "Big Daddy," and he is called that by her descendants today, though he's been dead for sixty years.[7]

A chance encounter, however, hints the Knights did not let the situation be. Mike Jennings, who sometimes worked at the stockyards in Fort Worth—a job, coincidentally, where he may have known John Wesley Hardin's younger brother, "Gip"—was riding on a train one day about 1907. The man sitting across from him engaged him in thoughtless conversation.

"He claimed he was a professional kidnapper on his way to a small town in Texas to retrieve a young girl for a wealthy California family. He asked Mike if he knew where Fredonia was...."[8]

Mike Jennings kept his head; he asked details and offered to "guide" the kidnapper. Taken into confidence, he confirmed the plot was directed at Laura, the Jennings family was the target, and the scheme was financed by the Knights. Three versions of what happened next have been uncovered, but the likely story is he excused himself and "telegraphed ahead to the next town. When the train arrived, the kidnapper was arrested by the sheriff."[9]

As things developed at Fredonia, Laura was not the only one to bend. The family compromised with her. In September 1905 Steve enrolled her (under the name Blanche, her middle name) in a private Catholic boarding school, the exclusive St. Mary's Academy For Girls in Austin, Texas. There was probably no better place to instill discipline in a young girl than such a place. Though her marks hint at her intelligence that first year ("Lessons 99%,") there is a hint she had adjustment problems: "Amiability 70%." It was the lowest score in the entire school. A mark for "order" was only 71%. The summer of 1906, she was back in Fredonia; then she returned to St. Mary's in the fall. That year, enrolled under her first name, Laura, she did better: "Order 88%, Lessons 98%." No score was given for amiability.[10] Though she registered for the 1907–1908 term, she did not graduate, reason unknown. Next would be a music school, at which she is said to have excelled.

A second compromise was that Laura was encouraged to continue her talent in music. Steve bought her a piano and had it shipped to to Fredonia, but when it was uncrated, it was so badly out of tune, Laura couldn't play it. The family imported a piano tuner from Austin, and he stayed until she was satisfied.

The piano and schooling must have worked. Laura was tamed—or at least resigned–to her new role. She was also, by that time, fond of the Jenningses, and she must have realized they were trying to do the best they could. On November 25, 1907, she sent Mary Ann Jennings a postcard. "Dear Auntie," she wrote. "This is the last time I am going to write you. You haven't written to me once. I re'd a letter from Lin last week. Hoping you will let me hear from you soon, I am your niece. LBJ" On the front of the card she added, "I hope you will all have a happy Thanksgiving. Please write to me! With love. LBJ."[11] She addressed the postcard to Miss M.A. Jennings, "Antler's Hall," Fredonia, Texas, probably a joking reference to the rural nature of the home.

Another compromise was made by the family shortly thereafter. Steve bought a small house in the town of Fredonia and moved himself and Laura there. This fortuitous move gave Laura a chance to socialize with others. She made a few friends and participated in some of the life of the village. Even so, her headstrong nature led her into a conflict of parental control. There are hints unwelcome or unworthy suitors vied for her time, and Steve learned he couldn't fully trust her alone with boys her age. If anything happened or not is unknown, but it seems unlikely. Probably the Jenningses were overprotective rather than justified in their scrutiny of Laura's affairs. The careful chaperoning continued. She was not allowed out without a companion. This must have been irritating, but she seems to have accepted it.

This tight control—plus the unknown effect of her traumatic childhood—made Laura uncommonly close-mouthed. She was taught to ask no questions. Friends have recalled she could be pleasant, formal, and a good listener. She forged life-long friendships. She is said to have taken great pleasure in music, and laughed quietly but with mirth. She could be sarcastic, gossipy, and had a temper, but she also seems to have been good-natured and caring. The Jennings family came to trust her, and she was granted freedoms and responsibilities greater than her age.

Despite her gentle Williams grandparents, despite her mother's influence and the Knights' tender nurturing, she was a Jennings in the end.

Steve Jennings on a horse in Fredonia, Texas, about 1930. Courtesy of Wilda Fay Jennings.

Samuel and Mary Knight, about 1900.

John Selman, Jr. said, "She wasn't skinny like most women of today. She had a pair of hips. But of course, hips were stylish in those days." Photograph taken in San Francisco about 1896–1897. From the original in the author's collection.

"Hazel" Williams testifying in a child abandonment case in San Francisco, April 1903.
Though she was working the streets as a prostitute, Helen was in her prime here.
From The San Francisco Examiner, April 23, 1903.

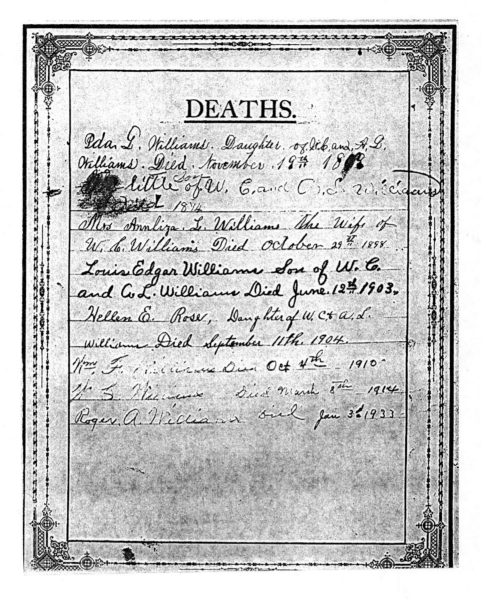

DEATHS.

Eda L. Williams. Daughter of W.C and A.L. Williams. Died. November 19th 18~~98~~

~~little~~ Son of W. C. and A. L. Williams ~~Died~~ 1894

Mrs Annliza L. Williams the Wife of W. C. Williams Died October 29th 1898

Louis Edgar Williams Son of W. C. and A. L. Williams Died June. 12th 1903.

Hellen E. Rose, Daughter of W. C & A. L. Williams Died September 11th. 1904.

Wm. F. Williams Died Oct 4th 1910

W. S. Williams Died March 8th 1914

Roger. A. Williams died Jan 3d 1933

The Bill Williams family bible recording the death, "Hellen [sic] E. Rose, daughter of W.C. and A.L Williams, died September 11, 1904." This is the only time the name "Rose" (for Mrose) was used when referring to Helen. Courtesy of Glenn Wilkins.

Laura Jennings, about 1925 with her grandfather Michael, father Steve, and son in Fredonia.
Courtesy of Joyce Capps.

Laura Jennings and her children in Fowler, California about 1925.
Courtesy of Glenn Wilkins.

25
THE WOMAN IN FREDONIA
ABOUT 1905 OR 1906

"At mention of his name, she spun on her heel and
walked out. She never stopped there again."[1]

We don't know when it happened exactly, nor even where. We don't know what was said, or who spoke first, but an extraordinary meeting occurred in Mason County, Texas, in 1905 or 1906. Lacking an account of the meeting, we can imagine it happened in summer, and knowing Texas, the ground was so hot even snakes had to stand up and walk. We don't know the locale, but it may have been a general store. Without details written or remembered, we must use our imaginations to fill in the gaps.

Suppose this: Laura may have come to pick up a few items. Rarely out of Mary Ann's watchful sight for more than a moment, she walked into a store. There were other women about, and, as always, a few men loitering over conversations. Laura knew most of the people, but there were visitors too.

One of these was a woman who spent a lot of time in Fredonia, Dr. Baze's wife. A talkative woman with an erect carriage and penetrating eyes, she was one of the leaders of Mason County society. Though there were rumors of strife in her marriage, her husband was an up-and-coming practitioner. Dr. and Mrs. Baze had lived in Fredonia for several years, though they now called the county seat of Mason home. Dr. Baze's brother and sister-in-law lived in Fredonia still, and the two couples often traveled the fifteen miles to spend time together.[2] Dr. Baze's wife was well-known and respected in Fredonia, and though there were whispers about her, she was oblivious to all gossip. There was something regal and matronly about her.[3]

Laura had seen Dr. Baze's wife before. This well-bred woman was present at Fourth of July picnics, weddings, and funerals. She was known to be charitable and kind-hearted. She was a shrewd dealer in land and cattle, but her dealings were honest and above board. Although she seemed to have few friends, no one had a harsh word for her. Everyone respected her, which says a lot for a young woman who was only about twenty-eight years old.

The woman may have nodded deferentially in her direction, but Laura surely realized she herself was a mere teenager in a country town in central Texas, certainly not someone of the status of the older, worldly-wise wife of Dr. Baze. Mary Ann Jennings was probably distracted, the men were talking cattle prices, the ladies were gathered around the millinery, and in that scarce moment of privacy, the great woman may have waved her near. It was to be one of the most remarkable encounters of the Old West.

There's no witness alive today who can recall what was said between the teenager and this doyenne of Mason County society, but it went a long way toward shaping the rest of Laura Jennings' life. In just a few words, perhaps hastily whispered before Mary Ann could intervene, Dr. Baze's wife created a bond with Laura that would last forever. They shared something no one could ever understand, no matter how hard they tried.

"What?" Laura must have wondered.

"John Wesley Hardin," the woman may have whispered, and with that, she established the unique bond that would unite these women of Fredonia for the rest of their lives.

Dr. Baze's wife and Laura Jennings were among the last women who had known Hardin personally. Laura had met him as a child when her mother had carried her across a bridge from Juarez, Mexico, to El Paso to hire a lawyer. Dr. Baze's wife had known him as a teenage bride, for her maiden name was Callie Lewis.[4]

We don't know if the two women ever grew close, though they shared this intimacy between them. We don't know if they had an opportunity to sit down, share memories, and offer each other hope and support. We do know Laura Jennings learned from the example of Carolyn Baze. She learned in Fredonia, as in London, Texas, there would never be redemption from the past. She would only have a chance to be herself by leaving, by getting out from under the protective thumb of Mary Ann, away from the fretful eye of her father, away from the whispers of neighbors who knew about her.

Dr. Baze's wife gave Laura the inspiration to live life on her own terms.

Carolyn Baze had outlasted the scandal of her youthful marriage to John Wesley Hardin. She had achieved respectability by marrying into it, and it was the lesson she offered Laura Jennings. Live a modest, restrained life in some little town; don't talk about your past, and don't tolerate those who wish to; wait years in silence, and people will stop talking. Silence is the best way to handle scandal. This was the pattern to follow, and Laura would take advantage of it in exactly the same manner as the woman who became her mentor, Caroline Baze.[5]

By age 14, Laura, who always wore a hat and gloves whenever she went out,[6] was disliked by a lot of Fredonia for putting on airs. Not only was she being educated at an exclusive Catholic school in Austin, but when she was home on holidays, she was treated like a princess. One Sunday, she accompanied a friend to a Baptist church to see what it was like. The sermon ended up being about her piano playing, and especially that she played secular tunes on the Sabbath. When she returned home, Laura told her father what had happened. Angered, Steve said, "I'll take care of that sorry old S.O.B.!"[7] and he marched off to teach the minister a lesson.[8] "My husband said he beat him with a piece of wood. Growing up, I heard it wasn't that bad [… and] he used a [buggy] whip. I heard [the minister] never spoke about Laura again."[9] The incident must've been mortifying for Laura.

The Jennings clan began to relax their control over her. Laura was given a pistol for protection, but she admitted years later she almost shot her foot off in an accident.[10] She also learned to drive a car and was soon better at it than her father. Even so, happiness did not come to her door. Nearly all who remember her have commented on her sadness during these years, and the most common story told of her is each evening, she would climb a ladder onto the roof of the house to watch the sun set, thinking of California and Papa and Mama Knight. It was a curious and mournful continuation of her grandfather's long-ago custom of watching the sunset after a day in the fields. It was at such times he sang *a capella* in Gaelic, but whether Laura remembered her grandfather holding her as a baby and singing is unknown. One resident is adamant each time Laura went up on the roof, her father would pour himself a glass of whiskey[11] and sit on the porch, drinking.[12] Another resident says she was told Steve always waited by the foot of the ladder, to be sure his daughter got down safely. "One day he was burning trash, and he burned that ladder up. I don't recall hearing if Laura [...] mounted the roof again."[13]

At this point, we must remind ourselves it was a harsher world then, and Steve and Laura Jennings's difficult relationship and the compromises they made are beyond our understanding. Of one thing we can be sure, however, is Steve felt, and Laura respected the fact she was indulged almost beyond patience. With the passing of her painful childhood, Laura blossomed into a young woman. She began to have suitors. The Jennings clan relaxed, and she was given that most precious of gifts: privacy.

And so it was, that, in an unguarded moment one day, Laura met her uncle Charley Bratton[14] at a funeral in Fredonia. Charley had been in Cartwright, Arizona, when her mother had taken her there in 1895. He had played with Laura as a little girl, and he remembered her mother well. He and Laura found a seat in the shade and sat down to talk about old times.

"You've grown up to be a beautiful young lady," Charley complimented her. "You look just like your mother now."

"Thank you," Laura remarked. "That's the first time anyone has said anything nice about my mother."[15]

Charley must have looked beyond, farther than the farms, granite boulders, and live oak trees of Mason County, beyond the cattle and cowboys of Texas and New Mexico, to the irrigated fields of Arizona, the vineyards of California, the goldfields of Alaska, and the people of the past. They were becoming memories by then. The Old West was gone, the outlaws were dead, the tragedy had ended, and only the sorrows remained. He looked at her, a pretty woman on the verge of establishing her own life, despite her setbacks and traumas, and he said, "Oh, I could tell you a lot of nice things about your mother."[16]

EPILOGUE
A BITTER BREW

"I've blowed my coffee, and now I'm going to
drink it."[1]

S everal towns mentioned in this narrative are no more. Wolfton, Seven
Rivers,[2] and Phenix[3] died not long after Martin Mrose. In a break with the
past both political and emotional, Eddy, county seat of Eddy County, New
Mexico, changed its name in 1899; today it is known as Carlsbad.[4] Cartwright,
Arizona, was absorbed so completely by Glendale a few people claim it never
existed.[5] Serbin, Texas, is a few houses and a church. In Mason County, Texas,
Wagram, Adullam, and Blue Stretch are gone forever. Fredonia is a quarter the
size it was a hundred years ago, and it takes each of its losses personally. Where
it was once full of progress and optimism, today it has lost its last store. To even
get a sense of the people once living in the area, one must visit the cemeteries
and read the familiar names: Jennings, Williams, and Ellison, still there, all at
peace now.

As for other people mentioned in these pages:

Annie Williams, Helen and Hardin's feisty landlady in El Paso continued
in the hotel business for some years after Hardin's death. She ran the Herndon
House through 1899, but the 1900 El Paso City Directory lists her at the Santa Fe
House a few blocks away. By then, her sister, Mrs. Maggie Boyd, and Maggie's
one-year-old son, Leroy, were living with her and her children. In 1902 Annie
was at the Columbia Hotel, and she and her children remained there until at least
1907. There is no further mention of her after that time, and it is unknown what
became of her.

Callie Lewis, the willful, teenaged second wife of John Wesley Hardin,
never succeeded at affairs of the heart. Sometime in 1910 she and her second
husband, Dr. Perry Allan Baze, separated. In 1911, he deeded their house to her,
and they had little to do with each other after that. On March 2, 1915, Callie
divorced her husband, citing abandonment and adultery. She never remarried.

Her contacts with the Jennings family continued; she did business with them, and she often inquired after Laura.[6]

It would be satisfying to report Steve Jennings went on to material success and happiness after his long quest for his daughter, but such is not the case. It appears he ruined himself financially seeing she received an education, first at St. Mary's Academy, then at a music conservatory in Chicago. After that, he was a middling rancher and cattleman in the Hill Country of Texas. A lifelong Catholic, he never considered divorcing Helen, but he did court his friend Ab Hayes' sister, Frances Carolyn "Dollie" Hayes. For eleven years he dated her, reportedly promising to give up his religion for her. Even so, family legend has it that at her own wedding Laura turned to her friend, Lucie Green, to whisper there never was so lonely a man as her father, and she urged Lucie to marry him.[7] It is unknown how this was accomplished, but quite suddenly Steve broke off with Dollie Hayes and, at the age of 47, married Lucie Green, a thirty-year-old Protestant considered the beauty of Mason County. Though the breakup was characterized as friendly, years later, Dollie burned a stack of letters she had saved since her courtship with Steve Jennings.[8]

It would also be nice to say Steve learned from his ordeal, that he had matured with age and experience. Unfortunately, that is not the case. Given a rare second chance, he carried on much as before. He was hard, stingy, profane, distant, harsh, and mean-spirited with his new wife and children.[9] At the same time, his relationship with his parents and siblings can be characterized as bizarre. Even so, Steve and Lucie had two sons, the younger half-brothers of Laura, both of whom went on to success. Steve Jennings died August 29, 1956 and is buried in Mason County. Lucie is buried beside him.

Bill Williams went on with his life.[10] In 1900 he married a widow twenty-four years younger than himself. By 1906, faced with deteriorating health and finances, he had to seek a Confederate pension. In 1909, his second marriage failed, and he moved to the home of his son Lon in Fowler, California, where he lived the rest of his life. It is said he took great pleasure in his remaining children and grandchildren, but, so far as is known, he rarely mentioned his eldest daughter again. In 1913 he became ill and was hospitalized in Fresno, and he died there on March 8, 1914.[11] During a period of windy and unusually cold weather, his body was returned to Georgetown, Texas, and he lies at Berry Creek near his first wife and other family and in-laws.[12]

Samuel and Mary Knight lived productive lives of privilege, charity, and patronage in San Francisco. During the 1906 earthquake and fire, Samuel worked tirelessly with the San Francisco Chapter of the Red Cross, which he had helped found in 1899, to shelter, feed, and resettle thousands left homeless after the disaster. In 1937 he was honored for 39 years work with the Red Cross. In addition, he was a founder and on the Board of Trustees for the town of Hillsborough, California, service interrupted by three years with the Army, including time in Europe after World War One. Mary Knight was involved in charitable work, but she is best remembered for her support of the arts.

One of their nephews recalled, "Mary Knight genuinely loved children. Samuel did too. He's the only adult I ever met who would sit down and have long conversations with a child. [...] Mary Knight hosted Easter Egg hunts and other events; there were often fifty children or more [there]. She enjoyed that. [...] She loved having children around. They were both wonderful people."[13]

When Samuel Knight died on January 28, 1943, the courts in San Francisco adjourned for three days in his memory. Mary Knight died at the Biltmore Hotel in Santa Barbara on March 12, 1953. The Knights are buried at Colma, California.

Having touched the hallowed feet of history when she was a little girl, Laura Jennings lived the rest of her life quietly. She did not often speak of her childhood.[14] It's possible she dreaded what neighbors might say, for she lived in small towns where the only excitement was gossip, but probably she did not speak of these events because the traumas were so great. As an excuse, though, she cautioned not to ask questions out of respect for her father and what he might think.[15]

Laura spent the rest of her life in Texas, and it was there she died December 30, 1986, at the age of 95. Typical of how she is remembered by those who knew her is she was "a person you know [that] has suffered an awful lot in life. There was allus [sic] something untouchable about her."[16]

Helen Elizabeth (née Williams) Jennings, known to history as Helen

Beulah Mrose, wound up a prostitute, a vagrant, and a petty thief in California. The fact is we can never really understand what caused Helen to lead her life that way. We can only wonder at the guilt and regrets she must have endured. She ran away from her marriage and took up with another man. Even though treated well by him, she was guilty of complicity in the conspiracy to murder him for his money. She was instrumental in the death of her lover, John Wesley Hardin, too, and her erratic and self-destructive behavior ruined her relationship with her family and hastened her own mother's death. Finally, she gave up her daughter, Laura.

It's not what others do to us that is so wounding; it's what we do to ourselves that hurts so much. Her life filled with regrets, Helen Beulah must have found the traumas too great. To constantly swim upstream is to be eternally battered by the current, and so it was with her. Bad choices, wrong choices, no choices at all led her into a downward spiral from which she never recovered. Living in Sacramento under the alias Helena Grace Rose,[17] she collapsed in an alley on September 11, 1904.[18] It was about four months after learning her daughter was back in the custody of the Jennings family in faraway Texas, and it was slightly less than ten years since her departure from her marriage to Steve Jennings. She was just 31 years old and had survived Martin Mrose and John Wesley Hardin by only nine years.

Laura traveled to California in the early 1970s, perhaps looking for a trace of the Knights and her mother's final resting place.[19] It is likely she went to Sacramento, but it is not known if she found much information. Nevertheless, it has been learned during research for this narrative that Helena Grace Rose was buried in New Helvetia Cemetery, established on land donated by the great California pioneer, John Sutter. In 1955, the cemetery was condemned and thousands of remains were dug up, moved to East Lawn Cemetery, and reburied in a mass grave.[20] Unfortunately, there is no specific record what happened to Helen's body, and so her final resting place is, today, officially unknown.

Seventy years after John Wesley Hardin's death, his desolate grave in El Paso's historic Concordia Cemetery was finally marked with a simple stone.[21] It has since become a tourist attraction, but very few of the curious glance two spaces north to the grave of Martin Mrose.[22] "Uncle" John Selman, Sr., the man who murdered Hardin, is buried not far away.[23]

Today, a hundred years after the events of this story, descendants of Helen Beulah Mrose and Laura Jennings still live in Texas ... but the pain and memories are even yet too great to bear, and most prefer not to speak about what happened so long ago.

APPENDIX ONE

> "I have seen the lone horseman disappear over a
> hill…."
>
> —Cecil Bonney

What happened to some of the men mentioned in this story:

George Scarborough, **Jeff Milton**, and **Frank McMahan** were tried for murdering Martin Mrose. Though others were involved in the conspiracy, when the case against these three came up for trial April 28, 1897, the judge directed the jury to vote for acquittal, and the men were released.

"Uncle" John Selman's trial for the murder of John Wesley Hardin ended in a hung jury, and he was never retried. Known in El Paso for his close ties with the Mexican community, Selman was mysteriously assaulted on El Paso Street five days after the trial by three Mexican toughs. Severely stabbed in the affray, he was never the same again. Two months later, he was shot by George Scarborough behind the Wigwam Saloon in El Paso, two years to the day after Selman had killed Baz Outlaw. Selman died the next day, April 6, 1896. The day after that, the murder charge against Selman in the Hardin shooting was dismissed. One of the first people on the scene after the Selman shooting was a barfly named Cole Belmont, who retrieved Selman's pistol and kept it. Belmont was arrested some time later for theft, but in the end, his testimony proved crucial, and Scarborough was acquitted. Belmont was assessed sixty days in jail for stealing the pistol. Putting up $4,000 bond for Scarborough in this case was J. L. Whitmore, who had beaten Helen Mrose's attempt to gain control of Hardin's estate.

George Scarborough was tried for two murders, Selman and Mrose, and though he got off both times, his reputation was destroyed. Facing intense criticism, he resigned his position as a U.S. marshal. He was alleged to have been one of the train robbers of the Santa Fe Pacific train at Grant, New Mexico, in November 1897. Though this was untrue, it demonstrates how far his reputation had sunk. Obtaining work as a range detective, he was shot by a rustler in Arizona. He died on April 5, 1900, four years to the day after shooting John Selman, Sr.

"Young" John Selman, Jr., (also known as "Marion" Selman) had difficulty with women. His grappling arrest of Helen Mrose led to the shooting of Hardin; similarly, his clumsy relationship with a sixteen-year-old Mexican girl was a prelude to the killing of his own father. Not long after this, Marion Selman killed a man in Brownwood, Texas. In 1898, he joined the Texas Eleventh U.S. Cavalry and was sent to the Philippines. Wounded in action during the Moro Insurrection, he returned to the U.S and lived and worked across the West. Born January 30, 1875 in Fort Griffin, Texas, he died of a heart attack March 31, 1937 in Rockdale. Selman is buried near Bertram, Texas.

Pat Garrett, killer of Billy the Kid during the Lincoln County War, was shot by Wayne Brazel on February 29, 1908. Controversy has surrounded this murder, for lurking on the edges of a possible conspiracy is the ominous figure of Jim Miller, who had dealings with Garrett in the last days of his life. Garrett is buried in Las Cruces.

Bud Frazer, former sheriff of Pecos, having tried twice to kill Jim Miller, was shotgunned to death by Miller in Toyah, Texas, on September 14, 1896. The resulting trial was moved to Eastland County on a change of venue and, in January 1899, Miller was found not guilty. Originally buried in Toyah, Frazer now rests in Fort Stockton, Texas.

Barney Riggs, involved in a bitter divorce with his wife Annie, the sister of Bud Frazer, was killed by Annie's son-in-law, Buck Chadborn, in Fort Stockton, Texas, on April 7, 1902. Riggs was unarmed. Chadborn was charged with second-degree murder but found not guilty.

John Denson and his friend **William Earhart**, "two as unscrupulous cut-throats as ever smothered an infant at his mother's breast," both of whom had "witnessed" the shooting of Bud Frazer by Jim Miller three weeks before, tried to conclude the Miller-Frazer feud by killing Barney Riggs, Frazer's brother-in-law. Instead they were outgunned by Riggs on October 3, 1896 in Pecos, Texas. Incredibly, a witness to this shooting was Cole Belmont, the man who had stolen a dying John Selman's pistol in El Paso a few months before. Riggs was tried in El Paso but found not guilty.

Jim Miller was lynched in Ada, Oklahoma, April 19, 1909, the same day a New Mexico jury declared Wayne Brazel not guilty of the murder of Pat Garrett. As the mob prepared to swing him off his feet, Miller shouted, "Let the record show that I have killed fifty-one men—!"

Green Denson, John Denson's brother, the man who had acted as Hardin's intercessor with Callie Lewis Hardin in Junction, Texas, and a "well known gambler" according to the *Daily Statesman*, was killed in a drunken brawl in Austin, Texas, January 9, 1899 by Sam Magnus. He is buried in Oakwood Cemetery.

Jim Clements, Hardin's first cousin who had come to Phenix to escort John Denson back to Kimble County after his release from jail in Eddy, was mysteriously murdered May 22, 1897—possibly by his brother-in-law, Tom Tennille. His body was never found.

Mannie Clements, John Wesley Hardin's first cousin, once removed, a man who may have been the "bagman" in the Pat Garrett murder conspiracy, was killed by an unknown assailant in a crowded Coney Island Saloon in El Paso, Texas, on December 29, 1908, only months before the Brazel murder trial began. He is buried at Evergreen Cemetery in El Paso.

Jefferson Davis Hardin, John Wesley Hardin's younger brother, was killed by John Snowden, the son-in-law of his cousin, Benjamin C. Hardin, near Clairemont, Texas, in November 1901.

Bob Ford, killer of Jesse James, and the man later intimidated by Martin Mrose, was killed by Ed O'Kelly in Creede, Colorado, on July 8, 1892. He is buried in Richmond, Missouri. Though O'Kelly was sentenced to life in prison for killing Ford, his sentence was commuted, and he was released in 1902. O'Kelly was shot and killed by a policeman January 13, 1904, in Oklahoma City.

Lon Bass, the deputy who forced Hardin to back down during an aborted holdup of a gaming table in Phenix, New Mexico, moved to Arizona. On the night of February 8, 1903, Bass assaulted Arizona Ranger William W. Webb, who shot and killed him.

James Leslie "Les" Dow, Eddy County sheriff, was shot in the mouth by former sheriff Dave Kemp in Eddy, New Mexico. After surgery to remove broken teeth, he bled to death on February 19, 1897. Kemp was charged with murder and tried in Chaves County, New Mexico, in March 1898, but was acquitted when Bill Smith testified the shooting was in self-defense. Dow is buried in Carlsbad.

David L. Kemp, a fellow convict in Huntsville at the time Hardin was incarcerated there, moved to New Mexico, became a friend of Martin Mrose, and was the first sheriff of Eddy County. He relocated to Lipscomb County, Texas. Among Dave Kemp's neighbors was Dillon Bridges, whose wife, Annie died in August 1903. Annie was the sister of Carolyn (Callie Lewis) Baze. On January 4, 1935, Dave Kemp died of a heart attack. He is buried at the Heart Cemetery, south of Booker.

William H. Smith, a constable in Eddy county involved in a near shoot-out with Les Dow in Seven Rivers, and who solicited John Wesley Hardin's help in the John Denson assault case, then was involved in a messy divorce with Eulalia Terrassas, and the star defense witness in Dave Kemp's murder trial in Roswell, New Mexico, was himself involved in a shooting in Texas while making an arrest in 1899. He and another Mexican woman appear together on the 1900 Census in Phenix.

Gipson "Gip" Hardin, John Wesley's last brother, was convicted of killing his best friend during an argument in February 1900 but served only a couple years at Huntsville Prison, then worked in the stockyards in Fort Worth. In 1918, while shipping horses to Europe for the U.S. Army in World War One, Gip Hardin was killed in an accident.

Beauregard Lee, the dashing Santa Fe Railroad detective who arrested Martin and Helen Beulah Mrose in Chihuahua, Mexico, was killed by outlaws in 1900, according to family tradition, but where, and under what circumstances he died, is unclear.

The Eddy brothers recovered from the Panic of '93. In 1896, they promoted a rail line from El Paso into the Tularosa Basin. They established the town of Alamogordo and the resort of Cloudcroft; as the railroad crept toward promising coal fields, the Eddys established Carrizozo, Capitan, Vaughn, Roy, and Tucumcari. In later years, C.B. Eddy continued his investments all over the country; J.A. Eddy retired to Salida, Colorado, where he became the first mayor. C. B. Eddy was a big influence on a young Conrad Hilton. He told him, "Connie, if you want to launch big ships, you must go to where there is deep water." Hilton did, and he became a success in the hotel business. C.B. Eddy died of natural causes in St. Vincent's Hospital in New York City on April 13, 1931. He is buried in Milford, New York. J. A. Eddy died in Denver, on November 10th. He is buried in Salida, in a plot overlooking the beautiful mountains he so loved. Twelve miles northwest of Salida is Eddy Creek, one of the few outward signs the Eddy brothers passed that way.

Victor Queen, Martin Mrose's friend, returned to Eddy. In April 1896, an Eddy County grand jury refused to indict him for cattle rustling, a pretty good indication how they would have handled Mrose's case too. Queen resumed his life in New Mexico. Working as a timber supervisor at the Burro Mountain Copper Company near Silver City, where he was considered a "valuable and useful man" according to the *Silver City Enterprise,* Queen was shot twice from behind, then shotgunned as he turned around outside a boarding house in the little town of Central on December 13, 1904. He was unarmed.

Tom Fennessey abandoned his wife and investments after the murder of Mrose. Tom's father, Ned Fennessey, died in Refugio, Texas, in 1901; in 1903 his and Tom's ranches were seized and sold by the sheriff. Tom's share of the proceeds was held in escrow, which led to a curious series of lawsuits in 1905. His wife Adah tried to claim a third of his estate. Both of her children, plus Mabel, Tom's daughter by his first wife, united against her. Adah said her husband "had recently died." The children denied that but offered no proof. In 1910, Mabel filed *ex parte* to gain control of her share of her father's estate. Tom Fennessey signed a document supporting her claim, which probably means she had known where he was the whole time … in San Antonio. Later that year, Tom signed a power of attorney to sue over the seizure and loss of his ranch, a ranch which still bears the Fennessey name to this day. The document was signed in San Antonio, where Fennessey was an attendant at the Southwestern Insane Asylum. Fennessey died January 20, 1922, of natural causes. He is buried in an unmarked grave in San Antonio within sight of the last resting place of Carolyn Baze.

Frank McMahan, one of Mrose's killers, wound up working as an immigration inspector. He died of natural causes in Yuma, Arizona, March 6, 1940 and was buried in San Diego, California.

Jeff Milton, another of Mrose's killers, but a man who may have rehabilitated his reputation through a long law enforcement career, died of natural causes in Tucson, Arizona, May 7, 1947.

Dee Harkey, Mrose's adversary, died of natural causes on June 16, 1958, in Carlsbad, New Mexico. He had outlived everyone in this story except Laura Jennings and Carolyn Baze.

APPENDIX TWO

Spelling:

Martin Mrose

A lthough one historian claimed Martin Mrose was illiterate, there are enough signatures like that above to prove he could sign his own name. To date, about three dozen signatures and several affidavits have been found, and, though heavy-handed, all handwriting samples are clear and stylistically written. It was quite common in the 1890s for illiterates to add their marks to documents with an "X."

Even so, Martin Mrose always signed his name, which shows not only could he write, but he could read, and he was particular about the spelling of his surname. Other evidence—for instance, a letter addressed to Helen discovered on his body, letters which she said he'd sent her in the weeks before his death, a letter reported at the post office in Eddy, and a letter (one of several from Juarez) George Scarborough produced in court, suggest Mrose sent personal letters. Who would have written them but him?

Unfortunately, there was, and still is, confusion over the spelling of his name. There were, apparently, no standardized spellings of the family name before his time, which is complicated by the fact that most Poles, Czechs, and Wends dropped the suffixes -ko, -ka, -ky, or -ke in America. In every case where Martin Mrose was present when his name was written—standing in front of county clerks, with friends, in newspaper stories prior to his departure from Eddy County—his name is spelled as above. Mrose must have spent a lifetime correcting people's spelling of his name, and the version he used was M-r-o-s-e. Consequently, his spelling has been used throughout this narrative. *It is the author's contention that if the man himself spelled it this way, future historians and writers should too.*

The author has noted these variations of the name of Mrose during research and gives them here to aid historians who follow:

Mroz—The name on the Baptism Registry at Annunciation of the Blessed Virgin Mary Catholic Church, St. Hedwig, Texas, for the children of Valentin and Barbara Maros. Property and other records in the Bexar County Courthouse in San Antonio, however, show that the family itself did not spell the name this way. The spelling is confined to church records, most of which are written in Latin, so it's conceivable the priests wrote it this way to be more Latin. Even so, later Polish and Czech immigrants in the Chicago area in the 1900s spelled it this way too. The name means "frost," and it was also a nickname for a white-haired man or one of an icy or unsociable disposition.

Maros—The spelling most commonly used on records about the St. Hedwig family.

Mros—Name carved on Barbara's (Polish) headstone, St. Hedwig, Texas, and on Wilhelm's (Wendish) grave, Fedor, Texas. In addition, Valentine Maros, who abandoned his wife and children and left them destitute in 1884 in order to take up with a Mexican woman, used this spelling in Blanco County, where he settled from 1884–1889 and 1890–95. Returning to Bexar County in 1895, he still appears to have used this spelling. In 1898, Barbara Maros filed for divorce after a series of assaults by her husband, and in court documents, she and her husband used this spelling. At least one descendant of Valentine's relationship with the other woman used Mros as a middle name. This version is also common in Wendish and Czech records in Bastrop and Lee counties.

Maroz—The Bexar County Texas Grantor/Grantee Index, lists a deed granted by Alex Maroz to Barbara Maroz, his mother.

Mroſs—Baptism records of St. Michael's Catholic Church in San Antonio, Texas, use this archaic spelling for the baptism of Martin Mroſs, born November 15, 1861 to Valentine Mroſs and Barbara Blow [sic]. This summa or "long s" (ſ) spelling might be encountered in other documents prior to 1880. Originally, the author thought this was proof of Martin Mrose's origin among the Poles of St. Hedwig. Each child in this family is not represented in baptism records, but a cross-check of first communion lists, instruction rolls, and confirmation records lists each of the known children except this one. Inconceivable he was a runaway before his first communion, the author is convinced he was one of the large numbers of child mortalities common in the Nineteenth Century. At the same time, the Mroſs child is too young; Martin Mrose indicated in affidavits that his birth was in 1856. Even more significantly, Barbara Mros testified in her divorce petition in 1898 that all seven of her children who had reached maturity were alive and living with her at that time. The children were: Mariam, Alex, Thomas, Julianna Catherina, Frances, Lucia Josefa, and Frank. For these and other reasons, the author is convinced "Martin Mroſs," died as a child and is not the later desperado Martin Mrose.

Mruss/Mrass—Valentine and Barbara Maros' son, Alexander George's Baptism record, St Mary's Catholic Church, San Antonio.

Mrosk—Lee County, probably the family of Wilhelm Mros.

Mrosack—A Wendish woman, Hanna Mrosack married Matthaus Wukasch in Serbin, Texas. Also spelled Mros and Mrose.

Maroske—Wends in Bastrop County using this spelling.

Meros—Various individuals on the 1880 census. Except for the St. Hedwig family, all others were born in Texas or Alabama.

Merose—Eve Ball, in her book *Ma'am Jones of the Pecos.*

M'Rose—*El Paso Daily Herald*, August 9, 1895, affidavit of Dr. Alward White, signature of Helen M'Rose on partnership statement with Hardin, and in numerous other places. This is probably the most common misspelling of the name. In Eddy County, after Martin's death, the *Pecos Valley Daily Argus* spells it this way.

M'rose—*El Paso Daily Times*, August 23, 1895.

McRose—*El Paso Times*, May 8, 1949, and caption scrawled at bottom of the famous photograph, "Mrs. McRose and kid."

Morose—Dee Harkey, as told to J. Evetts Haley. A common variant.

Morse—Noted it only in one instance: a letter reported at the post office for Martin Morse in *The Eddy Argus*, July 14, 1893.

Mrosr—(or Mron) A clerk's difficult handwriting within a bill of sale of Mrose's remaining stock to William McClendon prior to Mrose's ill-fated departure from Eddy. The written name at the bottom of the document, however, is clearly Mrose.

Monrose—W.H. Burgess, as reported by J. Evetts Haley and Chesley Hervey in Vandale Collection.

Min-yose—Bob Beverly, in a letter dated May 11, 1944 to J. Evetts Haley says, "Martin Monroe, *or as it was pronounced by he, himself, Min-yos* ...." Beverly's spelling is the closest anyone got to phonetically describing the correct pronunciation of the name, where the Germanic /x/ is a voiceless vilar fricative. In the International Phonetic Alphabet, the surname would be written /m/ /i/ /x/ /o/ /s/.

Munroe—Bob Beverly, in a letter, "The VVN Steers Go to Colorado," now in the Haley Collection, and in a letter to J. Evetts Haley, in the same collection. Also Mrs. Jerry Dunaway in a letter to Haley in 1937, wherein she calls him "Marvin" Munroe.

Monroe—Bob Beverly, in a letter, May 11, 1944 to J. Evetts Haley.

Moose—a direct but misspelled reference to Martin Mrose in the Index to Court Cases, Eddy County Clerk's Office.

Marose—A.P. Black in *The End of the Long Horn Trail*. Also, Thomas Maros used this spelling for registering his brands in Blanco County in the two years he lived there with his father and his father's common-law wife. The spelling is also used in the Civil Docket Book "A," Fifth Judicial Court, Eddy County, New Mexico, in the civil suit Ivy Cass vs. Laura A. Collier, Cornelius A. Collier, and Martin Marose.

Rose—*The Dallas Morning News* of July 1, 1895 reported on page one the "sensational killing of Martin M. Rose." Martin "Rose" was also listed in the 1885 Colorado State Census. Though it would seem this spelling would be a natural error to make, the spelling R-o-s-e is the rarest of all. It is, however, the name Helen Beulah died under in California.

Meraz—Baptism records for several individuals by this name and a marriage record at St. Hedwig. Meraz is Hispanic.

Mross—Valentine Mross, from St. Hedwig, was listed among emigrants arriving in Galveston, Texas, in 1855.

Monsk—The spelling used by *The Galveston Daily News*, November 26, 1883, in its report of the murders of Carl Keuffel and Wilhelm Mros in Fedor, Texas.

Mroska and Moreske—Bastrop County, Texas, Marriage Records. Later spelled Mros and Morose.

Martz—Not related to this story, but often encountered in research into the history of southeastern New Mexico. At the time of the Lincoln County War, Martin Martz, nicknamed "Dutch," or "Old Dutch," was an employee of John Tunstall's and an ally of Billy the Kid. Though the names are similar, Martin Martz predates the appearance of Martin Mrose in the same area of New Mexico by about five years.

Uros—the name on the published wedding registry of San Fernando Cathedral in San Antonio, obviously mistaken by a writer from a sharp or indecipherable "M." The entry notes the marriage of Valentin Maros and Barbara Ploch.

NOTES

Chapter 1—The Outlaw Cousin

1. Bill Longley in a letter to James Madison Brown, 1877, quoted by Doris Johnston from a copy given to her by Rodney Brown of Waco.
2. "Judge" Lemond was not a judge in Williamson County, according to District Judge Bill Stubblefield, who looked into it at the request of the author in December 1999. The only evidence of his being a judge is in Lavaca County during the Civil War, where he is listed as collecting funds for indigent widows and children. In true Texas tradition, he was called "Judge" the rest of his life.
3. The author first heard the story from Wilda Fay Jennings, the granddaughter of Virginia Gift Lemond, who was there that day.
4. Though modern kinship relationships have narrowed from the way in which those who lived a hundred years ago understood them, the author has often found such relationships did exist.
5. The author heard three versions of this story from descendants of those there that night. In two, only one other man was riding with Hardin. Another version, a more detailed account from Wilda Fay Jennings in an interview in March 1997 and repeated in a phone conversation in May 1998, said Hardin was with his "gang." Hardin was never known to have a gang, but in May 1874, on the run after killing Deputy Sheriff Webb, he did escape with at least one other man, James Taylor, who had been involved in the shooting of Jack Helms the year before. At any rate, to better understand the confusing relationships among the families of Gonzales County (though the Williams and Lemonds later settled in Caldwell and Williamson counties) see Marjorie Burnett Hyatt's *The Ties That Bind.*
6. Helen Williams was the granddaughter of the pioneering Williams and Ellison families of central Texas. She was related by blood and marriage to an extraordinary group of outlaws and lawmen.
7. Hardin visited the John W. Lemond family at this time.
8. Letter from Adriel Jacobs McGill to Dr. Richard C. Marohn, quoted in his book *The Last Gunfighter,* page 90.
9. On July 8, 1877, in Palo Pinto County, A.J. Williams married M.J. Ray; in Abilene in Taylor County, he married Lou Scott on November 11, 1884; in Shackelford County, he married Oceana Hart on June 28, 1887.
10. Pardon, Texas State Archives, case number 3898.
11. The charges of bribery are noted as cases #40, 69, and 81. Another entry in the Docket of the Jones County District Court was docket number 82, the State of Texas versus W.H. Smith for embezzlement of $42.50. W.H. Smith later went on to become constable of Eddy County, New Mexico.
12. Adella Barnes, in a letter to D.A. "Lon" Williams August 15, 1948, mentions her grandmother's trunk. This would be Frances Adella Bailey, wife of E. W. (Edmund Wade) Williams, the adopted brother of A.J. Williams. Lon Williams wrote back on August 20 that he did not know about the bond incident. The Adella Barnes letter is among the papers of Glenn Wilkins; the Lon Williams reply is from the papers of Dell Barnes.

13. Jones County Docket, page 25, entry 5.
14. This is not the W.H. Smith who enters this narrative later in New Mexico.
15. Extradition request in Territorial Governor Lionel Sheldon's papers from the Territorial Archives of New Mexico.
16. Letter Archie Jefferes to Homer Hutto, undated, quoted in Robert K. DeArment's biography, *George Scarborough*, p. 34.
17. R.E. Sherrill, *Haskell County History*, page 72.
18. R.E. Sherrill, "Colorful History of Haskell County is Recounted," Vandale Collection.
19. Archie Jefferes.
20. *The Galveston Daily News*, October 18, 1887.
21. *The Galveston Daily News*, October 19, 1887.
22. *The Taylor County News*, October 21, 1887.
23. *The Luling Signal*, October 27, 1887.
24. A.C. Williams sold out in Caldwell County and resumed his farming in Eastland County, where he spent the rest of his life.
25. R.E. Sherrill, page 172.
26. To be fair, the extended Williams family did not just contain outlaws, it also included well-known citizens like Captain Dan Roberts of the Texas Rangers; Sheriff James Eden Williams of Tehachapi, California; Chisholm Trail drover N.P. Ellison; Dr. Perry Alan Baze; President Abraham Lincoln; and later descendants Admiral Elmo Zumwalt, Audie Murphy, and Texas Governor John Connally.

Chapter 2—Lost Creek

1. Anonymous #1.
2. Information from Thomas and Wilda Fay Jennings, Ruth Jo Martin, *et al*, plus *San Saba County History, 1856–1983* and *Mason County Communities*.
3. The first Mary Ann drank lye and died; though it seems bizarre, the family bestowed the same name on the next girl born. How such a terrible accident could happen is explained by another pioneer, Sarah Harkey Hall in *Surviving on the Texas Frontier*, p. 16.
4. Thomas Jennings, March 10, 1997.
5. Jennings grant, Texas General Land Office, file #BEX-P, 2074. In 1910 Michael Jennings bought 14 acres (7 in San Saba County, 7 in Mason) for $2.50 an acre to round out the property.
6. The Comanches had been mostly neutralized by 1875 and were confined on reservations in Oklahoma. Nevertheless, bands of young warriors continued to raid into central Texas as late as 1879.
7. Sarah Harkey Hall, p. 27.
8. ibid, p. 44.
9. ibid, p. 52-3.
10. Lollie Roberts, February 2000.
11. Claims for Losses from Indian Depredations, Runge Papers, Texas State Archives, list losses from Comanche raids in 1876 and 1877, the years during which the Jenningses were establishing their homestead. There is not a mention anywhere of Jennings' losses. The family was noted for hog farming more than cattle raising. Most cattlemen did not feel hogs competed with livestock for forage, and so Michael Jennings's hogs roamed freely. A portion of the family income came from smoked meats, poultry, eggs, and dairy products. As such, they may not have been perceived as a threat to "fence-cutting" tensions, the violence of the

San Saba Mob, or the rustling on every side of them. Their dray horses and dairy cattle may have been safe simply because they were the wrong animals in a longhorn-driven economy.

12. To understand the climate of fear in San Saba County at the time the Jennings family lived there, see C.L. Sonnichsen, *I'll Die Before I'll Run*, p. 217.

13. Genealogists are aware of limitations studying the family of Abraham Lincoln. Aaron Williams, Jr., a dyed-in-the-wool Confederate, is known to have admitted his connection to Abraham Lincoln even during the Civil War. For this reason, the author believes Williams was indeed the first cousin of Abraham Lincoln.

14. Bill Williams served with Company "B," 4th Texas Regiment, 32nd Texas Cavalry from 1861 to the end of the war.

15. Thomas Jennings, November 1999.

16. Anonymous #2, December 1996.

17. *The Mason County News*, March 2, 1889, partially quoting from an earlier article in the *San Saba County News*.

18. Marriage license recorded at the Mason County Courthouse March 26, 1889.

19. San Saba County, Texas, League section 2800, Abstract #1954. In a proof of heirship filed in Llano County September 12, 1917, Steve Jennings described the property as Patent #541, Volume 30, 79 acres of land known as survey 2800, owned jointly by himself and his wife Helen *Eugenia* Jennings. This is the only reference to Helen's middle name, but Steve was often wrong, and the author feels her middle name was Elizabeth.

20. Bill Williams Family Bible, copy in author's possession. The author believes this entry is mistaken and the baby lived for three days, not three hours.

21. Bill Williams, op cit. This is probably the only accurate date for Laura's birth. As she grew up, Laura rarely gave her true age. Anonymous #1 recorded her birthdate as March 1, 1898, a date she got directly from Laura, who was sitting across the table from her. Laura claimed on her Social Security application in 1949 she had been born March 8, 1897, though the Social Security Death Index lists her birth as March 8, 1891—suggesting Laura corrected it at a future date. Wilda Fay Jennings said her father, Wilford C. Ellison (Laura's first cousin, once removed, who was born July 20, 1893) told her he was a couple years younger than Laura. Even so, Wilda Fay reported Laura consistently claimed she was "much younger" than Wilford. Curiously, the author can find no "delayed birth" records in any of the counties in which Laura is known to have lived, delayed birth being, of course, a legal way to nail down birthdates for those born before official record-keeping. Among the few pieces of information he shared with the author, Laura's son said he was "certain" his mother was born in 1892, but admitted in the same breath she had told someone else 1894. He said her daughter thought it was anywhere from 1890–1893. A niece thought Laura named 1890. Laura's death certificate lists her birthdate as 1892. On the census of 1910, Laura was listed as 19, therefore born in 1891; on the 1920 census, she claimed to be 27, or 1893; and on the 1930 census she claimed to be 33, or born in 1897. As if this weren't complicated enough, her baby brother—by oral tradition "Brian" Jennings—was recorded by Bill Williams as having been born July 1st and dying on July 3, 1893. He is buried at Union Band Cemetery in Mason County, his grave marked by a stone that reads, "Infant son of Steve and Helen Jennings, born April 3, 1891, died April 3, 1891." Finally, Jennings family tradition supports the Bill Williams bible in that Laura was 95 years old when she died, which again points to 1891. Her grave is marked by a headstone giving only her death date—and that is the only date that's certain.

22. R.E. Mather, *Scandal of the West*, p. 15

23. Bill Williams, *op cit*. Curiously, the Union Band Cemetery Association, under an official Historic Texas Cemetery placard, gives the history of the cemetery: "On March 31, 1891, T.H. and Priscilla Thomas conveyed one and one-half acres of this land to the trustees of the Union Band Missionary Baptist Church. Three days later, Steve and Helen Jennings' infant son was laid to rest here, the earliest marked grave at this site." It's clear the headstone is wrong, Brian Jennings having been buried July 3, 1893, rather than April 3, 1891. At the same time, by noting the baby was buried "in the city of the dead," Bill Williams gave a clue there were earlier burials, including Virgin Mary Jennings. It's possible the cemetery is older and more crowded than the Cemetery Association knows, unknown burials between Virgin Mary and Brian having occurred.

24. According to *The Eddy County Citizen*, January 9, 1893, there were 328,710 decrees for divorce in the United States in the twenty-year period from 1867–1886.

25. Mason County, Texas, Minutes of the District Court Index, page 25. Case recorded in Minute Book 4, p. 256, #377, October 1, 1894.

26. ibid.

27. Latham Miller interview with the author and Joyce Capps, September 9, 1997. There are numerous versions of Helen's departure from her marriage. For example, Elizabeth Jennings McLeod was quoted as saying Helen was stolen away by her lover from the farm in Fredonia. Other reports claim she ran off to engage a lawyer in the suit against her husband. The author believes Helen's departure was less romantic. She simply rode away with her daughter. She wouldn't have left at night, however, unless desperate. For that reason, the author believes she waited until an opportune time, borrowed a horse from her kinsmen, and headed west.

28. David Alonso "Lon" Williams, Helen's brother, and his family lived on the Upper Peñasco River until 1894. Lon was a freighter, and travelers through the area can still see the deep ruts cut by his freight wagons. For unknown reasons, he moved to Cartwright prior to February 23, 1895. Lon bought several tracts of land near Cartwright and Gila Bend, but in 1896–1897 he moved back to Mayhill, and in 1898 back to Cartwright, where he farmed and had dairy cattle. In 1907, a year after his father-in-law, Abram Glossbrenner moved there, D.A. Williams moved his family to Fowler, California.

29. Glenn Wilkins, letter to the author, February 19, 1999.

30. Ignacio de Jesus Ramirez interview.

31. In support of a train journey, rather than an arduous trek by horseback, Laura Jennings never said anything to her children about traveling across West Texas.

32. A hundred years afterward, the legend is becoming diluted. By coincidence, another young woman of Mason County was tainted by scandal and heartache at exactly the same time, and her story is better known. The author has encountered residents confused by the two stories, and some were blending them into one legend. In another twenty years, Helen Jennings would have been forgotten and the other woman's name attached to adventures not her own. The woman's name was Callie Lewis.

Chapter 3—The Cowboy

1. Bob Beverly letter to J. Evetts Haley, May 11, 1944.

2. For a discussion on the spelling of Mrose, see Appendix Two.

3. A.P. (Ott) Black, *The End of the Long Horn Trail*, p. 40. As written, 130 pounds, is unlikely. Most cowboys were between 120-150 pounds, lean and wiry. Mrose was bigger than anyone else. Contemporary descriptions of "big" men were often 180+ pounds, so it is the author's

feeling Black meant Mrose was 180. The discrepancy can best be explained by the similarity between a written 130 and a 180.

4. Stem Daugherty, interview with J. Evetts Haley, February 29, 1944.
5. Black interview, Vandale Collection.
6. Bob Beverly, op. cit.
7. Ignacio de Jesus-Ramirez, interview with the author.
8. Bob Beverly.
9. Ed Harrall interview with Hervey Chesley and J. Evetts Haley, June 13, 1939.
10. Frank Loyd interview with Hervey Chesley and J. Evetts Haley.
11. Charles Ballard, Vandale Collection.
12. Harkey, *Mean as Hell*, p. 129.
13. Dee Harkey interview, 1945, Vandale Collection.
14. In a letter to the author dated November 9, 1999, Regina and Allen Kosub, a San Antonio couple researching the Poles of Texas, said, "The divorce of Barbara and Valentin [Maros] after forty years of marriage was beyond unusual for this Catholic community. The records shows [sic] attempts began [sic] by Barbara to divorce Valentin soon after the 1895 death of Marcin [i.e. Martin.] The rancorous conclusion in 1899 was a decree granting a divorce. The court spelled the name Mros; the court's records were kept in English."

Unfortunately for any such attempt to link the divorce of Valentin and Barbara Maros to the death of their "son," the petition for divorce was filed October 27, 1898, and finalized on December 22nd. In her petition to the court, Barbara Maros (Mroz is the spelling used in the petition) said she had seven children as the issue of this marriage, and at the time of the petition *all were of mature years and living with her*, and she documented a life of physical and emotional abuse, including Valentin's 1884 abandonment of his family. Taking everything, including the utensils, livestock, and farm implements, Valentin left his seven children and wife destitute and moved to Blanco County, Texas, where he bought thirty-five acres along the Blanco River. In 1887, his son Thomas joined him, and they raised hogs and cattle until late 1889, when Valentin returned to St. Hedwig and lived for a time in his wife's house. Forcibly expelled after only a couple months, in the next two years "he was guilty of excesses, cruel treatment, and outrage towards [his wife] of such a nature as to render their living together unsupportable." In April 1897 he entered Barbara's home "and without the slightest provocation struck [Barbara] with his fists [...] with such violence [...] that had it not been for her two children, who immediately came to her rescue, [he] would have taken her life." Numerous witnesses were called to testify as to the veracity of these claims, including Barbara's family and a kinsman, Joe Kosub. In the end the court sustained all of Barbara's claims against her husband. Valentin's appeal over the property settlement was denied January 16, 1899.

15. Mrose's age is listed in only six places. The first is the 1880 census, Atascosa County, Texas, which lists him as eighteen years old and Polish. It's debatable whether Mrose himself provided this information, and it's likely that when the census taker rode up to the Sparks ranch, Mrose was working somewhere on the range. The 1885 Colorado census lists Mrose as Martin Rose, 23 years old, born in Texas, parents born in Europe. This entry again looks like he was not the source of the information, since he would have been more specific about his parents' origin. This may also mean he was out on the range.

Due to the loss of the 1890 census in a fire, we are left with only four other primary sources. In affidavits filed in his Desert Land application, *in his own handwriting*, Mrose said he was born in Texas, and records his age on one document as 37 and sometime later as 38 years of age. (A clerk, copying information for another affidavit in the file, misread Mrose's "7" and wrote 32 rather than Mrose's actual age of 37.) Working back from the later date and forward from the earlier affidavit, it's possible to narrow his birthdate to the period January 3 to April 23, 1856. The 1856 date is in agreement with his age in an account Milton Phillips made at the time he lived in Juarez.

16. Robert N. Mullin Collection. There are two instances when Mullin's research notes caused the author to wonder how much Mullin had learned over the years. (The other instance was the letter "E." for Helen's middle name, suggesting he knew "Beulah" was an alias.) Mullin appears to have been the only researcher who seriously investigated Mrose's origin north of San Antonio. Among his papers is a cryptic note, "Mrose was raised near Georgetown, Texas, north of Austin."

17. Most descendants of the Wends are Lutherans. The Wends established Concordia University and provided leadership of the early Missouri Synod in America.

18. For any historian or genealogist researching the Wends, the biggest problem arises from the fact the Wends themselves didn't know how to explain their ethnicity. When asked by census takers prior to the 1930s, they called themselves Poles, Prussians, Germans, or Bohemians. Among themselves, they were Sorbs. Wendish came as a compromise about the time first-generation immigrants were fading away, and second-generation Americans were struggling with their roots. Often confused in Texas with the prominent and larger group of Bohemians (Czechs) or the smaller, but vocal, Poles, the Wends tended to blend in with neighboring Germans, who shared Lutheranism with them. One researcher has said he is convinced that half of the huge and powerful German community of Texas was actually Wendish, but never recognized it themselves.

19. Pastor John Kilian, *Baptismal Records of St. Paul Lutheran Church, Serbin, Texas*.

20. Having gone through droughts, tornadoes, and floods while researching this narrative, the author can attest to the consequences of weather on agriculture in Texas.

21. Harkey said it was 1879 or 1880. In light of the difference in age between Mrose and Harkey, the earlier date is more likely.

22. A well known horse trader who had also gone on three cattle drives up the Chisholm Trail, Mahlon, listed as "McCawan" in the 1880 Census, was a stock raiser at a ranch at Weedy Creek, next to Z.H. Osborn and the Sparks family. Nearby was J.T. Stapleton.

23. 1880 U.S. Census lists the J.T. Stapleton family in Live Oak County, Texas. By 1884, the Stapletons were in Fredonia, and in 1890 they were in the town of Mason. Stapleton was probably Helen Jennings' lawyer in her divorce suit against Steve Jennings. In 1902, the Stapletons moved to El Paso, Texas. John and Mary Stapleton are buried in Evergreen Cemetery.

24. Interview, Vandale Collection, February 1945. In this interview Harkey calls Mrose "dusky." Every other historical description of Mrose notes he was blonde, fair-skinned, and blue-eyed, and the author feels the transcript for Harkey's interview, written from notes taken at the time, confused an "h" for a "d."

25. Mrose homesteaded two tracts of land, the first when he built a cabin and stretched a fence to join a section of fence owned by the Eddy brothers. It's unlikely a cowboy newly hired that year would be familiar enough with Eddy operations to capitalize on an opportunity beside their land.

26. Black, op. cit., p. 40.

27. Harry A. Epperson, *Colorado, As I Saw It*.

28. Sarah Harkey Hall, *Surviving on the Texas Frontier*.

29. Harkey, op. cit., p. 130.

30. G.K. Martin in reminiscences in *Old West* says of horse rustling, "Thefts which usually brought prompt action were those involving horses. When a horse came up missing, the owner got busy. He would scour the country, making inquiries about a certain colored horse of certain marking, weight, and height. People noticed strangers and their mounts as they came through the country. They were on the alert for cow and horse thieves, and were often instrumental in locating stolen animals. Horses were easier to locate and identify than cows and hogs, and thieves often paid dearly for them." With people so watchful, was it be possible for Mrose to steal a horse and *remain* in Live Oak County? For this reason, a "theft" is unlikely. At the same time, an examination of Live Oak and Atascosa County records reveals no complaints against Mrose.

31. A cowboy expression for *can't see* (before daybreak) and *couldn't see* (after sunset).

32. E.C. Abbott ("Teddy Blue"), *We Pointed Them North*, p. 60.

33. John D. Young and J. Frank Dobie, pp. 194-5.

34. Milton Phillips, *El Paso Daily Herald*, July 9, 1895, claims Mrose, Fennessey, and he were hired in March 1884, but 1880 or 1881 is more probable. (Fennessey was in Refugio County, Texas, in October 1878, then appears to have left during the spring of 1879 on a cattle drive.) Documents show C.B. Eddy and Tom Fennessey in southeastern New Mexico in 1883. In addition, C.E. Johnson's account in *The Trail Drivers of Texas*, says clearly in the spring of 1881, he and seven cowboys, including Fennessey, arrived in Dodge City. "[W]hile there we sold some saddle horses to a man named Eddy, who ranched on Seven Rivers, New Mexico. Finnessey and [...] two Williams boys went with him to his ranch, and I have never seen them since."

35. Mrose may not have been the only Wend to wind up in New Mexico. Two Wendish surnames, Fritsche and Lingnau, are also encountered during research on the Eddy-Bissell Cattle Company in the 1890s. Ernst Lingnau, a grandson of Matthaus and Hanna Mrosko of Serbin, Texas, born three years after Martin Mrose, moved to New Mexico in the 1880s.

Chapter 4—The VVNs

1. Bill McPhee, "The Eddy Brothers," manuscript, p. 2.

2. Even on range grass a two- or three-year-old longhorn could gain a pound or more a day.

3. Dwight G. Bennett, D.V.M., "Flying Horses, Driving Cattle, *and* Piroplasmosis," *Western Horseman*, p. 117.

4. The name has always been a source of amusement.

5. Historical Notes on "Pioneering the West" by Dr. F. Newton Reynolds, as related by I.N. (Newt) Bowers, p.22.

6. Lily Klasner, p. 330.

7. Fred S. Millard, *A Cowpuncher of the Pecos*, p. 36, p. 41.

8. Eddy family genealogists and the book, *The Eddy Family in America*, list C.B. Eddy's middle name as "Brevoort." Historical accounts say "Bishop." His father, John Eddy, did business under the name C.J. Bishop & Co., so "Bishop" is probably correct.

9. The Eddy brothers descended from one of the earliest settlers in America, Samuel Eddy, who arrived at Plymouth on October 29, 1630.

10. Amos and Harriet Bissell were parents of George Norman Bissell (1846–1901), who joined the Eddys in their investments in New Mexico and Colorado.

11. Amos Bissell was president of the Chemical Bank of New York, and some of its capital was

invested in the Eddy-Bissell Cattle Company. A son of one of the directors of the bank, Joseph Stevens, became another investor. Though some have speculated the Bissells and Eddys were related, they do not appear to be so.

12. N. M. Territorial Brand Book #9, Eddy-Chaves Counties, p.25.
13. McPhee, op cit., p. 5.
14. James F. Hinkle, "A New Mexico Cowboy on the Pecos," p. 354.
15. ibid, p. 13-14.
16. McPhee, op cit., p. 3.
17. Meaning "pleasing," "flattering," or "promising prospects."
18. Quoted in McPhee, p. 13.
19. A.P. "Ott" Black, op cit., See Bobbie H. Ferguson, pp. III-18, 19 for a discussion of the Eddys' land acquisitions.
20. Simmons, *Bayon Salado*, p. 242.
21. ibid, p. 243.
22. Colorado State Census, 1885, Park County, page 3. Mrose's relationship to the household was "servant," meaning he was an employee, rather than ranch owner. Martin "Rose" was also listed in the 1885 Index, Park County, Colorado.
23. The 1885 Colorado census gives details of the Eddy operation at Black Mountain. In addition to 1,100 acres, $10,000 in farm value, $300 in implements, and $50,000 in livestock, the Agricultural Schedule lists $1,000 paid in wages and 52 weeks of labor. This means the ranch, snow-covered or not, was a year-round operation.
24. Epperson, p. 57.
25. Nib Jones, in Eve Ball's *Ma'am Jones of the Pecos*, p. 201. A similar version comes from Bob Beverly in a letter to J. Evetts Haley, November 29, 1945.
26. A.P. (Ott) Black, p. 40. Most writers have attributed this incident to Creede, Colorado. Cripple Creek is more likely since the VVN's Black Mountain division was only ten miles west.
27. Epperson, p. 57.
28. Black, p. 40.
29. The land tracts are close to the VVN ranch. Mrose settled here September 13, 1884 and filed October 8. They are described as the south half of the Southeast Quarter of Section 23 and the west half of the Southwest Quarter of Township 15 South, Range 75 West.
30. The parcel is described as the south half of Section 5, Township 15 south and Range 26 East. It is a mile south of the Hagerman Canal and two miles north of Lake Arthur. The site shows great forethought, for it lies along the AT & SF railway and is crossed by today's Highway 2. The patent was recorded in the Chaves County Patent Book "B," page 434. Mrose contracted for water rights on February 21, 1894, recorded in Chaves County Mortgage Book C, p. 26. On June 28, 1894, Martin Mrose, an unmarried person (which helps date his marriage to Helen Jennings), sold property and water rights to William McMillan of St. Louis for $1,000, though he still owed some money as terms of a mortgage to the Pecos Irrigation and Improvement Company. In March, 1901, J.J. Hagerman, Mrose's "attorney in fact" and the mortgage holder, sold the land at auction in Roswell, New Mexico.

Chapter 5—The Woman and The Cowboy

1. Ignacio de Jesus-Ramirez, interview with the author.
2. Author's interview with Ignacio de Jesus. The interview was a secondhand retelling of his grandfather's life in Eddy County in the 1890s. Because of this, the author has used the

interview sparingly. Señor de Jesus was definite about Helen, Laura, and a horse. This is in keeping with the fact Helen had borrowed a horse from her kinsmen, the Millers in Fredonia, and ridden off. Did she ride all the way to New Mexico? Maybe. Ignacio was also definite the horse was "dead," and this was considered a joke in Eddy County, but remembered no details about it. The author has accepted these remarks that Helen and Laura arrived by "dead" horse as probably as close to the truth as we can get.

De Jesus' use of the word *"forajida"* during the interview has caused confusion. The author does not speak Spanish, but he is blessed with a number of Hispanic friends. The use of this word to describe Helen Jennings has caused comment among these native Spanish speakers. A Spanish dictionary defines the word as a woman outlaw, but none of the Mexicans view it that way. The consensus seems to be this is not an outlaw, but a runaway. At any rate, the author feels de Jesus meant a *desperate* woman, a little girl, and a dying horse.

3. To show how immense the Eddy ranch was, *The Eddy Argus,* February 2, 1894, reported the foreman had gone to a pasture 150 miles from the headquarters.

4. For a discussion of the New York, Colorado Springs, and New Mexican investors, see Stephen Bogener's *Ditches in the Desert.*

5. Cicero Stewart interview.

6. Territorial Brand Book #9, Eddy and Chaves counties.

7. Bobbie H. Ferguson, "... *AND THEY LAID THEM TO REST IN THE LITTLE PLOT BESIDE THE PECOS."*

8. Mrs. Jerry Dunaway, in a letter to J. Evetts Haley, June 23, 1937.

9. *The Eddy Argus,* March 9, 1894, called it, "A prohibition that prohibits."

10. G. L. Seligmann, *New Mexico Historical Review,* April 1992.

11. Francis Tracy, Sr., "Pecos Valley Pioneers," *New Mexico Historical Review.*

12. *The Eddy Argus,* January 31, 1891.

13. Interview with Kate Blau.

14. See Lee C. Myers' "An Experiment in Prohibition," *New Mexico Historical Review,* vol. 40, #4, 1965.

15. *The Carlsbad Current-Argus,* October 29, 1989.

16. *Eddy Current,* March 24, 1893.

17. *The Eddy County Citizen,* November 19, 1892.

18. *The Eddy Current,* April 21, 1893, reported favorably on the Silver King Saloon. Kemp and Lyell assembled a brass band that was arguably the best group of musicians west of St. Louis. Strolling musicians, traveling troubadours, piano players, acrobats, boxing matches, magic shows, and jugglers provided entertainment there. The saloon was very successful.

19. ibid.

20. *The Eddy County Citizen,* November 19, 1892, reported the two gamblers, Billy and Ben Thompson, Jr., working at Bennett's Legal Tender. Ben Thompson, Sr., of course, was a famous gunman and former city marshal of Austin. His brother Billy and son often traveled the gambling circuit, but their time in Phenix was short. Ben Thompson, Jr., died of tuberculosis in San Antonio on September 9, 1893.

21. *The Eddy Argus,* June 8, 1894.

22. *The Pecos Valley Argus,* October 5, 1894.

23. In case #154, Criminal Docket Book "A" and Fifth Judicial Court Records, the indictment was misdated as 1895, even repeating the mistake in stating the crime occurred December 20, 1895. For more information on this case, see Chapter Thirteen.

24. *The Eddy Argus*, November 24, 1893. A spurious version of the Harkey meat market story is related by Marc Simmons in his book *When Six-Guns Ruled*. In this version, not based on Harkey or the truth, Simmons says, "Harkey disarmed his rowdy customer, marched him to the railway station, and forced him to leave the country."

25. Harkey's arrest was reported in the *Pecos Valley Daily Argus* of April 26, 1895. In fact Harkey had legally married Sophie New in Beeville, Texas, on August 4, 1886.

26. Stem Daugherty, February 29, 1944, interview with J. Evetts Haley.

27. Dee Harkey interview with J. Evetts Haley, February 24, 1945.

28. The marriage could have taken place anywhere from March to November, based on other accounts. The author places the marriage in November, for that is when Mrose got final proof on his Desert Land Entry, and it is a month after Helen had withdrawn her suit against Steve Jennings in Mason County.

29. See *The Carlsbad Current Argus*, December 21, 1926.

30. Mrs. Jack B. Patterson, *Queen, New Mexico*, pp. 26, 27.

31. *Eddy Argus*, March 31, 1893.

32. ibid. April 13, 1894.

33. See *The Eddy Argus*, August 4-11, 1893, for information and maps of the destruction.

34. The author has been unable to find the original of this famous letter. It is quoted, in part, in Keleher, p. 201.

35. Philip J. Rasche, "The Life and Death of Lon Bass," p. 9. See also the Eddy County Deed Record Book 3, pp. 417-8. Ed and Ellen Lyell sold their Phenix house and several lots to Dave Kemp.

36. The stage to Roswell departed at 8 a.m., arriving at 7 p.m. The return journey departed at 5 a.m. and arrived in Eddy at 5 p.m.

37. *The Eddy Argus* of January 26, 1893 gave detailed directions how to grow Egyptian corn. A second article on the same page identified Egyptian corn, milo maize, and red kaffir as varieties of non-saccharine sorghum. Irrigated, the crops produced up to thirty bushels per acre on the first cutting, then good fodder at four tons per acre. Contemporary reports of Egyptian corn ten feet tall are not uncommon, and this success was, without doubt, why Martin Mrose chose Egyptian corn as his irrigated crop.

38. At first, the cultivation of sugar beets showed promise, and in 1894 J.J. Hagerman built a sugar plant. Two years later, the plant burned and sugar beet cultivation dwindled.

39. Peter Hurd, Introduction to Cecil Bonney's *Looking Over My Shoulder*.

40. G. L. Seligmann, New Mexico Historical Review, April 1992.

Chapter 6—The Celebrity

1. Doris Lila Holinshead, *Impetuous Hardin*, p. 40

2. Sheriff William H. Hutchinson and Deputy A.J. Perdue, both of Escambia County, Florida, assisted by Lieutenant John B. Armstrong of the Texas Rangers, Special Detective Jack Duncan, William Dudley Chipley, the Railroad Superintendent, and twenty deputies made the arrest.

3. Speights survived the shooting, one of few State Policemen to do so. An account of the shooting is in Chuck Parsons, "Gunfire in Hemphill," *True West*, December 1999.

4. Richard C. Marohn, p. 120.

5. *The Freeborn County Standard*, August 28, 1895.

6. Quoted in Louis Nordyke, p. 200.

7. Texas Ranger T.C. "Pidge" Robinson, in a letter to the *Daily Democratic Statesman*, September 24, 1874.

8. Historically, the number of men this gunman killed is unimportant, but it's possible he killed more than he lists in his autobiography. F.M. Fly, a lawyer who knew him, said, "He admitted to 48, and I personally know of several he didn't admit. I don't doubt that [he] killed any less than 100 men." John Selman Jr. said the gunman "had the reputation of having killed some twenty-five or thirty men. I've found since that that was a very conservative estimate."

   On the other hand, Bruce V. Lander, an Englishman who has devoted some time to studying the body count, said in an article in *NOLA*, "[T]he simple fact remains that only nine of [the gunfighter's] killings can be named with certainty." He expounded on this in a letter to the author dated May 6, 2001, "My main writing interest is World War Two combat [...] and as such I have applied the rules that qualify fighter pilot[s'] claims. [U]nder these rules I fear [he] fails to meet the criteria for the majority of his claims."

   A hundred years ago, however, nearly every unexplained murder in Texas was blamed on this gunman. The people who knew him best put great credence in the reports of his murders. His autobiography was intended to *lessen* the damage to his reputation, not enhance it. It was intended to *justify* the murders, not list the truth. He was concerned with how he would be remembered. For this reason, he probably omitted murders he didn't care to recall twenty years later, fifteen of which had been spent in prison. For this reason, the autobiography must be taken with a grain of salt.

   With the autobiography as a guide, the author sees a minimum of 48 killings—the same as Fly. Using the same autobiography, Dr. Richard C. Marohn lists 42 killings. Leon Metz, who starts off numbering the murders in his biography of Hardin, loses steam in mid-book. On page 284, he says, "A primary question regarding his autobiography is not 'Did he kill all those people he claims he did,' but 'How many other deaths did he neglect to mention?'" For this reason, the author's opinion is the autobiography is probably 1/3 too conservative. Thus, the figure 60 may be closest to the true number of murders.

9. Rex Beach, *Personal Exposures*, p. 97.

10. Harkey, *Mean as Hell*, pp. 71, 72.

11. London *Spectator*, probably July 1, 1875

12. Strangely, though this gunfighter had an awful reputation, an aspirant for his fame was arrested in Clay County, according to the *Austin Democratic Daily Statesman*, January 7, 1876. The man, whose real name was Gillespie, was brought to Austin where he was identified.

13. The *Houston Daily Post*, August 21, 1895.

14. ibid.

15. He has been the subject of articles, lectures, and books. He still holds a fascination for many people.

16. A fortuneteller, according to the *San Antonio Daily Express* of August 23, 1895, told the prisoner, "He would get to be a good man in the penitentiary, but when he got out he would kill two men and then get killed." As the reader shall see, the author believes the fortune teller was half right....

Chapter 7—The Dangerous Child

1. J.G. Hardin, quoted in *The Life of John Wesley Hardin As Written By Himself*, p. 33. Page numbers refer to the common University of Oklahoma Press edition available today.

2. Leon Metz, "The Ghost of John Wesley Hardin," *Roundup*, February 1998.
3. Donaly Brice, who visited the site with researcher Barry Crouch in July 2000, noted the Hardin farm is delineated by four pecan trees, one at each corner of a pasture, and the Hardin home/church/school was in the middle.
4. Mattie H. Smith interview with C. L. Sonnichsen, June 17, 1944.
5. It was here, presumably, that he met Victor Queen, with whom he had a friendship later. Queen was related to Hardin by marriage.
6. One prominent Methodist minister, Anthony Bewley, was hanged in Fort Worth in 1860 on suspicion of provoking slaves to rebel.
7. James G. Hardin bought a slave from his mother's estate for $750 in 1863.
8. See *Brushmen and Vigilantes* for an understanding of politics and atrocities in northeast Texas during the Civil War.
9. Barnett Jones was the son of Hardin's cousin, Martha Jones. Since Hardin claimed kinship to "cousins," the exact genealogical relationship is important.
10. Hardin, pp. 12, 13.
11. Hardin's killings began in 1868; Bill Longley's began about a year earlier. Among parallels in their careers is the fact that Longley shot up a circus. Hardin did too. One can't help but wonder if it weren't the same unfortunate circus.
12. Bill Longley to Milton Mast, October 29, 1877, quoted in Fuller, *Adventures of Bill Longley*.
13. Hardin, pp. 15, 16.
14. Rebecca White interview, May 15, 1978, Hardin file, Gonzales County Records Center and Archives.
15. R.E. Mather, *Scandal of the West*, p. 45, referring to an incident in Hardin's autobiography, p. 16.
16. Texas Ranger T.C. "Pidge" Robinson, in a letter to the *Daily Democratic Statesman*, September 24, 1874.
17. Simp Dixon was killed by soldiers in Limestone County.
18. Hardin, p. 18.
19. Records from the Adjutant General's office, Texas State Archives, indicate the killing of Jim "Smalley" occurred near Marshall, Texas, January 22, 1871.
20. Hardin, p. 33. The irony of this is Hardin gleefully includes his father's statement in his autobiography, revealing himself, therefore, as incapable of understanding the heartache he caused his family.
21. Hardin, p. 15.
22. Hardin, p. 34.
23. Hardin said, "I never had any troubles except in Texas," during an interview with the *Galveston News*, September 3, 1877. Twice he denied killing in Oklahoma and Kansas, yet in his autobiography he proudly details several murders there.
24. One man who knew Hardin at this time said in the *San Antonio Daily Herald*, August 23, 1895, Hardin "had a grudge against a certain fellow in Atchison and saw a man lying in a room whom he thought was his enemy, and Hardin shot the man while the fellow was asleep."
25. Hardin, pp. 62, 63.
26. p. 64.
27. p. 65.
28. pp. 66, 67.
29. pp. 68-70.
30. p. 73.

31. p. 80.

32. p. 82.

33. Obed Mast Christian married Elizabeth Green in Gonzales County, on March 22, 1860. Elizabeth Green was the first cousin, once removed, of Helen Mrose, one of the subjects of this book.

34. Elizabeth Christian, typewritten story in Hardin file, Gonzales County Records Center and Archives. Also Doris Johnston, unpublished manuscript, quotes her, "John Wesley Hardin spent at least two days in their household and saved her and Mrs. Tip Davis from death."

35. J.P. Billings interview, quoted in Parsons, *Bowen and Hardin*, p. 134.

36. Gonzales County Marriage Book "B," p. 364. #1576, lists the marriage of "W. Handen" and Jane Bowen. The license was issued on February 27th, and the marriage was performed on February 29, 1872 (a leap year) by T. F. Rainey.

37. Hardin's purpose isn't known, but a clue may lie in Hobart Huson, p. 195, "Hardin is said to have had relatives at Victoria; and, according to Lyman B. Russell and Mrs. Burmeister, there was a St. Mary's family with whom the desperado was intimate. They state Hardin made several visits to St. Mary's and lived with said family there. He is also said to have gambled in the gambling houses at St. Mary's, Rockport, and Refugio." Judge Rea, quoted in Huson, identified Hardin's St. Mary's friends as the Chambliss family.

38. It's possible Hardin's father revealed his son's hideout to save him from being caught and hanged by a mob. This scenario is outlined in a letter from Mrs. Walter Meyers, Jr. to Chuck Parsons, August 29, 1969.

39. Alan Richmond, *Texas Pistoleros*, date unknown.

40. Jim Taylor was arrested in Austin, Texas, on January 30, 1875, according to *The Austin Daily Democratic Statesman*. He was killed in 1876.

41. Thaddeus H. Swift and his wife Irene were hacked to death by Mexican sheepherders the night of June 8, 1874, about four miles from Refugio. The murders set off a vengeful spree by posses who killed an unknown number of Mexicans, sparking an exodus of thousands of others across the border into Mexico.

42. Hardin's parents moved to Hill County. Of Hill County, Elizabeth Hardin recalled in a letter September 21, 1879, "The people are living a century behind the times."

Chapter 8—The Hellhole of Texas

1. John Wesley Hardin, p. 118, speaking of his arrest in Pensacola, Florida.

2. Dr. Marohn, in his biography of Hardin, was at a loss to explain Lora Edney's role, saying she "was probably a trusted friend."

3. Taylor was probably the man who accompanied Hardin on his visit to the Lemond farm, mentioned in Chapter 1.

4. John H. Swain, January 13, 1853–December 19, 1877, is buried in Smith County.

5. Hardin, p. 111.

6. p. 113.

7. Hardin, p. 125. On the same page, Hardin claims he served twenty-five years for the killing of Webb, an exaggeration, for he served only seventeen years, fifteen of which were at Huntsville. It's surprising, however, how many superficial writers have picked up on this and repeated it in their writings.

8. Convict Record Ledger, p. 212.

9. One unidentified fellow inmate of Huntsville recalled in a *San Antonio Daily Herald* article,

August 23, 1895, that Hardin informed on his co-conspirators. The man also described a beating which Hardin received. After the second crack of the whip Hardin "yelled for mercy and commenced spilling briny tears."

10. Hardin, p. 127.

11. Another man, Charles C. Campbell, wrote a graphic account of a beating. Said Campbell, "The prison laws say that thirty-nine lashes shall be the extreme limit of punishment for any offense; also that convicts shall not be struck above the belt, and yet that old cock-eyed reprobate of hell stood there and hit me at least sixty lashes from my neck to the bend of my knees, all the time cursing me in the vilest manner and calling me all the most diabolical names which he could conjure up. [...] The law forbids the skin being broken on a prisoner in whipping, but after that unspeakable monster finally let up on me my entire body and legs were saturated with my own blood, and for two weeks I lay on my face unable to turn over."

12. T. U. Taylor described being taken as a boy to view "outlaw row"—an unusual treat, *Frontier Times*, August 1925.

13. Sallie Campbell is mentioned in a letter from Hardin to his wife, March 14, 1878; Hardin names her brother as George Campbell of Sumpter.

14. Prison Conduct Register, Prisoner #7109, p. 212.

15. J. W. Hardin to Jane Hardin, June 3, 1881.

16. *Beeville Bee*, January 3, 1891.

17. She is buried at Asher Cemetery near Mound City, Texas.

18. For an account of Jane Hardin's life while her husband was in prison, see the *El Paso Herald*, August 30, 1895.

19. See Barry Crouch.

20. *The Mason County News*, February 24, 1894.

21. Marjorie Burnett Parsons, "The One That Got Away," *Gonzales County, Texas, Marriage Licenses Issued, 1829–1900* and Louis Nordyke, *John Wesley Hardin: Texas Gunman*, p. 127-8. The story is undoubtedly true. It was so much like Hardin to forgive the old blacksmith and declare friendship, but there is no mention how Lackey felt, a man who had had a friend shot to death by Hardin and then suffered a debilitating facial wound himself before being forced to flee and hide in a lake. Perhaps Lackey did forgive Hardin, but the story tells much about Hardin. He probably walked away from the encounter chuckling over his sportsmanship, and he thought enough of the incident to include it in his autobiography. It must be noted, however, that Hardin's visit with Lackey may have been the result of ulterior motives. In the contested sheriff's race in Gonzales County, Hardin's enemy, Bill Jones, may have solicited Lackey's support as one of Hardin's victims and as a black businessman. See a letter, John Wesley Hardin to Jim Clements, October 4, 1894. For more information, see the author's article "A Shooting—Much Exaggerated."

22. Jo Foster, unpublished 1986 genealogy of her family.

23. Unknown author, in the Hardin file, Gonzales County Archives. It was the custom to leave an empty chamber under the hammer of a loaded gun. Only five cylinders would be loaded; therefore, if Hardin shot eight times, he left himself two loaded chambers.

24. Letter to Jim Clements, October 4, 1894.

25. The date comes from a January 14, 1895 letter and bill from A.O. Hamon to John Wesley Hardin about an overdue bill "up to the time you left."

26. Jennie Hardin, who married John Ross Lyons, had no children. Hardin's other children had offspring, but none of Wesley, Jr.'s had descendants so John Wesley Hardin's paternal genealogical line is now dead. Mollie Hardin, who married Charles Billings, had twelve

children, so all descendants of John Wesley Hardin are through the Billings line. One of these was Edith Billings (1898–1958) who married Elmer Spellman. Edith inherited letters and other effects. Elmer Spellman had the letters photostated at the University of Texas; later his son donated most of the originals to Texas State University, where they form the bulk of the Hardin Collection. The photostat collection at the University of Texas (the Hardin Papers) is more complete, but both collections are invaluable resources used by researchers today. Transcriptions of many of these letters are to be found in *The Letters of John Wesley Hardin* by Roy and Jo Ann Stamps.

Chapter 9—The Flirt

1. Callie Lewis's father, in a letter to Hardin dated March 4, 1895.
2. Hardin may have made inquiries about starting a law office in San Angelo. See *The Dallas Morning News*, December 19, 1894.
3. Bill of Sale, E.F. Schlickeisen to John Wesley Hardin, August 10, 1894, an eight-year-old buckskin horse for $25 legal fees; and letter, Ferdy Bishop to Hardin, April 14, 1894 in answer to Hardin's inquiries about selling horses in Polk County. Hardin also accepted a new wagon, a team, and another saddle horse in trade for legal services in October 1894.
4. At Noxville, about where Highway 479 crosses the James River, Creed Taylor and his family settled in the Blue Mountains after the unpleasantness of the Sutton-Taylor Feud and the HooDoo War. Twelve miles north, across the Llano River, was London, home of Callie Lewis. Hardin's younger brother, Jeff, was close to Creed Taylor and his family. In 1897, he married May Taylor, Creed's daughter.
5. London was named after the hometown of the Pearl family, according to *Families of Kimble County*, p. 234, but the author feels it was named after Lewis. The problem comes from Lewis' inconsistency. Sometimes he called himself Lon or Lem, he applied for a homestead in Montana as Londin L. Lewis, and he told census takers he was Lemuel L. Lewis. His poor handwriting has given us a variant "Len," and still the confusion goes on. Sometimes he called himself "Captain," and other times "Major." In short, he must have been what Texans call "a pill," and the best guess is his name was Lemuel Londin Lewis.
6. *Families of Kimble County*, p. 234.
7. Callie's headstone lists her birth as July 23, 1882. This is wrong. Callie was actually born July 23, 1879, making her fifteen years old at the time she met Hardin.
8. Hardin Papers, University of Texas.
9. Hardin Papers. Though there have been rumors Hardin "won" Callie in a card game with her father, the author feels correspondence between Callie and Hardin shows the relationship was based on Callie's flirtatiousness and not a deal between her father and Hardin.
10. Marriage License, Kimble County, Texas, January 8, recorded January 12, 1895.
11. This story is common in Mason and Kimble counties today. On page 451 of *Families of Kimble County*, Jo Foster, who did a commendable job collecting information and stories on the Hardins, says it was Gip who prepared the woodshed, " ... about 6x8 feet ... all it would hold was a bed." The author, however, is of the opinion it was Jeff Hardin who prepared the woodshed.
12. Hardin's first wife was also fifteen when he married her.
13. Note January 18, 1895, in the Hardin Collection.
14. The author has taken liberties with the Lewises' letters in this chapter. Their spelling, grammar, and punctuation would interrupt the flow of the narrative. For the most part, the author has

corrected these mistakes, except where they are most charming.

15. Stella Gipson Polk, "The Saga of John Wesley Hardin," *The Cattleman*, p. 188.
16. Anonymous #2. Two other long-time residents of Mason County who knew Callie Lewis in later years have quoted the figure of one month. Ruth Jo Martin told the author that it was "exactly one month." Jane Hoerster, in a conversation, said she was sure it was "about a month." Finally, Anonymous #2 expounded on her comments two years later when she said, "I knew [Callie Lewis] quite well, you know, and we *never* talked about it. But one day, in passing, [she] mentioned her second marriage. Oh, I didn't say anything! And she said, 'You know, I was married once before, but only for a month.' And again I didn't say anything. [It's] the reason we remained friends for so long, you see." Finally, a letter from Callie's sister Annie, dated February 4, 1895, is playfully addressed to "Mr. Hardin and friend," about a month after their marriage.
17. Barry Crouch, "That Good Citizens Ask It." The wounds were also mentioned in detail in the August 20, 1895, *El Paso Daily Times*.
18. Strangely, the author ruined his left arm in a fall while researching this book. He now shares this unique feature with John Wesley Hardin, Dave Kemp, and Annie Londonderry, and to some extent, he shares a loss of mobility with Jesse Rascoe too; historian Betty Dorsett Duke has the same ruined arm, somewhat matching one of her subjects, Zerelda James. Do historians have to pay for being close to our subjects? It's cause for speculation for those historians who follow....
19. Hardin Papers.
20. Hardin Collection, op. cit.
21. ibid.
22. Hardin Papers.

Chapter 10—The Trouble in Pecos

1. Jim Miller, in a telegram urging Hardin to come to Pecos.
2. Glenn Shirley says in his biography of Miller, "In 1874, when he was eight, his grandfather and grandmother were found murdered in their home at Evant. Jim was arrested for this double slaying, but never prosecuted."
3. In 18 Texas Court of Appeals 232, there are over thirty pages of testimony in this case.
4. Mrs. Kimbrough interview with C.L. Sonnichsen, August 14, 1946.
5. John McEwan Formwalt, born in Mississippi in 1848 and died in 1928 in Granbury, Texas, was from a family of Texas pioneers. Formwalt was the first sheriff of Runnels County, serving from February 16, 1880 until November 4, 1890.
6. *The Ballinger Eagle*, April 2, 1887.
7. Undated clipping in vertical files at El Paso Library, probably from a 1924 *El Paso Times*, gives an unflattering and inaccurate account of Frazer and the election of 1894. The article is significant, though, for it shows the election was a referendum on Frazer.
8. See Ellis Lindsey and Gene Riggs' *Barney Riggs*.
9. *El Paso Daily Herald*, April 11, 1895.
10. The *Eddy Argus*, April 13, 1894.
11. *El Paso Daily Herald*, April 11, 1895.
12. Dr. Marohn got the chronology wrong. He wrote the shooting of Miller was in retaliation for the shooting of Gibson.
13. Hardin Collection.

14. Mrs. Kimbrough interview with C.L. Sonnichsen, August 14, 1946.

15. Hardin Papers.

16. The Queen family called him Victor. In newspaper accounts he was "Vic." The author decided it was a formerly well-understood joke. Nearly every newspaper of the era was full of gossip about the royalty of Europe, there being, of course, few celebrities. Among the more popular subjects of discussion was "Queen Vic," or Queen Victoria of England. Reversed, "Vic" Queen may have been a playful jab at a well-liked Eddy County cowboy.

17. Smith and Denson were first cousins. Since Denson was Hardin's first cousin, once removed, that meant Smith was only slightly related to Hardin—but in Hardin's mind, that was enough to call on someone for favors.

18. Helen, it will be remembered, was a two-year-old child at the Lemond home in Berry Creek the night Hardin and Jim Taylor sought refuge after killing Deputy Sheriff Charlie Webb.

19. Hardin, p. 130.

20. Pardon applications, certificate of prison conduct, and other documents, Texas State Archives. Among these is a telegram mentioning Kemp's information to authorities before his release.

21. Letter D.L. Kemp to John Wesley Hardin, Hardin Collection.

22. Robert J. Casey, p. 323.

23. Though the author has been unable to establish a familial connection with Dave Kemp, well-known El Paso attorney Maury Kemp was Frazer's attorney and the judge was Wyndham Kemp.

24. Dated June 2, 1895, the original is at Texas State University. The author has corrected Miller's spelling and punctuation.

Chapter 11—The Desperadoes

1. Eva Pendleton Henderson, *Wild Horses*, p. 16. In a later interview in *Eddy County New Mexico to 1981*, Eva, whose uncle was Lon Bass, expanded on the doll story.

2. *The Eddy Current*, March 13, 1895.

3. Harkey, p. 114.

4. *The Eddy Argus*, May 12, 1893.

5. Report of the Eddy County Grand Jury, published in *The Pecos Valley Argus*, November 23, 1894.

6. See *The Eddy Argus*, September 24, 1897, when U.R. Christmas was sentenced to three years in prison, and the October 15, 1897, edition that says the case was the very first conviction for cattle stealing. Dee Harkey exaggerated this incident so badly he named the wrong cattleman. Unlike most of the others Harkey lied about in his book, this one was still alive when the book was published, and he sued Harkey into poverty.

7. Cicero Stewart interview with Louis Blachly, December 20, 1953.

8. Kate Blau interview with the author, March 12, 2000.

9. Judge Charles R. Brice of the New Mexico State Supreme Court, a friend of Harkey's, was solicited to write a foreword to Harkey's book to add credibility. He was deeply hurt when the book was proven to be lies. The only published source of how Brice felt about Harkey is in Cecil Bonney's book, pp. 156-7, "[T]hat box is filled with promissory notes which Dee Harkey has given me over the years. And the whole batch is not worth ten cents. I am going to destroy them one of these days. I do not want to die and have my wife and others know what a damned fool I have been."

10. Harkey's granddaughter in letters and conversation with author.

11. *Criminal Docket Book A, Eddy County, Fifth Judicial District Court*, case #125, November Term, 1894. The warrant was served on Mrose by outgoing sheriff Dave Kemp on November 17, 1894. Mrose pleaded not guilty and was ordered to appear at the February 1895 term. The case was dismissed in April. Strangely, Marohn says on p. 222, "A warrant was issued for [Mrose's] arrest but Sheriff David L. Kemp could not find him in Eddy County."

12. Although Mrose sold his ranch in Eddy County, he did not do the same with the land he had just "proved" under the Desert Land Act.

13. Final Proof Affidavit for Martin Mrose dated April 25, 1894.

14. *El Paso Daily Herald*, July 9, 1895.

15. A possible document of the Edmunds Act witchhunt is improbably included in the Hardin papers documenting the marriage of Trinidad Fuentes and Manuela Rodriguez in Mexico.

16. Undated letter, J.F. Cunningham to J. M. Daugherty, Center for American History, Austin.

17. Bob Beverly interview with J. Evetts Haley, June 22, 1937. The *1991 Brand Book of the State of New Mexico* does not list either the Seven Ladders or the 4X in use today.

18. Todd Barber was related to Helen. Born in Caldwell County, Barber moved with his family to Williamson County and then to San Saba County, just north of the Jennings homestead at Fredonia. Until Barber's death in 1919, he was a frequent visitor to San Saba County and knew the Jenningses.

19. Ivy Cass vs. Laura A. Collier *et.al*, case #60. Another civil suit naming Mrose was a disagreement over a promissory note by Francis G. Tracy against Fred Peitz and Martin Mrose. This suit was dismissed at the expense of Tracy.

20. Eddy County Record of Marks and Brands, N.M. State Archives.

21. Stem Daugherty interview with J. Evetts Haley, February 29, 1944.

22. *The Eddy Argus*, June 23, 1893.

23. *The Eddy Current* of March 20, 1895 reported he had sold his stock to W.J. Barber and taken the outgoing train. This is wrong, but may be evidence Helen took the train.

24. Fifth Judicial District Court, case #154, Eddy County. The appearance bond is signed by Martin Mrose and is one of the better examples of his signature, of which more is said in Appendix Two.

25. William E. Bass married Susan Iona Chism, a descendant of the great cattleman, Jesse Chism, in San Patricio County, Texas, in 1872. They moved to New Mexico in the 1880s and by 1895, they ranched north of Eddy. San Patricio and Refugio counties were tightly knit Irish settlements along the Texas coast. The Fennessey family was prominent in both counties, so it is not unreasonable to suppose Tom Fennessey knew William Bass and may have brought him to New Mexico.

26. Eva Henderson, p. 16.

27. Such dolls were in vogue. With ceramic heads and hands, the dolls were a marvel: lie the doll on its back and its eyes would close, hence the name "Sleepy Doll." Most were made in France or Germany. They were expensive in 1895, and they are expensive collectors items today.

28. Curiously, in her teenage years, Eva Bass had a gelding named "Red Bird." Whether this was a common name at the time is unknown, but the horse Martin Mrose rode in Atascosa County, Texas, in 1880-or so Dee Harkey claimed-was also named Red Bird.

29. Named for his grandfather, John Stemler Daugherty, he was nicknamed "Stem." Born in Denton, Texas, in 1869, he worked in west Texas as a cowboy, rancher, and justice of the peace. He was an example of a pioneer with one foot on either side of the law. He claimed

in a 1944 interview, "Frank Jackson, of the Bass Gang, used to work for us. [He] was not a cowboy." Stem's friendship with other outlaws is well known.

30. Stem Daugherty, February 29, 1944.
31. Midland County, Texas, Bills of Sale, Book 2, page 7.
32. *El Paso Daily Herald*, May 7, 1895.
33. *The Eddy Current*, March 23, 1895.
34. The only historical source for a reward from the Live Stock Protective Association was in *The El Paso Daily Times*, April 12, 1895, "A reward of $1,000 is offered [...] and $250 by his bondsmen."
35. *ibid.* "It seems that the accused had formerly been useful to J. M. McKenzie, charged with cattle stealing. Mrose had testified to selling the cattle to McKenzie, which he [McKenzie] had been accused of stealing. When Mrose left Midland, it was on a gray horse belonging to one of the McKenzies."
36. The El Paso newspapers routinely recorded the movements of law officers and other bounty hunters throughout the region. In the next three months, every one of these dangerous men put in an appearance, seeking a way to get Martin Mrose.
37. *El Paso Daily Herald*, July 1, 1895. Helen was interviewed only reluctantly, and the reporter says he had to use "considerable persuasion" to get her to talk.
38. Helen Bond Melton, in conversation with the author in 1998.
39. Certainly, he didn't steal a horse from his friend Dave Kemp. In a time of suspicion, Kemp wouldn't have wanted to be accused of aiding and abetting a fugitive. Most probably, he reported the horse stolen to cover himself. No charges were ever filed over the "stolen horse."
40. A former resident of Carlsbad, Mrs. E. Delaney, gave exactly the same quote in a conversation with the author, except for the word "sons-a-bitches" at the end. Interestingly, though Mrose was well known in Eddy and had been mentioned in the newspapers many times before, from this time on, his name was misspelled in Eddy papers. Was this in response to his threat?
41. C.B. Goforth, in a letter to the author. In a later conversation in El Paso, he was hazier on details, but did state his grandfather believed Sheriff Walker never wanted to see Mrose arrested.
42. *El Paso Daily Herald*, May 7, 1895.

Chapter 12—Beauregard Lee

1. Beauregard Lee, quoted in *El Paso Daily Herald*, August 9, 1895.
2. Beauregard Lee's age is listed on the 1900 census, Colfax County, New Mexico as 31.
3. Ironically, this was an area Mrose knew well, for the VVNs' cattle trail through Trinchera Pass crossed the area on its way to Walsenburg, Colorado.
4. Their move to town may have had something to do with the *Gorras Blancas*, or White Caps, a Hispanic vigilante group that focused on fence-cutting to protest such large enclosures of land as the Maxwell Land Grant.
5. Today, it's 632 S. 2nd, a change necessitated by a brick building housing shops that block the front of the Victorian home.
6. Email to the author from Beauregard Lee II, June 26, 2000.
7. Beauregard Lee II and his wife Sue remember a photograph of Beauregard Lee wearing a sombrero. Sue told the author, "He was a very handsome man." The photograph, apparently, has since been lost.

8. Probably her stockings or hose, which indicates, for the time, a pretty thorough—and questionable—search.

9. *El Paso Daily Herald*, August 9, 1895.

10. *El Paso Daily Times*, April 12, 1895.

11. Published timetable from 1890. Whether trains improved their speed from an average 20 mph in the intervening five years is doubtful, and, in fact, it was probably worse, for the El Paso papers often mentioned the Mexican trains were "delayed" due to wash-outs and other problems

12. Laura never mentioned Mrose's arrest later in life. At the same time, she discouraged questions about her childhood in deference to "what her father would say." We are left to wonder if she even remembered Martin Mrose, instead confusing him in her childhood memories with her father, Steve Jennings. The flight from posses, the trauma of the arrest, the confusing and troublesome appearance of lawmen trying to make deals with her mother in a Mexican hotel, all became, in her youthful mind, part of a vague, undefined scandal, and she protected this scandal the rest of her life.

13. The two accounts differ as to where the revolver was hidden. Helen Beulah, however, has come to be such a symbol of sexual abandon and desire, that the author—and others—see her pulling it from her bosom rather than from the train seat. Nevertheless, the mechanics of that trick challenge the imagination. Helen was known, later, to pull a pistol concealed in a secret pocket in her dress. The pistol she pulled in Mexico was probably hidden in similar fashion, somewhere just below her breasts.

14. Harkey, *Mean as Hell*, p. 132.

15. As a constable, Harkey had to submit a detailed list of arrests in what was called a "warrant," or an accounting sheet. Though an April warrant doesn't seem to have survived, his search for the fugitive Martin Mrose would have taken place in March 1895. Significantly, in Harkey's Warrant #596, Eddy County record #864, submitted for that month, a warrant which was reviewed and approved by county officials, there is not a single listing of any expenses involving Martin Mrose or Victor Queen.

16. Mexican authorities may have jailed Queen as early as March 26th.

17. *The Silver City Enterprise*, December 16, 1904.

18. *Juzgado,* Spanish meaning a panel of judges, a courtroom, or a jail, gives us the English "hoosegow."

19. Helen Mrose, quoted in the *El Paso Daily Herald,* July 1, 1895.

20. The author has spoken with the Mexican consulate in Austin, Texas, and with the Mexican Attorney General's office in Mexico City about the arrest. Even in pre-Revolutionary Mexico the arrest was highly irregular. Chief Haro was out of his jurisdiction, and a messy arrest on a train would have attracted local police. The only legitimacy the arrest had was through Beauregard Lee, a railroad detective, on railroad property.

21. Dr. Marohn, in his biography of Hardin, in note #24, p. 232, quotes an article, "Mrose and His Money, They Cause Contention in Old and New Mexico, Tom Fennessey's Narrow Escape," *Pecos Valley Weekly Argus*, April 26, 1895." The author has been unable to locate this article. *The Pecos Valley Daily Argus* does not contain any article with this title. What Dr. Marohn had discovered, therefore, remains a mystery.

22. The Mexicans were circumspect about the money. The status of the arrest, legal or illegal, obviously worried the officials. A receipt was issued, the money was deposited in a safe manner, and mentions of it made in all the files.

23. After being released from jail, why did Victor Queen wait so long to come back across the border to face the music in New Mexico? Also, in the two weeks Mrose was in Mexico

before his arrest, what was he doing? The author's theory is Mrose was shopping for a ranch somewhere in Chihuahua. Say he bought one … what would have happened to the ranch after his arrest? Fennessey and Queen would have known about it. It's possible one or both of these men tried to gain control of the ranch in order to sell it. Did they succeed? A Mexican historian working through the property records of the state of Chihuahua should be able to find records.

24. Copy in author's files. Another document, a letter from the Mexican Secretary of State, says, in part, "This Secretariat told the Governor [of Chihuahua] on April 18th to order the return of the money to Mrs. Bulna [sic] Mrose which he had taken from her." So, Helen was without her money for a period of about twelve days.

25. Laura was confused in several key details in her story, recalled ninety years after they occurred. This point, the hair-cutting and dressing as a little boy, is among the most troubling. Laura believed her hair was cut specifically because she was meeting John Wesley Hardin, an attorney, over trouble her mother was having with her father. The author has come to believe Laura confused the timing of the event in the overall sequence of her story. This is most evident in the fact Laura never mentioned Mrose, a man who doted on her from the moment he met her.

The hair-cutting incident is significant for historians due to the fact Helen had a photograph taken of her daughter and herself. During the last fifty years, the photograph has been the basis of speculation Helen's child was a boy named "Albert." The author has an original of the photograph, inscribed on the back "Aunt Hellen and Laura Jennings."

26. See author's article "Broken Heart, Broken Dreams."

Chapter 13—The Hoosegow

1. Martin Mrose and Victor Queen in a letter to President Porfirio Diaz of Mexico.
2. The *Eddy Current*, April 27, 1895, reported District Attorney Franklin was in Juarez to advise Sheriff J.D. Walker on the extradition of Mrose. The *El Paso Daily Herald* of April 29 reported Mrose and Queen would stay in jail 30 days longer, having applied for naturalization, and the May 3rd *El Paso Daily Herald* claimed the *habeus corpus* application by Mrose and Queen had been refused.
3. *El Paso Daily Herald*, May 30, 1895.
4. Mexico changed the city's name in 1888 to honor Benito Juarez, whose headquarters were in that city during the struggle against Emperor Maximilian.
5. Despatches from United States Consuls at Ciudad de Juarez (Paso del Norte) 1871–1906, in the Benson Collection.
6. Letter from Consul A.J. Sampson to Assistant Secretary of State William F. Wharton, October 31, 1891.
7. ibid.
8. ibid.
9. ibid, April 28, 1890, decrying the meager rations (6 tacos a day) of American prisoners in the Juarez jail. The Consul General at Nuevo Laredo added at the bottom of the letter, "I can state from my own observation that the same conditions obtain in all the prisons in northern Mexico."
10. Petition of P.O. Saunders to the U.S. Consul at Monterey, Mexico, October 8, 1895. During his confinement, he said his diet consisted of "coffee and cold bread for breakfast, tortillas and soup for dinner, tortillas, coffee, and beans for supper."

11. Correspondence contained within the dispatches of the consul at Juarez in October 1891.
12. There are two requisition entries in Governor Thornton's papers, but unfortunately the whole series of legal papers from Thornton's term from 1893 until July 1896 are missing, including Mrose's and Queen's extradition requisitions.
13. Larry D. Ball, *Desert Lawmen*, pp. 219-20.
14. *El Paso Daily Herald*, June 3, 1895.
15. A second reason for seeking legal help at this time may have been to settle affairs with Steve Jennings, back in Fredonia, Texas. Laura Jennings once said Helen Mrose's purpose in seeking out Hardin was for help against Laura's father.
16. Mrose's translator—and possibly his attorney—was Sebastian Vargas, and his letter to the President of Mexico is, in the opinion of translator Dr. Debra Shipman, amateurish and riddled with grammatical errors.
17. The *Times* use of "a stranger in town" may not have been entirely the choice of the editors. It has long been seen as a way the newspapers insulted Hardin, but the reality may be different. Said the editor of the *Times* on August 8th, "People who want to see their opinions in print should not object to allowing the reporter to use their names. Names are the real meat of a news item, and a man should always be manly enough to speak out in meeting and let people know where he stands." The *Weekly Phoenix Herald* may have cleared up this mystery forever, when, in an article based on an interview with Hardin, it said, "[T]he name of the party is suppressed for the reason that he is now a quiet and law-abiding citizen and is sensitive of notoriety."
18. Ann Carroll, *El Paso Herald-Post*, November 27, 1973.
19. Harkey, p. 94.
20. Harkey, pp. 94-5
21. *The Gonzales Inquirer*, June 6, 1895.
22. Gladden first met Hardin in the Travis County Jail in Austin, Texas, while Hardin was being held for trial, and, later, while he awaited word on his appeal.
23. El Paso County Memoranda of Court Cases, Volume 2, p. 17.
24. *The El Paso Daily Herald*, May 25, 1895. The two parts of the quotation are in reverse order for narrative reasons.
25. *El Paso Daily Times*, November 18, 1896.
26. George Scarborough married Mollie McMahan of McCulloch County, Texas, on August, 30, 1877. Her brother, Frank, would marry Alice Hunter, J. Marvin Hunter's sister, in El Paso on September 2, 1895.
27. The spelling of Outlaw's first name is controversial. The author has decided to spell it "Baz" based on Robert W. Stephens' discussion of the spelling in *Bullets and Buckshot in Texas*, p. 33 and 34.
28. *The Gonzales Inquirer*, August 22, 1895.
29. Joe Parrish, p. 81.
30. W.D. Allison to John Wesley Hardin, Hardin Collection.
31. *The Arizona Daily Citizen*, June 19, 1895, p. 4. The *El Paso Daily Times*, June 17, 1895, gives additional details. Mart Hardin was alighting from a buggy when the pistol fell from his pocket. It is important to remind the reader at this point that holsters as we know them were not common. Pockets and belts were as likely to contain pistols as holsters and gunbelts. The bullet that struck Mart Hardin entered under the right shoulder blade, passing through the "thoracic activity," and lodged in the muscles of the neck. Mart Hardin shot himself on June 15th. According to the *Western Liberal* newspapers of the 21st and 28th of June, plus

July 12th, John Wesley Hardin and Helen Beulah Mrose, as luck would have it, were in Lordsburg on their way back from Arizona, and they took the wounded Mart Hardin to El Paso for treatment.

32. Letter, Victor Queen and Martin Mrose to President Porfirio Diaz, June 5, 1895

33. Article 19 says, "No one's detainment may exceed 3 full days without the justification of a writ or order giving a cause for imprisonment.... All mistreatment in arrests or within prisons, all annoyances that are inferred without legal motive, all taxes and *contributions to the prisons* [author's emphasis] – are abuses that the laws must correct and the authorities punish severely."

Article 20, finalized in the Law of December 14, 1882, and also cited in the letter, says in Part Two, "In all criminal justice, the accused has the following guarantees: "That the depositions must be taken inside of/within 48 hours, to be counted from [the time of] the order or decree of the judge."

34. This political officer was Jesus Najera, the "Political Chief of Bravos," about whom Mrose and Queen bitterly complained in a telegram on June 7th, "We are prisoners through his fault alone."

35. Letter from Jesus Najera to the Mexican Supreme Court, May 24, 1895.

36. By this time Queen was tied to Mrose as an "accomplice."

37. The author experienced a prized bull that disappeared on a leased property. Though he looked everywhere for sign, it was two years before he found the bull's bones in a thicket of "Devil's shoelaces," where it had become entangled and died—only seventy-five yards from the gate. Another time, a favorite horse disappeared on a cultivated pasture, and it was a year before the author found its bones only two hundred yards from a busy feedlot.

38. District Judge Jesus Najera op. cit., May 24, 1895.

39. Najera, *op.cit.*

40. There were no requisitions issued for either man from the State of Texas. Most likely, the confusion among Mexican authorities was caused by the fact that New Mexican officers were scarce during the extradition proceedings, but nearly a dozen prominent Texas lawmen were interested in Mrose's return to American soil.

41. The decision was written in the form of an order from the Mexican Supreme Court dated June 6, 1895.

42. *The El Paso Daily Times*, April 24, 1895.

43. This unknown friend may have been quoted in a *San Antonio Daily Herald* article, August 23, 1895. He said, "I was in Mexico one night with him when a policeman started to arrest Hardin for carrying a gun. The policeman made a break for his gun, but he didn't have time to pull it. Hardin hit the Mexican in the face and then pulling his gun told the Greaser to get out of town...."

44. The Eddy Current, April 27, 1895. Another account of this encounter was given by W.H. Burges to J. Evetts Haley fifty years later. It is badly flawed and not taken into account here.

45. About two weeks after this incident in Juarez, Milton suffered the embarrassment of having his effects garnished for nonpayment of bills. See *The El Paso Daily Herald*, May 7, 1895.

46. See *The El Paso Daily Herald*, June 6, 1895. Two "ifs" the author will pose to the reader: if John Wesley Hardin was firmly in Martin Mrose's employ after all; and if Hardin had anything to do with the Mexican legal maneuvering or sought the help of Sebastian Vargas, then the non-extradition of Martin Mrose and his release from a Mexican jail were Hardin's greatest legal triumphs. This may mean Hardin was a better lawyer than anyone has figured.

47. *The El Paso Daily Herald*, July 1, 1895.

48. The Mexican Supreme Court decision and the case files of Martin Mrose and Victor Queen are contained in the Archives of the Mexican Supreme Court, Institute of Federal Justice, Mexico City, D.F., in Box 362, file 12 (2nd Part), exp. 914, and Box 361, file 10, exp. 839. The author wishes to acknowledge the generous help of Miguel Bonilla Lopez, Secretario General del Instituto de la Judicatura Federal, and Carlos Baez Silva, Licenciado, who assisted him in gaining access to these important case files.

49. Letter, Jesus Najera to the Mexican Supreme Court, June 7, 1895, included in the case files of Martin Mrose and Victor Queen.

50. Sheriff J.D. Walker returned to Eddy soon after Mrose and Queen's release. He told *The Eddy Current* (June 13, 1895) the men had been released because 1.) The evidence was insufficient to convict, 2.) Governor Thornton had failed to certify the official before whom the papers were sworn was qualified, 3.) The Mexican consul at El Paso had been by-passed and didn't sign the papers, and 4.) Mrose and Queen were "citizens of Mexico." Said the newspaper, "Mrose may now walk the soil of Mexico a free man, but the business has cost him dear. When he went to Juarez he possessed $3,400 in American certificates of deposit and drafts. When he was turned loose he was a 'busted community.' His woman is said to have flown with a better looking man and refuses to have anything to do with Martin."

51. As the reader will soon see, Helen Beulah was not in El Paso at the time Mrose was released and did not return to the city until June 16. By then, events were developing quickly. One account, however, in the *Western Liberal* of June 21, 1895, theorized Mrose was released because of bribes paid by "a woman who was deeply interested in Mrose."

52. And what happened to Mrose's money? Dr. Debra Shipman, who worked through the Mexican Supreme Court documents at great length, said, "No mention in any of the documents about money on Mrose, only 1800 taken from his wife." Since Mrose's money was not referred to at the time of his arrest, that means he had gotten rid of it sometime between his crossing of the Rio Grande River and his arrest. After being released from jail, Mrose made at least one trip out of Juarez. The author believes this means Mrose had a ranch in the state of Chihuahua.

53. Though mentioned in period newspapers, only Louis Nordyke picked up on the fact so many men gathered in support of Mrose. Since they were not under suspicion or indictment, they freely crossed into El Paso to report developments.

54. It was at this time that Martin Mrose and Tom Fennessey posed for a photograph together. Fennessey's defiant look and the curious bulges under Mrose's jacket are indications of their resolve.

Chapter 14—The Woman and The Gunfighter

1. Teddy Blue, *We Pointed Them North*, p. 48.
2. The famous photograph, Mrs. McRose and Kid, taken about this time, does NOT show Helen at her best, but rather, at her worst. She was worried, hadn't eaten or slept well in a month, and was afraid of what was happening with Martin Mrose in jail and what might happen if Steve Jennings caught wind of her being back in Texas. Modern writers have commented the picture shows a plain young woman; historical accounts are unanimous she was a great beauty.
3. Owen P. White, *Lead and Likker*, pp. 7- 8.
4. This is one of the great Freudian slips of the Old West. Of course, he meant "all right."
5. John Selman, Jr., "Young John" manuscript, p. 114.

6. Edna S. Haines, "John Selman of El Paso" manuscript, p. 96.
7. Cunningham, *Triggernometry*, p. 60; Haley, *Jeff Milton*, p. 232; Robert J. Casey, *The Texas Border and Some Borderliners*, p. 325; and Sonnichsen, *Pass of the North*, p. 321.
8. Haines, p. 124.
9. John Marion Selman, manuscript "Young John," p. 113.
10. *El Paso Daily Herald*, May 13, 1895.
11. Robert J. Casey, p. 325. Elsewhere in his book, *The Texas Border*, Casey calls Helen, "the beautiful blonde relict," "the lovely blonde," and "a handsome woman."
12. Most observers remembered them as dark blue.
13. Edna S. Haines, "John Selman of El Paso" manuscript, p. 95.
14. Hardin, p. 104.
15. *Arizona Gazette*, February 24, 1895.
16. *The Arizona Daily Gazette*, May 9, 1895.
17. *The Arizona Daily Gazette* of July 17, 1895 says, "Last September there were about 1500 persons living on the [Gila] Bend. In singles, pairs, and families they have moved away until there is but a handful remaining. The outlook for the city is not very flattering unless the dam litigation ceases and gives place to repair." By the fall of 1895, Bill Williams was finished in the Gila Bend. He and his wife returned to Williamson County, Texas. Lon Williams, Helen's brother, continued farming alfalfa at Gila Bend until the early part of the twentieth century, hauling hay to his dairy at Cartwright. Lon Williams may have had a small home at Gila Bend. In later years, his children recalled playing with Native American children from the nearby reservation. About 1907, Lon Williams sold out and moved to Fowler, California.
18. An approximate date can be given for Bill Williams' trip to El Paso. On the May 18th "Letter List," a list of names of those receiving mail like today's General Delivery, the *El Paso Daily Herald* lists W.C. Williams as having received a letter.

Chapter 15—The Saloons

1. The name of the saloon where George Scarborough killed A.J. Williams, Helen Mrose's uncle on October 3, 1887.
2. Refrigerators were selling well. See the *El Paso Daily Herald*, April 8, 1895.
3. Stroke, kidney disease, congestive heart failure; pulmonary tuberculosis, tuberculosis of the spinal column, tuberculosis of the neck lymph nodes; childbirth, smallpox, and influenza, respectively.
4. John Selman, Jr., manuscript, p. 113.
5. *El Paso Daily Herald*, May 4, 1895. On page two, the *Herald* adds, "John Wesley Hardin, who the *Tribune* named as the 'stranger' of the *Times* and the 'visitor' of the *Herald's* account, [...] does not deny making a gun play at the Gem, but stated that the *Herald's* report of the affair was wrong in so far as we stated that when he demanded his money, everybody left the room but himself and the dealer. He states that several gentlemen stayed in the room."
6. *Cameron Herald*, May 2, 1895.
7. ibid. In the bill of sale, Hardin paid a thousand dollars for a share in the Wigwam, plus a half interest in his as-yet-to-be-published autobiography. As you shall soon see, he also gave Helen Beulah a half-interest—leaving him nothing of his own manuscript.
8. Major Burgess.
9. *El Paso Daily Herald*, May 6, 1895, p. 1.
10. See the *Western Liberal*, May 31, 1895, for a long article on Milton's financial troubles.

11. ibid, May 16, 1895. Jones' comment about Justice Howe was especially embarrassing, for Howe was a law-and-order justice against gambling.

12. *El Paso Daily Times*, July 4, 1895.

13. *El Paso Daily Times*, June 30, 1895.

14. *El Paso Daily Herald*, July 2, 1895.

15. Joe Parrish, pp. 76, 77.

16. *El Paso Evening Telegraph*, April 8, 1896.

17. *El Paso Times,* August 11, 1895.

18. Letter, R.M. Glover to John Wesley Hardin, May 18, 1895.

Chapter 16—The Note to Albert

1. Helen Beulah Mrose, The Terrassas Injunction, Hardin Collection.

2. *Eddy County Marriages*, book 1A, p. 11 and Brides's Index.

3. The Terrassas Injunction is a curious documentation of a hypocrisy that characterized Hardin's actions after his release from prison. In jail he paid lip service to the idea of family; when released, he pushed family away at every opportunity. He did it with his children; he did it with his cousins in Kimble County, and he did it with Jim Miller. Another example is with Bill Smith, a relative who had assisted in the negotiations over Denson's bail in Phenix. Smith had written Hardin and probably hosted him when he arrived in Eddy County. Smith may have introduced him to Martin Mrose, Victor Queen, Dave Kemp, and even Helen Beulah. Hardin's thanks was this injunction to prevent Smith and his woman from bringing her daughter to their home in Phenix.

4. The divorce between Augustin Terrassas and his wife Eulalia was granted May 29, 1895. Custody of the girl named in the so-called Terrassas Injunction, ten-year-old Eulalia, was granted to her father. Another daughter, Carlota, was a bit older, and she chose to be under the custody of her uncle, rather than accompany her mother to New Mexico. The *El Paso Daily Times* of May 30, 1895 gives a good description of the divorce/wedding. The *El Paso Daily Herald* said, "It appears that Smith had married Señora Terrazas not knowing her husband was living, and when husband number one suddenly turned up, the action of yesterday became necessary." The marriage did not last. Smith divorced Eulalia in February 1896 on grounds of her drinking, abuse, and desertion, for she had moved back to El Paso. The divorce was granted on April 14, 1896, about a year after the first divorce scandal.

5. *El Paso Daily Herald*, May 30, 1895.

6. Eddy County Civil Case #279. W.H. and Eulalia Saldaña Smith's relationship must have been tempestuous. The *Eddy Argus* of March 26, 1897, reported their having a baby!

7. *Arizona Daily Star,* June 15, 1895, noted the arrival of John Wesley Hardin and "wife." One of the extended Williams family at Cartwright was Charley Bratton, who told numerous interviewees he saw a marriage license for Hardin and Helen. Anonymous #2 says Bratton was quite clear he met Hardin in Arizona. Other Williams family members are adamant Helen married Hardin. The *Weekly Phoenix Herald* of June 20, 1895 says Hardin, "a quiet man with a quiet and charming wife, ... has been a visitor in Phoenix for some weeks and has just left us." One other reason for the trip to Arizona may have been to drop off Laura with her grandparents, for the little girl is not mentioned in El Paso newspapers again until October 1895.

8. *Eddy Current*, July 5, 1895.

9. *El Paso Daily Herald,* August 9, 1895.

Chapter 17—The Santa Fe Dump

1. Martin Mrose, quoted by George Scarborough in the *El Paso Daily Herald*, July 1, 1895.
2. Ironically, the Santa Fe Dump is now in Mexico. The Rio Grande River and the border between the U.S. and Mexico has shifted in the last hundred years as a result of floods. The border is now several blocks north of where it was. Today, Mexican government buildings between the current Santa Fe Bridge and Chamizal Park cover the site of the former Santa Fe Dump.
3. This time frame is based on several facts, which Brad Armosky, public information officer at the University of Texas's McDonald Observatory and *StarDate* magazine, was kind enough to assist with. The moon was in its first quarter phase and appeared half full on June 29, 1895. Its azimuth was at 259 degrees from true north, or 11 degrees south of due west. On this date, the moonset was at 12:09 A.M., but one has to factor in the mountains. To do this, the author gained access to the roof of a *cantina* in Juarez to measure the horizon with a protractor. The mountains at 259 degrees azimuth cause the perceived horizon to vary from the true horizon by 25 to 30 degrees, about a half hour's difference. For this reason, a bright half moon in a cloudless sky would appear to set about 11:40 P.M. A walk across today's pedestrian walkway takes three minutes, about what it would have taken across the Mexican Central Railroad bridge, plus another three to the Santa Fe Dump, which would make the time of the shooting 11:46 P.M., plus or minus three minutes.
4. From the official death registry "El Paso County Deaths, 1894–1900," page 66.
5. Affidavit of Dr. Alward White contained in records of the case #1902, volume 4, 34th District Court. According to this affidavit, Scarborough carried a .45; McMahan and Milton used shotguns. Since Mrose was hit by five bullets of "large" caliber, did Scarborough hit Mrose all five times, keeping in mind, of course, that experienced gunmen only loaded five chambers of a sixshooter? This seems unlikely, leading to the theory at least *two* men used sixshooters, a theory supported by White's comment two other penetrating wounds may have been made by a gun of smaller caliber. In this case, a .32 or .38 seems likely. If all this is true, that means there were at least two other shooters. Might this mean John Wesley Hardin and Helen Mrose participated in the murder? The possibility is intriguing, especially in regard to George Look's comment, "Then Hardin got to him first...."
6. *El Paso Daily Herald*, July 1, 1895.
7. From his age in his own handwriting in his Desert Land File.
8. Judge Brice interview.
9. *El Paso Herald*, July 1, 1895.
10. F.M. McMahan, Deputy U.S. marshal, being sworn, testified as follows: "I went to the Santa Fe dump this side of the Mexican Central bridge and was stationed with Milton alongside of a trail leading up to the dump. At the appointed time, Scarborough and M'Rose came up the trail. From where I was stationed, I could easily recognize the man behind to be M'Rose. When nearly opposite us, Milton and myself ordered M'Rose to throw up his hands and consider himself under arrest. He made no move to throw up his hands, but began drawing his revolver from the front of his pants. I saw the revolver and also heard it click as he was cocking it. About that instant, there was a shot fired and I thought it was from M'Rose's revolver and I began shooting. I fired two shots and M'Rose fell, then got up. I then fired two more shots and he fell back on the embankment. I do not know how many shots were fired by all. When the shooting was over, Scarborough asked me to go after a doctor and the sheriff. I went to the county jail and told J.C. Jones, Deputy Sheriff, that Scarborough, Milton

and myself killed Martin M'Rose in attempting to arrest him. I then telephoned Dr. White and asked him to come down to the Mexican Central bridge, that there was a man badly hurt. In company with Jones, I then returned to the place where the shooting occurred and a few minutes later Dr. White arrived in a carriage. [...] The doctor pronounced M'Rose dead."

11. Charles Newman, quoted in interview between W.H. Burgess and J. Evetts Haley, February 29, 1944.

12. ibid.

13. While the author sees credible details within this testimony, the reader must take it with a grain of salt. There are two things wrong with it. First, it's hearsay evidence. Second, the Mexican smugglers were never identified nor interviewed by anyone other than Victor Queen.

14. A.P. Coles letter dated December 20, 1939, Vandale Collection.

15. *El Paso Herald*, July 1, 1895.

16. *El Paso Daily Herald*, August 9, 1895.

17. *El Paso Daily Herald*, July 1, 1895.

18. Robert K. DeArment, *George Scarborough*, p. 277, n. 53.

19. *El Paso Herald*, July 1, 1895.

20. Letter from Judge W.D. Howe, December 20, 1939, in Vandale Collection.

21. *El Paso Daily Herald*, July 1, 1895.

22. *El Paso Daily Herald*, November 20, 1895.

23. Victor Queen, *El Paso Herald*, July 1, 1895.

24. Maury Kemp, December 20, 1938.

25. Sheriff J.D. Walker, quoted in *El Paso Daily Herald*, July 1, 1895.

26. *El Paso Daily Herald*, July 9, 1895.

27. *Western Enterprise*, August 24, 1933, an article on Scarborough's career.

28. Charles Ballard interview in Vandale Collection.

29. Major Burgess, Vandale Collection.

30. Owen P. White, *Lead and Likker*, p. 7.

31. Letter from Judge W.D. Howe, December 20, 1939.

32. Note to himself by J. Evetts Haley at end of Dee Harkey interview, February 24, 1945.

33. *Western Liberal, July 5, 1895.*

34. August 22, 1895, page 2.

35. Epperson, p. 57.

36. W.H. Burgess, op. cit.

37. George Look Manuscript.

38. September 3, 1895, *El Paso Daily Herald.*

39. The *El Paso Herald*, May 7, 1895, says Milton's effects were garnished for nonpayment of bills, and the *El Paso Daily Times*, May 5, 1895, reported Milton had returned from Mexico, after running away from his bills. Even so, the October 17, 1895 edition of the *Herald* reports Milton was conned out of $500. Where did he get $500 so quickly?

40. *The Eddy Current*, July 11, 1895.

41. *El Paso Daily Times*, August 8, 1895.

42. *El Paso Herald*, July 1, 1895.

43. Article from *The El Paso Daily Herald*, quoted in *The Eddy Current*, August 22, 1895.

44. Letter Victor Queen to Bula Mrose.

45. Haines, p. 100.

46. *The Eddy Current*, July 11, 1895. The *San Antonio Daily Herald*, July 1, 1895, says, "Mrs. Mrose did not attend the funeral, and by advice of her counsel, refused to contribute to its expense."
47. *El Paso Daily Herald*, July 3, 1895.

Chapter 18—Helen Beulah

1. Editor, *El Paso Herald*, August 2, 1895.
2. Whoever wrote the preface to the original edition described the book as "given to the public with little, if any, alteration from the manuscript." If true, the stylistic differences between the book and Hardin's last known letters are an indication of another's work on the manuscript, in other words, Helen Beulah.
3. Undated letter, J.A. Lipscomb to Hardin.
4. Letter J.D. Hargis to Hardin, July 28, 1895.
5. J. Marvin Hunter and Noah Rose, *The Album of Gunfighters*, p. 122.
6. J. Marvin Hunter, *Frontier Times*, September 1925, p. 17.
7. The stage required twelve hours to travel fifty miles, the advertised time. The cracking whip and running horses portrayed in films are myths. Four miles an hour, a simple walk for the team, seems to be representative of the real speed of stages.
8. Ed Bartholomew, *Wild Bill Longley*, pp. 26-7.
9. Letter, Otto P. Kroeger to Joe Barbisch, November 20, 1894.
10. *The El Paso Daily Herald*, July 2, 1895.
11. Ruentes-Chaney case, Reeves County, Texas.
12. Edna S. Haines, "John Selman of El Paso," p. 122.
13. Haines, p. 122 -3.
14. Note the difference between Selman's account and the newspaper story. There were two restaurants on San Antonio Street in 1895. The American Kitchen, run by Bob Chin Wo at 103 San Antonio Street, faced the English Kitchen at 106 San Antonio, operated by Yee Charley Tong, and it was *this* restaurant Helen hurrahed. Therefore, when young Selman spotted trouble through the window, he probably saw a Chinese man with a long pigtail, his hands in the air as he faced the blonde and her two pistols.
15. *El Paso Herald*, August 2, 1895, one of several times Helen's ability to curse made the newspapers. Since she certainly hadn't learned to do this from her parents, it may have been a legacy of her association with men in New Mexico and El Paso.
16. *El Paso Daily Times*, August 2, 1895.
17. *El Paso Herald,* May 6, 1895, Hardin's arrest by Sheriff Simmons and the report from the *Herald* of May 16, plus the *El Paso Times* of May 17 show he had only one gun and was fined $25.
18. *The Eddy Current*, August 15, 1895. Unfortunately, another account by the *Pecos Valley Daily Argus* does not survive.
19. Helen Bond Melton conversation with the author.
20. *El Paso Daily Times*, May 28, June 5, and June 7, 1895. Separated from her husband, a woman listed as a "widow" in a city directory was not uncommon. J. Marvin Hunter's editor at the *Graphic*, W.W. Bridgers' wife, Melissa, was a "widow" too.
21. Joe Parrish, pp. 76-77.
22. Parrish, "Boy and the Gunslinger," p. 44.
23. ibid.

24. *El Paso Herald,* August 20, 1895.

25. There was a report she attempted suicide after Mrose's death.

26. *El Paso Herald,* August 7, 1895.

27. *El Paso Herald Post* reported the peace bond was rediscovered June 27, 1940.

28. Haines, p. 121.

29. Haines, p. 120.

30. *The Houston Daily Post,* August 21, 1895.

31. *El Paso Daily Times,* August 7, 1895.

32. Major Burgess interview with Earl Vandale, December 19, 1938.

33. Noted in Marohn, p. 256.

34. *El Paso Times,* August 12, and *El Paso Herald,* August 13, both from the *Chicago Herald-Post.*

35. On the train was a probable acquaintance. The *Arizona Daily Gazette* of August 14, 1895, reported, "C.H. Philbrick and family, who left [Eddy] some four weeks ago by wagon for Phoenix, Ariz., sold out the wagon in El Paso and went from there by train to Phoenix, tarrying a short time at Deming." After her breakup with Hardin, Helen was probably distraught. Philbrick had been a saloon owner in Phenix and was on good terms with Dave Kemp, W.H. Smith, Lon Bass, and others. It's likely the Philbricks encountered Helen on the train, especially since they detrained together at Deming. If so, it's possible the Philbricks gave Helen emotional support as she thought about hurrying back to El Paso.

36. *The El Paso Herald* of August 14, 1895, reported "Mrs. Martin M'Rose left for California this morning. Wes Hardin saw her off."

37. *El Paso Daily Times,* August 20, 1895.

38. Hardin moved from the Herndon House after breaking up with Helen Beulah. He took lodgings at the Melrose House, 207 N. Stanton.

Chapter 19—The Unlamented

1. Helen Beulah Mrose, hearsay, but quoted by both Gary G. Williams and Anonymous #1, who never met each other. A similar quote ("I'm a widow twice over.") has been attributed to Charley Bratton, who was in Cartwright at the time she was there.

2. Anonymous #1 and Gary G. Williams. The author heard two other versions differing somewhat in details, but both may have originated from Anonymous #1, so the author discounted them.

3. The Maricopa and Phoenix Railway.

4. Eddy County Civil Cases, Case #241.

5. *El Paso Herald,* August 20, 1895.

6. Marohn, p. 255.

7. Three years after John Wesley Hardin's death, his first cousin's widow, Mary Clara (neé Parks) Hardin owned and operated a boarding house at 211 Texas Avenue, around the corner from the Acme Saloon.

8. L.H. Hubbard correspondence in Robert N. Mullin Collection.

9. *El Paso Daily Times,* August 20th.

10. ibid.

11. *El Paso Daily Herald,* August 22, 1895.

12. *El Paso Daily Times,* August 20th.

13. Owen P. White, *Lead and Likker,* p. 9.

14. Billy Smith quoted in the *El Paso Times,* March 3, 1933.

15. Haines, p. 124–5.

16. *El Paso Daily Times*, August 20.

17. *El Paso Daily Herald*, August 22, 1895.

18. Richard Burges interview, December 19, 1938.

19. *The (Dallas) Daily Times Herald*, August 20, 1895.

20. *El Paso Daily Herald*, August 21, 1895.

21. *El Paso Daily Times*, August 20th.

22. Wild Bill Hickock was killed in Deadwood, S.D. while supposedly holding a "Dead Man's Hand;" the ace of spades, ace of clubs, and two black eights. Hardin's dice roll, all sixes might be termed the "Dead Man's Roll."

23. *El Paso Daily Herald*, August 20, 1895.

24. ibid.

25. The George Look manuscript, El Paso Public Library.

26. Phillip J. Rasch, "The Life and Death of Lon Bass," *The NOLA Quarterly*, p. 9.

27. Jack Martin, *Border Boss*, p. 155.

28. Major Burgess interview with Hervey Chesley and J. Evetts Haley, Vandale Collection.

29. *Houston Post*, later reprinted in *El Paso Times*.

30. William Wallace Mills, *Forty Years at El Paso, 1858–1898*.

31. Annie's story was previously reported in Chapter 19. Both Annie and Jailer Jones were quoted in the August 23rd edition of the *El Paso Daily Herald*.

32. *El Paso Daily Herald*, August 21, 1895.

33. *San Antonio Daily Light*, August 20, 1895.

34. Quoted in the *El Paso Daily Herald*, August 24, 1895.

35. *The Taylor County News*, August 23, 1895.

36. *Western Liberal*, August 23, 1895.

37. *El Paso Daily Herald*, August 21, 1895.

38. *The Hondo Herald*, August 23, 1895.

39. Not wanting to beat a dead horse, but this article is another reason the author doesn't believe J. Marvin Hunter met Hardin in Mason, Texas, in 1895. (See Chapter 18) There surely would have been a sentence or two in this article that Hardin had dropped by trying to pitch a book, etc. With no mention at all, one must conclude Hardin never went to Mason, Texas.

40. *El Paso Herald*, August 21, 1895.

Chapter 20—The Estate

1. *El Paso Daily Herald*, October 1, 1895. The poem continues:
But now I am prepared,
You can be sure,
To wage the fall campaign,
And secure
A beau who will attend me
To parties,
And will send me
Pretty flowers and all the candy
I can endure.
Won't that be nice?

2. Laura Jennings interview.

3. Beauregard Lee is listed on the 1900 census as "divorced."

4. During World War Two, he played for Spike Jones and The City Slickers.

5. Lee family history from Beauregard Lee II, grandson of Beauregard Lee of Raton.

6. *El Paso Daily Herald,* November 9, 1895.

7. *El Paso Daily Herald,* April 25, 1898.

8. Runge Papers, Correspondence File, Texas State Archives.

9. Edna S. Haines, "John Selman of El Paso," p. 100.

10. For stylistic comparison, see an undated example of Hardin's writing from a letter in the 1895 file of the Hardin Collection beginning with, "god grant that you may ask...."

11. *El Paso Daily Times,* August 27, 1895.

12. Joseph L. Whitmore was born about 1852. He died in El Paso in 1900. Roberta Whitmore was born about 1870 and died in El Paso in 1924. See the author's article, "Family Secrets at Concordia," for more information.

13. In direct competition with Whitmore, Teel filed his notice on August 21, 1895. Teel had been a character witness for Hardin in the May, 1895 term of the El Paso court when Hardin was charged with carrying a gun. Teel's relationship with Hardin is very curious. Teel was Doboy Taylor's defense attorney during the Sutton-Taylor Feud; Hardin was the Taylor's main gunman. Teel's appearance with Hardin twenty years later in El Paso ties Hardin to the Feud far longer than most historians have realized.

14. Estate of John W. Hardin, #261, August 21, 1895, filed March 21, 1896, University of Texas at El Paso, Special Collections.

15. For a complete inventory of Hardin's effects, see Marohn, pages 282-3.

16. *El Paso Herald,* August 26, 1895. In an article immediately under this, Helen is called "Mrs. J.W. Hardin of El Paso."

17. Judge Hunter is buried within feet of J.T. Stapleton, Dee Harkey's mentor from years before, at Evergreen Cemetery, El Paso.

18. *El Paso Daily Herald,* August 27, 1895.

19. *El Paso Daily Herald,* August 30, 1895. The suit, Helen B. McRose vs. J.L. Whitmore, was filed as #2192 in El Paso District Court.

20. Reported the *Cameron Herald,* September 5, 1895, "Mrs. B.M. Rose has filed suit at El Paso for possession of the manuscript of the life of the late John Wesley Hardin which she claims was assigned to her before his death."

21. This portion of the application is significant because it proves her absolute familiarity with the manuscript.

22. A proposal was once made to exhume Hardin's body. As the legal case seesawed back and forth, one simple fact was overlooked. Helen Beulah's descendants own Hardin's grave under Texas law.

23. Application of Helen B. Mrose in the case of J.W. Hardin, deceased, #262, El Paso County Court, J. Evetts Haley Collection.

24. University of Texas at El Paso, Special Collections.

25. *El Paso Daily Times,* October 2, 1895, "Mr. and Mrs. Williams are in the city from Austin to spend a few days with their daughter, Mrs. J.W. Hardin."

26. Denson arrived about the first of November. He is mentioned on in the *El Paso Herald,* November second. The *El Paso Daily Times* mentioned Gip Hardin's arrival on November tenth, followed, two days later, by Jeff Hardin.

27. *El Paso Daily Herald,* November 11, 1895.

28. *El Paso Daily Herald,* November 18, 1895.

29. *El Paso Daily Herald*, August 26, 1895.

30. ibid.

31. *El Paso Daily Herald*, December 4, 1895.

32. *El Paso Daily Herald*, February 10, 1896.

33. Minutes of the 34th District Court, Volume 8, page 525, February 10, 1896.

34. Letter from Judge W.D. Howe, December 20, 1939, in Center for American History. Selman was Judge Howe's constable; the men did not have a good relationship.

35. *The Williamson County Sun,* obituary dated November 3, 1898.

36. Marohn, page 282.

37. See the author's article and Ed Bartholomew's letter in the NOLA *Newsletter* about the missing volumes.

Chapter 21—The Horseman

1. Probably John Wesley Hardin, "Caught on the Fly," *El Paso Daily Times*, June 30, 1895.

2. No one will say who this might have been, but the tergiversator may have been A.B. "Ab" Hayes, Steve's best friend. Laura Jennings said Hayes provided invaluable help during Steve's search for her. Another possibility is suggested by the fact Bill and Ann Eliza Williams did not avoid Mason County after the flight of their daughter. This might mean neither they nor their family kept secrets from the Jenningses. If so, they were interested in retrieving Laura too. Another intriguing clue is the fact that as Steve searched, Bill Williams's resources declined. Did Williams finance the search?

3. Anonymous #1.

4. The departure of Steve Jennings from Fredonia was described to the author in June 1998 by Sonnie Jennings, whose uncle rode in the opposite direction that morning, but circled around to intercept him and hand him a dollar out of sight of prying eyes. This simple act of charity was considered so scandalous the man did not mention it, even to his own family, for forty years.

5. *The El Paso Daily Herald*, April 8, 1895, reported the young man had reached Phoenix and added the intriguing detail he had ridden from New York to California and was on his return journey!

6. Her journey was only indirectly inspired by the adventures of Nellie Bly, but was directly influenced by "Paul Jones," who left Boston on a similar journey in 1894.

7. From El Paso, Annie Londonderry rode north across the dreaded *Jornada del Muerto* to Albuquerque, Raton, Denver, Cheyenne, and Omaha. She ended her round-the-world adventure in Chicago on September 12, 1895, fourteen days ahead of schedule. See Peter Zheutlin's article in the May 2005 issue of "Bicycling" and his excellent book *Around the World on Two Wheels.*

8. *The Arizona Daily Gazette*, July 21, 1895.

9. ibid

10. "Texas Parade" January 1968.

11. Shelley Frear, "The 1893 Chadron to Chicago Cowboy Horse Race."

12. In not one of the many versions of the Jennings family story is the name Mrose (or Rose) mentioned. Every variation is Hardin took Helen away from Steve Jennings, and the Jennings family has focused on Hardin as the opponent ever since. When Steve rode west to claim his wife and daughter, hearing the names Martin and Helen Beulah Mrose and learning of their bigamous marriage in New Mexico must have been mortifying. Either he chose not to

mention it to his family, or the family discounted it. The likely reason for this is that the only status attendant to having a wife run off is that she ran off with someone famous.

Chapter 22—The Charmed Circle

1. *San Francisco Examiner,* May 25, 1900, announcing the sailing of the *Charles D. Lane.* "The steamer has the distinction of carrying the first cow that ever left for Nome. [...] A banner covering the cow bore the legend: 'Milk and Butter to Burn.'"
2. Also spelled Hevens.
3. *The New York Times,* April 17, 1866.
4. *The Daily Alta,* April 17, 1866.
5. *The New York Times,* op cit.
6. Born in 1834, in Rochester, New York and died there in 1907, she is buried at Colma, California.
7. Henry Huntley Haight, born in Rochester, New York, married Anna Bissell, who is undoubtedly connected to Amos Bissell and family, partners with the Eddy brothers in New Mexico and Colorado.
8. "Federal Control of Hydraulic Mining," October 1897 *Yale Law Journal.*
9. For more information, see the author's articles in *The Alaska Bar Rag* and the NOLA *Quarterly.*
10. The first version includes the greatest saloon brawl ever filmed, a free-for-all so exciting it became a staple of Western films for the next fifty years. The last version of *The Spoilers* climaxes with a spectacular fistfight between John Wayne and Randolph Scott—the second greatest brawl ever filmed.
11. Born in 1830, in New Hampshire, died in Menlo Park, California, in 1925. Not to be confused with Charles Benson Holbrook, head of the San Francisco SPCA, who was often mentioned in newspapers.
12. Mary Hurd Holbrook, born in 1870 in San Francisco, died in 1953.
13. Olive Holbrook Palmer, *Gazette,* November 1998. Invented by Hermann Wentzel, air clocks were tricky to install and trickier to maintain. Wealthy homeowners and government agencies were the main customers. When the Holbrook mansion was demolished in 1947, contractors salvaged the clocks from the walls.
14. Olive Palmer, *Gazette,* November 1998.
15. ibid.
16. *The New York Times,* July 7, 1895.
17. The Knight estate in Hillsborough, California, was sold to developers in 1954. The beautiful twenty-five-room mansion the Knights had built at great expense in 1898 was demolished, and seventeen ranch-style homes were built in its place in a development named "Knightslands."
18. Mary Knight bequeathed $20,000 to Yale to establish a chair in American History in honor of her husband. She also gave Yale his library of rare books. Unfortunately, Yale did not want Samuel Knight's papers dealing with the Red Cross, Ambrose Bierce, or items that might have shed light on Knight's important role in breaking the Crime of 1900.
19. The Pacific-Union Club, the Francisca Club, the Century Club, the Burlingame Country Club, San Mateo Polo Club, and the Claremont Club.
20. *The San Francisco Examiner,* September 1, 1904.

Chapter 23—Destiny Has Claws

1. Anonymous #1, speculating.

2. *The Sacramento Bee*, September 12, 1904.

3. The *Sacramento Union* of September 12, 1904, says, "When [Helen was] arrested Saturday night the woman had a letter in her possession that was written by her little daughter in Oakland. In it the child speaks of her grandmother's death...." Whether this denotes a regular correspondence between Laura and her mother is not certain. Laura's grandmother died on October 29, 1898, so the letter may have been an old one. The existence of the letter, however, shows Laura did have contact with her mother (and her grandfather Bill Williams) after she had been placed with the Knights, and it clarifies how Steve Jennings could have tracked his daughter to California.

4. *The San Francisco Examiner*, April 21, 1903.

5. *The San Francisco Examiner*, April 23, 1903. The article is illustrated with the last known image of Helen Beulah Mrose, stylishly dressed and confident.

6. ibid, April 21, 1903.

7. In the strictest sense, these children were not orphans, for "most were children turned over to the institution by poor lone mothers who could not afford to keep them." (Gordon, p. 6).

8. Gordon, p. 286-7

9. ibid, p. 296.

10. See *The San Francisco Chronicle*, November 8, 1903, and The *San Francisco Examiner*, June 10, 1900, for representative stories.

11. See the *El Paso Daily Herald*, August 22, 1895, and the *San Francisco Examiner*, September 1, 1903, for examples of child stealing. In the El Paso example, a little girl was stolen by a man from her mother in Kansas City and found in Providence, R.I. a year later. The San Francisco story was about a girl stolen from Hobble Creek, Utah, and raised by a miner. Years later, she tried to find her family but was unsuccessful.

12. See *The San Francisco Chronicle*, April 1, 1897. Mrs. Theodore Pillech's child was being kept against her wishes in Trieste, Austria. Mrs. Pillech appealed to San Francisco socialites in the Women's Industrial and Educational Union to support her long-distance fight for her daughter.

13. *The San Francisco Chronicle*, August 28, 1904.

14. *The San Francisco Examiner*, March 24, 1903.

15. *The San Francisco Chronicle*, May 8, 1904.

16. ibid, August 1, 1904.

17. ibid, August 14, 1904.

18. *The San Francisco Examiner*, November 1, 1900.

19. *The San Francisco Chronicle*, June 3, 1904.

20. *The San Francisco Examiner*, June 19, 1903.

21. ibid, June 10-11, 1903, plus the Fiest case in the *Examiner*, April 15, 19, and December 24, 1903.

22. *The San Francisco Chronicle*, January 6 and 29, and February 4, 1903.

23. *The Rocky Mountain News*, July 9, 1895.

24. *The San Francisco Examiner*, November 15, 1903.

25. ibid.

26. *The San Francisco Examiner*, June 30, 1903.

27. Laura Jennings, about 1982.

28. This conversation is based on hearsay, as noted by Sonnie Jennings, but Laura Jennings told a similar story. The silence of the Jennings family since this dramatic scene makes any breakthrough to the complete truth impossible. None of the living Jenningses today has any

knowledge how Steve Jennings found his daughter in California. How it was accomplished comes from hints through others. One hint was that the adoption was well-known, therefore may have been reported—and it's known Steve was well informed by newspapers during the years of his search. It's also known Laura corresponded with her grandfather, Bill Williams, and it's possible he cooperated with the Jenningses. The author, however, believes Steve must have found and talked to the only person who knew exactly what had happened: Helen.

29. Versions of the Jennings family story hint there was a hearing, during which Steve won custody of his daughter. Whether this was before the Superior Court, a justice of the peace, or a high-ranking Catholic official is unknown. The 1906 San Francisco earthquake destroyed court records; no newspaper accounts have been discovered either. A broke cowboy successfully winning his daughter back from one of the best lawyers in the country is amazing, but it may have something to do with the missing court documents of Helen's suit against Steve Jennings in Mason, County, Texas, in October 1894.

Chapter 24—Home Again

1. Anonymous #1, Conversation, March 1997, Mason, Texas.
2. Sonnie Jennings, questioned on this point four times, was definite the Jenningses rode the length of Fredonia on the way back to the homestead. Though such a route is impossible today and was probably so in their day too, she was so sure of it that it has been included here.
3. When relating her story, Laura remembered meeting John Wesley Hardin, but she recalled it was her mother's plan to engage him to write a letter to her father because of his behavior. Because of this, Laura may have confused her father and Martin Mrose all along. This may explain why she didn't talk about her childhood, even with her own children, for she may have believed things about Steve that were, in fact, wrong. It is sad to think, therefore, she may never have appreciated how her father found her and brought her home, nor may she have appreciated the cost to him and her family.
4. Sonnie Jennings.
5. Michael Jennings was illiterate, yet when he applied to buy fourteen more acres in 1910, he listed part-time employment as the assistant postmaster. While it's possible he had learned to read late in life, he has been remembered by his grandchildren Thomas and Jack Jennings and Ruth Jo Martin as being illiterate.
6. "I heard her speak about living in California once, but I don't recall hearing the name of the family that has [sic] her," Sonnie Jennings said in an interview in March 1997. Another interviewee, Wilda Fay Jennings, said, "I never heard the name. I don't believe anyone ever mentioned it. Steve would've had a fit!"
   Such a situation strikes the author as odd. Laura's life could have been improved by some contact with the Knights, but there is no evidence she took the opportunity. Given their well-known generosity, their wealth, and their affection for her, what harm would have come from initiating some contact? At the same time, what would have prevented the Knights from sending money for her education and expenses?
7. Steve is "Papa Steve" to descendants of his second wife.
8. Ruth Jo Martin, Mike's daughter, said her father never mentioned this incident in her hearing, but his reported actions on the train were "so very much like him!" She also admitted her father was close-mouthed about anything to do with Laura and Steve.
9. Sonnie Jennings. Though this incident looks easy to research, the author had difficulty locating

arrest records or newspaper accounts. Since this version comes directly from Laura, who claimed to know of it, some trace of the incident must still be waiting along the possible railway route from Fort Worth to Llano. Joyce Capps, in a conversation at Deer Creek in February 2000, said Mike Jennings, "told the kidnapper what a terribly mean man Steve was, so the kidnapper turned around and went home." A different version is Mike threw the man from the moving train. Another tale comes from Anonymous #2, who mentioned "Wells Fargo graves" north of the Jennings home. Asked what this meant, she said it was a secret when she was growing up, but she thought it had to do with the San Saba Mob. The author has not found any other reference to such graves; though such a connection is unlikely, Samuel Knight's father was an executive for Wells Fargo.

10. Records of St. Mary's Academy, Austin, Texas, school years 1905-07, preserved at the Catholic Archives of Texas, Austin, Texas.

11. Laura Jennings, copy in author's files.

Chapter 25—The Woman in Fredonia

1. Jane Hoerster, speaking about Carolyn Baze. Jane witnessed an incident in a store near the square in Mason. The shopkeeper had decided to tease Carolyn Baze about Hardin. Not amused, Carolyn left immediately without saying a word. Though Mason is but a small town, she never shopped in that store again. A similar story comes from Ruth Jo Martin, who told of a group of men sitting in a barber shop talking when Carolyn Baze came in and mounted the shoe-shine stand to have her shoes polished. While she was waiting, a stranger entered and said he'd like to meet the wife of John Wesley Hardin. He asked if any of the men knew who she was, and while the men hemmed and hawed, Carolyn Baze slid off her seat and slipped out the door. Only after she was gone did the men tell the stranger he had just missed her.

2. The *Mason County News* is a good source for information on the Lewis and Baze families during this period. From these accounts, it is possible to chronicle P. A. Baze's early career, living in London with his in-laws, his early shared practice with his brother in Fredonia, and his later independent practice in Mason.

3. The second wife of Doctor Baze (Bessie Donup) is most often referred to as "Mrs. Baze" in Mason County. Nevertheless, future researchers must use care in talking to oldtimers about whom they are speaking: the first wife ("Dr. Baze's wife") or the second one ("Mrs. Baze").

4. Callie (Lewis) Hardin married Dr. Perry Allen Baze in Kimble County, Texas, January 21, 1898. She was the second Callie Baze in the family, for her brother-in-law, Martin Baze, was also married to a "Callie." It is for this reason—and her desire to break with the past—that she started using her formal name. She was called Carolyn Baze the rest of her life.

5. One of the many frustrations encountered during research for this book involved confusions between Callie Lewis, Dr. Baze's wife, Helen Williams, Mrs. Baze, and Laura Jennings. In a tiny area of central Texas hardly twenty miles across, there was not just *one* woman touched by the scandal of John Wesley Hardin, but *three*. Because of this, the rumors and legends, at this late date, are blending together into one hazy story. The author often had to discount comments by interviewees that had confused the women. One Mason County resident claimed, "I have always heard that Wes Hardin caught the fancy of a pretty Fredonia girl, but her name was Caroline Lewis. Another story was 'Callie' Lewis was the same person from Camp San Saba, ten miles west of Fredonia. Other stories said Katemcy, 8 miles west, and London, 20 miles west of Mason. She was suppose [sic] to be a doctor's wife, Dr. Perry Baze

who practiced in all of the above towns [....] The girl he [Hardin] ran off with married the Dr. in 1897. Wes Hardin got killed in 1895, so, there you are. The dates just don't match up." Other people encountered in Mason and Kimble counties were similarly confused, one so-called "expert" even calling Perry Baze "Doc Bodenhammer."

6. Lollie Roberts, in a phone interview with the author, February 2000.

7. From a story related by Steve Jennings's daughter-in-law.

8. Probably Rev. Jonathan C.S. Baird. Baird was a controversial defender of the San Saba Mob, unpopular in the area.

9. Anonymous #1. Another interviewee, Sonnie Jennings, had heard of the incident, but said the enraged Steve Jennings was pulled off the surprised preacher before any damage was done.

10. Laura Jennings. Several interviewees have related she packed a pistol as late as the 1930s.

11. Four Roses brand, it has been reported.

12. Sonnie Jennings.

13. Sonnie Jennings. Quite a number of other correspondents, family members, and interviewees have also mentioned Laura climbing the roof in the evenings. For example, Thomas and Wilda Fay Jennings, who lived next door, told the author in November 1999 Laura was "regular as clockwork." Apparently, Laura's quixotic habit had ended by the time she married. Either the pain had lessened, she had outgrown the desire, or she was convinced her yearnings were hopeless. Laura herself mentioned the ladder climbing, but offered no details.

14. Charley Bratton (born 1878 in San Saba County and died in San Angelo in 1972) was the brother of William R. Bratton, who married Helen Jennings' sister Sallie, and he (Charley), by all accounts, was quite close to Helen. He told a number of people over the years that while living in Cartwright, he had seen a marriage license between Helen and Hardin. The author has scoured every courthouse between Phenix and Phoenix, from Albuquerque to Juarez, with no luck. There is one thing wrong with such a marriage: it would have come up during the fight over Hardin's estate. Even so, Helen may have purposely not claimed such a marriage because, by the time of Hardin's death, she knew the relationship was doubly bigamous because her suit against Steve Jennings had been dismissed and she was still legally married to him, and because she had learned during the suit for control of the estate that Callie Lewis Hardin still considered herself married to Hardin. Having gone through the disturbance in Phenix, New Mexico, when lawmen enforced the Edmunds Act, she may have been unwilling to be accused of breaking this federal law herself. Nevertheless, the author feels Hardin and Helen may have gotten married, due to three facts: the extent of Helen and Hardin's behavior together, the matter-of-fact nature of reports in the Arizona newspapers, and even more particularly, the acceptance by the Williams family of their daughter's escapades up until November 1895.

15. Although the author has agreed to keep most information about Laura's later life and family from the general reader, there is one detail indicative of her true feelings about her mother. The Jennings family actively discouraged any mention of Helen, but, even so, Laura insisted on naming her daughter after both the little girl's grandmothers. The family softened the impact of this decision—in the Southern fashion— by calling Laura's daughter by her first *and* middle name ever afterward.

16. Conversation witnessed by Ruth Nye and recounted by her to her sister Joyce Capps. Later recollections were expounded upon in a letter, also to Joyce Capps. In a conversation with the author on July 9, 2000, Joyce cleared up a few questions. "It was Old Man Charley Bratton," she said. "They met at a funeral. I don't remember which one. They sat and talked for an hour about what had happened to Laura."

Epilogue—A Bitter Brew

1. Peter Bader, quoted in Sonnichsen, pp. 95-6.
2. In the 1980s even its cemetery was moved. It is laid out in its original orientation at the Twin Oaks Cemetery near Artesia, N.M.
3. Begun in 1892, Phenix straddled the railroad tracks south of today's Carlsbad. The Stevens Motel and a shopping center have been built over much of it. The last permanent building, the "Phenix Adobe," was razed in August 1989. Contrary to what many locals believe, Phenix was not "cleaned up." Instead, after the Eddy brothers moved on, prohibitions against drinking, gambling, and prostitution eased. Many of the establishments and even the buildings of Phenix were moved into Eddy. Except for a few houses, most of Phenix was gone by 1900, absorbed rather than defeated. The last brothel was closed about 1910, so the wild town had lasted only eighteen years.
4. Renamed after a famous spring in Germany, Carlsbad became the center of a vast oil field. Today, oil and gas production, mining, and tourism are components of the region's economy unforeseen a hundred years ago.
5. Cartwright is today the intersection of 59th and Thomas, Glendale, Arizona. On the southwest side of the intersection is a former church established by Brooks, Ellison, and Williams family members, among others. Across the street, a school is also a leftover of the little town, but all the dairy cattle, irrigation canals, and houses are gone, replaced with the congestion of a modern residential/business district.
6. Carolyn Baze is buried at Mission Burial Park (South) in San Antonio. Unsure whether Laura attended the funeral in Mason or a graveside service in San Antonio, one interviewee, who didn't know of Laura's connection to Carolyn Baze, said she was surprised to see Laura and her daughter there.
7. Jennings family legend.
8. Joyce Capps.
9. "They say Steve [Jennings] was the meanest man ever lived, but I think his sister Miss Mary was." —Anonymous #1, among many who commented on Steve's irascible behavior over the years. One family story is that Lucie Jennings' attempted to keep her sons from being raised as Catholics. She declared she would go sleep out in the middle of a field rather than lose her boys to the strict variety of Catholicism the Jennings family espoused, and Steve replied he "would follow [her] out in the field and shoot [her] in the head first. Those boys are mine!"
10. About two years after the death of Ann Eliza Williams, Bill Williams married Mrs. Sarah Elizabeth (Miss Sallie) Towler. They had one son, Roger Aaron Williams (1901-1933). Property records show they sold the last of their properties in Williamson County in 1908/9, and by the 1910 census, Bill was living with his son D.A. Williams in Fowler, California. Miss Sallie died in 1942 and is buried in an unmarked grave in Batson, Texas.
11. Book 5, p. 345 of Fresno County, California Index to Deaths.
12. Bill Williams' obituary in *The Williamson County Sun*, March 19.
13. John G. Belcher, one of the Knights' nephews, in a phone conversation with the author in February 2000.
14. Laura's son said his mother never spoke to her own children about her childhood. If true, this may mean the only time she opened up was in a conversation with her niece in the early 1980s. Laura's son added that in the days following this conversation, Laura expressed regret to him and her daughter for saying anything about herself, her mother, her father, and John Wesley Hardin. Be that as it may, this short conversation resulted—a number of years later and after much heartache—in the book you are holding now.

15. Thomas and Wilda Fay Jennings, Ruth Jo Martin, *et al.*

16. Anonymous #1 interview, March 1998.

17. *The Sacramento Bee*, July 22, 1904, under the headline "Several Women Appear in Court," reports "Three other women who gave their names as Mary Doe, Grace Rose, and Mrs. Wilson, were victims of foaming intoxicants yesterday. They were each lectured by the [City Justice] Court and allowed to go free."

   This was one of several times "Grace Rose" appeared before the court. Such arrests show a remarkable leniency. Drunks and vagrants were usually given an hour to get out of town, but Grace Rose was tolerated. It was not enough to save her, however, and on September 12, 1904 the newspaper reported, "Grace Berry, who has more than once faced charges in the City Justice's Court ranging from petty larceny to vagrancy, lies dead at the Morgue. Officer Butler found the woman dying on a dirty mattress in a cottage located in the alley in the block bounded by L and M, Fourth and Fifth Streets yesterday afternoon. He called the patrol wagon and had the [woman] removed to the Receiving Hospital where City Physician Nichols attended her. His efforts were unavailing, however, as the woman died about six o'clock last evening. The woman was known here as Grace Berry, but her true name is supposed to have been Mrs. Grace Rose. She claimed to have had a mother and daughter, the former dying in Stockton about a month ago, leaving the Berry woman heir to an estate of $10,000. The deceased stated to the officers that she was in receipt of an income of $75 a month from her relatives, who gave her that amount to stay away from them. The Berry woman, or Mrs. Rose, as her true name is, was drinking yesterday afternoon in the house where she was found with a man named Charles Lessler. Lesles [sic] stated to Coroner Gormley that suddenly the woman seemed to faint and he called an officer when unable to do anything for her. The cause of the woman's death is not known, although it is believed by some of the officers that the woman took poison."

   Items worthy of note: first the names. Rose is obvious: Mrose. It was also the name her father entered in his family bible to record her death. The name Berry comes from her family's long association with the Berry family of central Texas, but why she chose to use their name eludes the author. As for the story of the $10,000, a version is from *The San Francisco Chronicle*, April 9, 1903, "Mrs. Williams will try to keep her daughter from Mongol Husband. The mother of the girl approached the Judge just before the case was disposed of, and, showing him a handful of bank notes and deeds, told him that they represented $10,000, which, by a will she exhibited, would all go to the daughter on her death. Then, turning to the girl, who was sitting quietly by, she said, 'It will all be yours, Grace, if you leave that Mongol....'" The author feels Helen read the story and added it to her repetoire.

18. Bill Williams' Family Bible lists her death date. Her death certificate, signed by County Coroner W.F. Gormley, lists the cause as "chronic alcoholism," and as such it was reported in *The Evening Bee*, September 13, 1904. The author, however, feels Helen killed herself, either with alcohol or poison.

19. Laura traveled to California at least twice. The author has three photos from Glenn Wilkins, whose mother, Lela Elizabeth Wilkins, was Laura's cousin. The photos show Laura and her children at the Graff Ranch, near Fowler, California in 1922, only 18 years after Laura was returned to the Jenningses in Texas.

   Little is known of a 1970s trip. Laura picked up a nearly blind cousin, Lois Freer, in Fowler, and the two old women disappeared for a few days. Laura's son knew nothing of the trip. Glenn Wilkins recalled their going somewhere, but he didn't understand the reason. Lois Freer mentioned the trip in a letter to Wilda Fay Jennings in 1981, and Laura also mentioned it, but gave no details. One can imagine the two women in San Mateo County and up in San Francisco on a sentimental journey. They probably didn't find a trace of Laura's mother in Sacramento, but perhaps they found and visited the graves of the Knights at Colma.

20. John Bettencourt and Anastasia S. Wolfe, City of Sacramento Department of Community and Visitor Services, City Cemetery, in letters to the author dated June 3, 1997 and October 16, 1997, and phone conversation with Patricia Vogel, Sacramento County Coroner's Office, July 7, 1997. On May 11, 1999 Mrs. Sibylle Zemitis of the California State Library, after checking available resources, concluded, "Helena Grace Rose is most likely buried at East Lawn Memorial Park." Dr. Bob La Perriere, Chairman of the City Cemetery Committee, concurred in a letter to the author dated July 13, 1999, "It is most likely that she was reinterred with the 4,691 'unknowns' the City of Sacramento buried at East Lawn Cemetery." Nancy Ehlers, in a letter dated August 25, 1999, says, "The beginning of the end of the cemetery began long before the idea of placing a school on the property was raised. The removal of headstones and monuments began as an ease-of-maintenance issue with the city promising to place flat markers so that lawn mowers could be run over them. [... T]he headstones and monuments were just set out in the street and many are now part of driveways or steps in the surrounding residential area. Very few flat markers were installed at New Helvetia, and as the weeds took over, the nearby residents complained of the eyesore. It was turned into a park for some years before the city offered it to the school district." Dr. La Perriere said he suspected there were "a few" bodies still remaining at the site of the school. Other Sacramento residents have the same opinion, one even naming today's playing fields as an area unexplored by the grave removal experts. Even so, the author feels Helen's body was recovered and removed to East Lawn.

21. Hardin is buried in Tier 8, Grave 13, Section 1, N.E. Addition of Concordia Cemetery.

22. Martin Mrose is buried in Tier 8, Grave 10, Section 1, N.E. Addition of Concordia.

23. Selman is buried in the Knights of Pythias Section of Concordia Cemetery, Tier 7, Lot 23, Grave 11, according to Beth Jones of the Concordia Research Committee in a letter to Leon Metz dated July 10, 2000.

BIBLIOGRAPHY

Primary Sources:

County records, including Complaints, Indictments, Warrants, Bills of Sale, Deeds, Birth, Marriage, Death, and other records from the following counties:

Texas—
Atascosa County (Jourdanton)
Bandera County (Bandera)
Bastrop County (Bastrop)
Bexar County (San Antonio)
Blanco County (Johnson City)
Burleson County (Caldwell)
Caldwell County (Lockhart)
Eastland County (Eastland)
El Paso County (El Paso)
Fannin County (Bonham)
Fayette County (La Grange)
Gonzales County (Gonzales)
Haskell County (Haskell)
Hays County (San Marcos)
Jones County (Anson)
Kimble County (Junction)
Lee County (Giddings)
Liberty County (Liberty)
Lipscomb County (Lipscomb)
Live Oak County (George West)
Llano County (Llano)
Martin County (Stanton)
Mason County (Mason)
Midland County (Midland)
Milam County (Cameron)
Ochiltree County (Perryton)
Palo Pinto County (Palo Pinto)
Polk County (Livingston)
Potter County (Amarillo)
Reeves County (Pecos)
Refugio County (Refugio)
Runnels County (Ballinger)
San Saba County (San Saba)
Shackelford County (Albany)
Taylor County (Abilene)
Travis County (Austin)
Washington County (Brenham)
Williamson County (Georgetown)

New Mexico—
Chaves County (Roswell)
Colfax County (Raton)
Eddy County (Carlsbad)
Lincoln County (Carrizozo)
Otero County (Alamogordo)

Arizona—
Maricopa County (Phoenix)
Pima County (Tucson)
Yavapai County (Prescott)

California—
Contra Costa County (Oakland)
Fresno County (Fresno)
Sacramento County (Sacramento)
San Mateo County (Redwood City)
Santa Barbara County (Santa Barbara)
San Francisco County (San Francisco)

Mississippi—
Winston County (Louisville)

Colorado—
Huerfaño County (Walsenburg)
Park County (Fairplay)

Documents in state libraries and archives:

Texas—Confederate pension applications, genealogical records, newspapers, letters, pardons, extradition requests, and other documents.
New Mexico—County records and territorial papers.
Colorado—Brands and court records.
Arizona—Property records, maps, microfilms, and manuscripts.
California—newspaper collections, books, and city directories.
Alaska—newspaper files and microfilms.
Minnesota—Manuscripts.

Federal Court Cases reported in:

United States Court of Appeals Reports (e.g. 60 CCA 155 and 57 CCA 444).
United States Reports (e.g. 180 US 536).
Supreme Court Reporter (21 Sup Ct 468) and (45 LED 657).
Alaska Reports I and II.

Federal Statutes:

The Homestead Act (12 Statutes at Large 392, May 20, 1862).
The Desert Land Act (19 Statutes at Large 377, March 3, 1877).
The Edmunds Act (22 Statutes at Large 30-32, March 22, 1882).

Federal Records:

The National Archives, Military/Civil Records and Land Entry Files.
Despatches from the U.S. Consul at Paso del Norte and the Consul General at Nuevo Laredo, Mexico.
Report of the Secretary of War to the Third Session of the Fifty-third Congress, Government Printing Office, Washington, DC, 1894.
U.S. Census reports, 1870–1930 for Texas, New Mexico, Arizona, California, as well as 1900 Nome, Alaska.

Foreign Records:

The municipal civil and criminal records of Ciudad de Juarez, Chihuahua, Mexico.
Case files of the Mexican Supreme Court.
Articles 19 and 20 of the Mexican Constitution of 1857.

Additional Texas Records:

Texas Court of Criminal Appeals (18 Texas App 232-260).

Memoranda of Court Cases, El Paso County, Texas, containing the Probate Papers of John Wesley Hardin.

Court Testimony in the State of Texas vs. John Wesley Hardin, Special Collections, El Paso Public Library and University of Texas at El Paso.

Passenger Ship List: the *Ben Nevis* 1854, Port of Galveston, Texas.

Records of Baptisms, Marriages and Confirmations from St. Paul's Lutheran Church, Serbin; Trinity Lutheran Church, Fedor; and St. Paul's Lutheran Church, Paige, Texas.

School, Confirmation, Death, Marriage, and Baptism records, The Catholic Archives of Texas, (Austin, Texas); The Catholic Archives of the Archdiocese of San Antonio; and the Catholic Archives of the Archdiocese of San Francisco.

Other Records:

The New Mexico Territorial Census and The Colorado State Census of 1885.
The W. C. "Bill" Williams Family Bible.

Collections:

Archivo Judicial de la Suprema Corte de Justicia de la Nacion, Instituto de la Judicatura Federal, Mexico City, Mexico.

The Nettie Lee Benson Latin American Collection, University of Texas at Austin.

The John A. and Charles B. Eddy Collection, Fray Angelico Chavez History Library, Santa Fe, New Mexico.

The Falls-Pickering Collection, Texas A & M University-Commerce.

The Gonzales County Records Center and Archives, Gonzales, Texas.

The J. Evetts Haley Collection and the Robert N. Mullin Collection at the Nita Stewart Haley Memorial Library, Midland, Texas.

The John Wesley Hardin Collection, Texas State University, San Marcos, Texas.

The Hardin Papers, Center for American History, University of Texas at Austin.

The Charles Holbrook Collection, California Historical Society Library, San Francisco, California.

The New Mexico County Archives (1860-1930), University of New Mexico, Albuquerque, New Mexico.

The Papers of Rex Ellingwood Beach, Special Collections, University of Virginia Library, Charlottesville, Virginia.

The Sacramento Archives and Museum Collection, Sacramento, California.

The C. L. Sonnichsen Special Collection, University of Texas at El Paso.

The Territorial Archives of New Mexico, New Mexico State Records Center and Archives, Santa Fe, New Mexico.

The Earl Vandale Collection, Center for American History, The University of Texas at Austin.

The Wendish Heritage Society Museum and Archives of Serbin, Texas.

Manuscripts:

Barnes, Dell, *The Williams Family*, unpublished genealogy.

Bogener, Dr. Stephen Dean, *Ditches Across the Desert: A Story of Irrigation Along New Mexico's Pecos River*, Dissertation, Texas Tech University, 1997.

Eilers, Kathryn Burford, *A History of Mason County, Texas*, master's thesis, 1939, Center for American Studies, University of Texas at Austin.

Foster, Jo, *Geography and Descendants of John Wesley Hardin*, Gonzales County Records Center and Archives, Gonzales, Texas.

Haines, Edna Selman, *John Selman of El Paso, as Told by my father, John Selman Jr.*, Special Collections, University of Texas at El Paso.

Haines, Edna Selman, and Selman, John Jr., *Young John*, Special Collections, University of Texas at El Paso.

Hamner, Laura V., *Personal Interviews in the Midland Area: "Interview with Mr. and Mrs. Hunter Irwin,"* Center for American Studies, University of Texas at Austin.

Hargrave, Tommy Ruth and Slack, Carroll Terrell, *"Helms Family Records,"* bound typescript, date unknown, Falls-Pickering Collection, Texas A & M University—Commerce.

Harkey-Schneider, Vada Beatrice, *The Harkey Family Tree*, self-published, date and location unknown.

Howard, Jed, *Phenix and The Wolf: Including The Saloon Battles of Eddy and The Dave Kemp Saga*, Carlsbad, New Mexico, date unknown.

Johnston, Doris, unpublished genealogy of the Williams family.

Lewis, Charles William, Jr., *Early Settlers in Carlsbad, New Mexico, and Vicinity*, self published, date unknown.

Look, George, *The George Look Historical Manuscript*, 1909, Border Heritage Center, El Paso Public Library.

McCown, Dennis, *A Comparative Analysis of the University of Texas Hardin Papers and Southwest Texas State University's Hardin Collection*, 2003.

McPhee, William Norvell, *The Eddy Brothers*, Roswell Public Library, Roswell, New Mexico, no date.

Melton, Helen Bond, *Carlsbad Chronologies*, Eddy County Library, Carlsbad, New Mexico, date unknown.

Selman, John Marion, *Young John*, Special Collections, University of Texas at El Paso.

Sievers, James L., *Selected Correspondence of John Wesley Hardin, From Capture Until Parole*, 1972, Thesis, Texas State University.

Typewritten stories of John Wesley Hardin from unknown family sources, the Hardin file, Gonzales County Records Center and Archives, Gonzales, Texas.

Newspapers

The Alamogordo Daily News
The Arizona Daily Citizen
The Arizona Daily Gazette
The Arizona Daily Star
The Arizona Weekly Star
The Arizona Republican
The Austin Daily Statesman
The (Austin) Daily Democratic Statesman
The (Austin) Daily State Journal
The Ballinger Eagle
The Bastrop Advertiser
The Booker News
The Boston Daily Globe
The Boston Evening Transcript
The Boston Herald
The Cameron Herald
The Carlsbad Current
The Carlsbad Current-Argus
The Daily Alta
The (Dallas) Daily Times Herald
The Dallas Morning News
The Eddy Argus
The Eddy County Citizen
The Eddy Current
The Elgin Courier
The El Paso Times
The El Paso Daily Times

The El Paso Daily Herald
The El Paso Herald
The El Paso Evening Telegraph
The El Paso Herald Post
The Fairplay Flume
The Freeborn County Standard, (Albert Lea, Minnesota)
The (San Antonio) Freie Presse Für Texas
The Fredonia Kicker
The Fresno Ensign
The Galveston News
The (Nome) Gold Digger
The Hondo Herald
The Houston Daily Post
The Houston Post—Dispatch
The Las Vegas (New Mexico) *Optic*
The Live Oak County Herald
The Lockhart Register
The Luling Signal
The Mason County News
The Mason County Herald
The Mason Herald
The New York Times
The Nome Daily Chronicle
The Oakland Enquirer
The Ochiltree County Herald
The Otero County News
The Pecos Valley Daily Argus
The Pioneer News Observer
The Raton Reporter
The Rocky Mountain News
The Sacramento Bee
The Sacramento Evening Bee
The Sacramento Union
The San Antonio Daily Express
The San Antonio Daily Light
The San Antonio Daily Herald
The San Angelo Standard
The San Francisco Call
The San Francisco Chronicle
The San Francisco Examiner
The San Saba County News
The Santa Fe Daily New Mexican
The Seattle Daily Times
The Seattle Post-Intelligencer
The Silver City Enterprise
The Texas State Democrat
The Taylor County News

The *Victoria Advocate*
The *Weekly Phoenix Herald*
The *Western Liberal*
The *Williamson County Sun*

Secondary Sources

Books

Abbott, E.C. and Smith, Helena Huntington, *We Pointed Them North: Recollections of a Cowpuncher*, University of Oklahoma Press, Norman, Oklahoma, 1939.
Altrocchi, Julia Cooley, *The Spectacular San Franciscans*, E. P. Dutton and Company, New York, 1949.
Ball, Eve, *Ma'am Jones of the Pecos*, The University of Arizona Press, Tucson, Arizona, 1969.
Beach, Rex Ellingwood, *Personal Exposures*, Harper, New York, 1940.
Bidal, Lillian H., *Pisacah: A Place of Plenty*, Robert E. and Evelyn McKee Foundation, El Paso, Texas 1995.
Bonney, Cecil, *Looking Over My Shoulder: Seventy-five Years in the Pecos Valley*, Hall-Poorbaugh Press, Inc., Roswell, New Mexico, 1971.
Bowden, Jesse Earle, and Cummins, William S., *Texas Desperado in Florida: The Capture of Outlaw John Wesley Hardin in Pensacola, 1877*, Pensacola Historical Society, Pensacola, Florida, 2002.
Caldwell, Lillie Moerbe, *Texas Wends: Their First Half-Century*, The Anson Jones Press, Salado, Texas 1961.
Campbell, Charles C., *Hell Exploded; An exposition of Barbarous Cruelty and Prison Horrors*, self-published, Austin, Texas, 1900.
Casey, Robert J., *The Texas Border and Some Borderliners: A Chronicle & Guide*, Bobbs-Merrill and Company, Indianapolis, 1950.
Chesley, Hervey E., *Adventuring With the Oldtimers: Trails Traveled-Tales Told*, Nita Stewart Haley Memorial Library, Midland, Texas 1979.
DeArment, Robert K., *George Scarborough: The Life and Death of a Lawman on the Closing Frontier*, University of Oklahoma Press, Norman, Oklahoma, 1992.
Dixson, Walter Clay, *Richland Crossing: A Portrait of Texas Pioneers*, Peppermill Publishing, Everman, Texas 1994.
Dobie, J. Frank, *A Vaquero of the Brush Country*, Little, Brown & Company, Boston, 1943.
Epperson, Harry A., *Colorado: As I Saw It*, 1944.
Ferguson, Bobbie H., *...And They Laid Them to Rest in the Little Plot Beside the Pecos: Final report on the Relocation of Old Seven Rivers Cemetery, Eddy County, New Mexico*, Bureau of Reclamation, Denver, Colorado, 1993.
Floren, Lee, *John Wesley Hardin: Texas Gunfighter*, McFadden Books, New York, New York, 1962.
Gordon, Linda, *The Great Arizona Orphan Abduction*, Harvard University Press, Cambridge, Massachusetts, 1999.
Haley, J. Evetts, *Jeff Milton: A Good Man With a Gun*, University of Oklahoma Press, Norman, Oklahoma, 1948.
Hall, Sarah Harkey, *Surviving on the Texas Frontier: The Journal of an Orphan Girl in San Saba County*, Eakin Press, Austin, Texas, 1996.

Hardin, John Wesley, *The Life of John Wesley Hardin: From the Original Manuscript, as Written by Himself*, Smith & Moore, Seguin, Texas, 1896.

Harkey, Dee, *Mean As Hell, The Life of a New Mexico Lawman*, Ancient City Press, Santa Fe, New Mexico, 1989.

Henderson, Eva Pendleton, *Wild Horses: A Turn-of-the-Century Prairie Girlhood*, Sunstone Press, Santa Fe, New Mexico, 1983.

Hinkle, James F., *Early Days of a Cowboy on the Pecos*, First National Bank of Roswell, Roswell, New Mexico, date unknown.

Hughes, Alton, *Pecos; A History of the Pioneer West*, Pioneer Book Publishers, Seagraves, Texas, 1978.

Hunter, J. Marvin, editor, *The Trail Drivers of Texas*, University of Texas Press, Austin, 1924.

Hyatt, Marjorie Burnett, *The Ties That Bind: Families of Precinct Five, Gonzales County, Texas 1850-1900*, The Clan McBean Press, Cut and Shoot, Texas, 1980.

Keleher, William A., *The Fabulous Frontier: Twelve New Mexico Items*, The University of New Mexico Press, 1962.

Kimble County Historical Commission, *Families of Kimble County*, Volumes I and II, Junction, Texas, 1985.

Klasner, Lily, *My Girlhood Among Outlaws*, University of Arizona Press, Tucson, Arizona, 1972.

Lindsey, Ellis and Riggs, Gene, *Barney K. Riggs: The Yuma and Pecos Avenger*, Xlibris Corporation, 2002.

Lipscomb County Historical Commission, *The History of Lipscomb County, Texas 1876-1976*, Lipscomb, Texas, 1976.

Marohn, Richard C., *The Last Gunfighter: John Wesley Hardin*, Creative Publishing Company, College Station, Texas, 1995.

Mason County Historical Commission and Mason County Historical Society, *Mason County Historical Book 1976*, Mason County, Texas, 1976.

Mason County Sesquicentennial Committee, *Mason County Communities, 1986*, Texas Genealogical Library, 1986.

Mather, R.E., *Scandal of the West: Domestic Violence on the Frontier*, History West Publishing Company, Oklahoma City, Oklahoma, 1998.

McManus, J., *Bastrop and Lee Counties, Texas: Wend Colony 1854*, published by Frances T. Ingmire, St. Louis, Missouri, 1985.

Metz, Leon, *John Selman, Gunfighter*, University of Oklahoma Press, Norman, Oklahoma, 1966.

—— *John Wesley Hardin: Dark Angel of Texas*, Mangan Books, El Paso, Texas, 1996.

Millard, F. S., *A Cowpuncher of the Pecos*, unknown, but probably *Frontier Times*, J. Marvin Hunter, editor, Bandera, Texas.

Miller, Rick, *Bloody Bill Longley*, Hennington Publishing Company, Wolfe City, Texas 1996.

Mills, William Wallace, *Forty Years at El Paso: 1858-1898*, published by Carl Hertzog, El Paso, Texas, 1962.

Myers, Lee C., *The Pearl of the Pecos: The Story of the Establishment of Eddy, New Mexico, and Irrigation on the Lower Pecos River of New Mexico*, Southeastern New Mexico Historical Society, 1999.

—— *Eddy County ... A Fond Look Back, Memories of Other Years*, self-published, date unknown.

Nordyke, Lewis, *John Wesley Hardin: Texas Gunman*, William Morrow & Company, New York, New York, 1957.

Parrish, Joe, *Coffins, Cactus, and Cowboys: The Exciting Story of El Paso, 1536 to the Present*, Superior Publishing Company, El Paso, Texas 1964.

Parsons, Chuck and Parsons, Marjorie, *Bowen and Hardin*, Creative Publishing Company, College Station, Texas 1991.

Parsons, Marjorie Burnett, *Gonzales County, Texas, Marriage Licenses Issued, 1829–1900*, self-published, Smiley, Texas, 1993.

Pickering, David and Falls, Judy, *Brushmen and Vigilantes, Civil War Dissent in Texas*, Texas A & M University Press, College Station, Texas, 2000.

San Saba County Historical Commission, *San Saba County History, 1856–1983*, San Saba, Texas, 1983.

Simmons, Virginia McConnell, *Bayou Salado: The Story of South Park*, Century One Press, Colorado Springs, Colorado, 1966.

Smith, Clifford Neal, *Nineteenth Century Emigration of "Old Lutherans" From Eastern Germany (Mainly Pomerania and Lower Silesia) To Australia, Canada, and The United States*, German-American Genealogical Research Monograph Number 7, Westland Publications, McNeal, Arizona, 1980.

Stephens, Robert W., *Bullets and Buckshot in Texas*, self-published, Dallas, Texas, 2002.

Unknown, *Eddy County, New Mexico: 1981–Present*, Carlsbad, New Mexico.

Unknown, *History of Texas Together With a Biographical History of Milam, Williamson, Bastrop, Travis, Lee, and Burleson Counties*, The Lewis Publishing Company, Chicago, 1893.

White, Owen P., *Lead and Likker*, Minton, Balch & Company, New York, 1932.

Zheutlin, Peter, *Around The World on Two Wheels: Annie Londonderry's Extraordinary Ride*, Citadel Press, 2007.

Articles and Other Publications:

Bauman, Richard, "The Magical Touring Sack of Flour," *True West*, August 1999.

Beach, Rex, "The Looting of Alaska," *Appleton's Booklovers Magazine*, Vol. VII, January–May 1906.

Bennett, Dwight G., D.V.M., "Flying Horses, Driving Cattle, *and* Piroplasmosis," *Western Horseman*, vol. 64, #2, February 1999.

Black, A.P. (Ott), "The End of the Longhorn Trail," *The Selfridge Journal*, Selfridge, North Dakota, no date.

Frear, Shelley R., "The 1893 Chadron to Chicago Cowboy Horse Race," *Old West*, Spring 1998.

Fuller, Henry C., "Adventures of Bill Longley," Baker Printing Company, Nacogdoches, Texas, date unknown.

Hale, Leon, "F.M. Fly as a Young Man Knew John Wesley Hardin," unknown publication, 16 July 1962.

Hinkle, James F., "A New Mexico Cowboy on the Pecos," *Frontier Times*, May 1938.

Knight, Samuel, "Federal Control of Hydraulic Mining," *Yale Law Journal*, New Haven, Connecticut, Vol. 7, October 1897–June 1898.

Lander, Bruce, "John Wesley Hardin: Was He Really the 'Fastest Gun in Texas?'," *Quarterly of the National Association for Outlaw and Lawman History*, Volume XXV, No. 2, April–May 2001.

Marohn, Dr. Richard C., M.D., "John Wesley Hardin, Adolescent Killer: The Emergence of a Narcissistic Behavior Disorder," *Adolescent Psychiatry: Developmental and Clinical Studies*, University of Chicago Press, vol. 14, 1987.

McCown, Dennis, "The Death of Helen Beulah," *True West*, May 1999.

—— "Two Women," *Quarterly of the National Association for Outlaw and Lawman History*, Volume XXIII, No. 2, April–June 1999.

—— "The Search For Martin Mrose," *Quarterly of the National Association for Outlaw and Lawman History*, Volume XXIII, No.4, October–December 1999.

—— "… despite big losses …, The Last Shooting of the Old West," *Quarterly of the National Association for Outlaw and Lawman History*, Volume XXIV, No 4, October–December 2000.

—— "The Crime of 1900," *Quarterly of the National Association for Outlaw and Lawman History*, Volume XXV, No. 4, October–December 2001.

——"The Crime of 1900 & Its Role in the Establishment of Civil Law in Alaska," *The Alaska Bar Rag*, May–June, 2002.

—— "Family Secrets at Concordia," *Quarterly of the National Association for Outlaw and Lawman History*, Volume XXVI, No. 4, October–December 2002.

—— "Broken Heart, Broken Dreams," *Quarterly of the National Association for Outlaw and Lawman History*, Volume XXVII, No. 4, October–December 2003.

—— "Wes Hardin, Dennis McCown, and Ed Bartholomew," *Newsletter of the National Association for Outlaw and Lawman History,* vol. XXVIII, No. 2 (April 15, 2003).

—— "The Vagrant's Grave," *The WOLA Journal*, Summer 2003, vol. XII, No. 2.

—— "John Wesley Hardin's Last Love," *Wild West*, December, 2004.

—— "The Cowboy Rock Art of Trinchera Pass," *Wild West*, April, 2008.

—— "A Shooting—Much Exaggerated," *The Journal* of the Wild West History Association, Vol. IV No.5, October 2011.

Metz, Leon C., "The Ghost of John Wesley Hardin," *Roundup Magazine*, Vol. 5, number 3, February 1998.

Mullin, R. N., "In El Paso, John Wesley Hardin Tried to Live Down His Gunman Reputation, but His Flaws, Society Trapped Him," *The Southwesterner*, December 1972.

Parrish, J. Kittrell, "Boy and the Gunslinger," *Texas Parade: Telling the Story of Texas Since 1936*, January 1968, pp.43-45.

Parsons, Chuck, "Gunfire in Hemphill," *True West*, December 1999.

Polk, Stella Gipson, "The Saga of John Wesley Hardin," *The Cattleman*, August 1977, pp. 186-188.

Rasch, Phillip J., "The Life and Death of Lon Bass," *The NOLA Quarterly*, Vol. XIV, Numbers 3 & 4, 1990.

Selman, Bill, "Harden [sic] Had Four Six-Guns to Beat," *Southwesterner*, Vol. 3, #12, June 1964.

Sherrill, R.E., "Colorful History of Haskell County is Recounted," unknown publication, date, Earl Vandale Collection, University of Texas at Austin.

Spiller, Wayne, "His Brother's Long Shadow," *True West* magazine, February 1972.

Zheutlin, Peter, "Chasing Annie," *Bicycling*, May 2005.

Lectures

Crouch, Barry, "That Good Citizens Ask It: The Pardon of John Wesley Hardin," delivered as part of the John W. Stormont Lectures on South Texas at Victoria College, Victoria, Texas, February 5, 1999.

McCown, Dennis, "A Surprising Genealogy of Central Texas," delivered at the historic Archer House during the 28th Annual Rendezvous of NOLA, The National Association for Outlaw and Lawman History, Northfield, Minnesota, July 27, 2001.

—— "The Vagrant's Grave," delivered at The International Congress on Outlaw-Lawman History, Sacramento, California, July 25, 2002.

—— "Three Things You Didn't Know About John Wesley Hardin," delivered at the 31st Annual

Rendezvous of NOLA, The National Association for Outlaw and Lawman History, Reno, Nevada, July 22, 2004.

—— "Bloomers: An Adventure Story," delivered at the 34th Annual Rendezvous of NOLA, The National Association for Outlaw and Lawman History, Rapid City, South Dakota, July 28, 2007.

—— "I'll Leave That For You To Decide: The True Story of Laura Jennings," delivered at the Prince Solms Chapter, Sons of the Republic of Texas, April 21, 2012, New Braunfels, Texas.

A Symposium

"The Deadliest Gunfighter in Texas History," by Donaly Brice, Dennis McCown, and Chuck Parsons, delivered at the Dr. Eugene Clark Library, Lockhart, Texas, January 21, 2010.

A Novel

Beach, Rex, *The Spoilers*, Harper and Brothers, Publishers, New York, New York, 1905.

A Poem

Holinshead, Doris Lila, *Impetuous Hardin*, Naylor Company, San Antonio, Texas, 1962.

Interviews and Noteworthy Correspondence:

(N.B. Anonymous interviews were used mostly for colorful quotes. The story these interviewees told was verified through other sources. Many other interviewees refused to allow anything they said to be used or quoted publicly, and the author has honored their wishes, *with deep regret.*

Anonymous #1 (Member of one of the families who, for reasons of his/her own, wished to remain unknown.)

Anonymous #2 (Member of one of the families who, for various reasons, wished to remain unknown.)

Rodger Barnes
Edward E. Bartholomew
John G. Belcher
Kate Blau (Mrs. Max A. Blau)
Tyre Harris Brown II
Joyce Capps
Mrs. E. Delaney
C.B. Goforth
Arthur Jennings Hill
Virginia Spivey Hill
Jane Hoerster
Francis Louise "Sonnie" Jennings
J.W. Jennings, Sr.
Laura Jennings
Thomas Jennings
Wilda Fay Jennings
Beauregard Lee II

Ruth Jo (Jennings) Martin
Leonard Joe McCown
John McPhee
Helen Bond Melton
Latham Miller
Dr. Victoria Parr
Leon A. Perriraz
Stella Gipson Polk
Ignacio de Jesus-Ramirez
John Starling "Lollie" Roberts
Clara Strzelcyk
Bea Tschatchula
Marguerite Capps White
Gary G. Williams
Glenn Wilkins
Dorothy Wilkins
Charles Wukasch

INDEX

Williams, James Eden, Sheriff Tahachapi County, CA, 277n26

Williams, Martha Ann, 21

Williams, Roger Aaron, 314n10

Williams, Sallie, marries William R. Bratton 313n7

Williams, Sarah, 184

Williams, Thomas, Jr., 184

Williams, Thomas, Sr., 184

Williams, William Crawford, "Bill," 29, 34-5; photo 84; 93; Civil War service, 278n14, 278n21, 279n23; 149, 161, 191, 261,2; gives up in Gila Bend 300n17 & 18; arrives in El Paso, 207-8; supports daughter 307n25; supports Steve Jennings? 308n2, photos 83, 84

Williamson County, TX, 93

Williamson, W.T., deputy, 60

Wilmarth, Rae, 134

Wilson Rye Whiskey, 58

Wilson, Frank, Sheriff Comanche County, 70

Witt family, 119

Wo, Bob Chin, 304n14

Wolfton, NM, 59, 260

Women's Industrial and Educational Fund, 310n12

Yale University, 234, 237, 309n18

Young, John D., 282n33

Zemitis, Sibylle, 316n20

Zumwalt, Elmo, Admiral, 277n26

CPSIA information can be obtained at www.ICGtesting.com
Printed in the USA
LVOW08s1154191113

361909LV00002B/42/P